R. S. Thain

Songs for the Service of Prayer

R. S. Thain

Songs for the Service of Prayer

ISBN/EAN: 9783337243739

Printed in Europe, USA, Canada, Australia, Japan

Cover: Foto ©Thomas Meinert / pixelio.de

More available books at **www.hansebooks.com**

SONGS

FOR THE

SERVICE OF PRAYER,

COMPILED BY

R. S. THAIN,

ASSISTED BY

LEADING PASTORS
OF DIFFERENT DENOMINATIONS.

CHICAGO:
F. H. REVELL, 148 AND 150 MADISON STREET.
Publisher of Evangelical Literature.

I have thoroughly examined Mr. Thain's compilation, SONGS FOR THE SERVICE OF PRAYER, offering such suggestions in the way of changes and additions as I judged advisable. The work so fully meets my views of what a Prayer Meeting book should be, that I do not hesitate to give it my most hearty endorsement and approval, and trust that it may prove a blessing to many assemblies of the saints in the worship of the King.

ABBOTT E. KITTREDGE,

Pastor 3rd Presbyterian Church, Chicago

I have examined somewhat carefully Mr. Thain's compilation of hymns, and take great pleasure in commending it to the churches of the land. The fact that it has been prepared with sole reference to the social Prayer Meeting, gives the collection a very great advantage. There is afforded thus an unusually wide range of hymns and tunes peculiarly adapted to such gatherings.

I think the compilation will be found especially rich in hymns endeared to Christian hearts, and greatly owned of God in comforting His people, establishing their faith, inspiring their zeal. Whatever the excellencies of other collections, I make no doubt this will prove one of the best. I trust it may be greatly blessed in magnifying the gospel of the grace of the Lord Jesus Christ.

EDWARD P. GOODWIN,

Pastor 1st Congregational Church, Chicago.

The assistance which I rendered Mr. Thain in this work has been mainly confined to a very careful examination of the sheets when nearly ready for the press, resulting in offering such suggestions as would increase the acceptableness of the book for the blessed Service of Prayer. for which it is designed. It is hoped that the labor of love for the Master done by Mr. Thain may commend this book to other Christian hearts as it has to those who have aided him.

WM. M. LAWRENCE,

Pastor Second Baptist Church, Chicago.

PREFACE.

—:o:—

In compiling Songs for the Service of Prayer, the object has been to furnish a book containing hymns and tunes specially adapted to use in the social meetings of the Church ; to this end, tunes of a purely congregational character, and hymns filled with prayer, praise, and worship have been selected.

The classification by subjects will be found very thorough. We believe that this feature will commend the book to Pastors. In many cases abridgments have been made, where the elimination of stanzas would not mar the hymns for prayer-meeting use, thus affording space for a larger number of hymns.

Nearly all of the old favorites, and the best of the modern Gospel Songs will be found in the work. For the use of the large number of copyrighted pieces, acknowledgments are gratefully tendered to the owners of the same; and for the kind co-operation of the Reverend gentlemen who cheerfully gave so much of their valuable time to a thorough examination and revision of the work, and to Mark Ayres, Esq., to whose rare judgment and experience much of the excellence of the work is due, the compiler tenders his most hearty thanks.

Richard S. Thain.

Chicago, Nov. 24th, 1880.

J. E. White, Music Typographer & Stereotyper,
Battle Creek, Michigan.

TABLE OF CONTENTS.

Songs for the Service of Prayer.

PRAYER.

WHAT A FRIEND. *C. C. Converse, by per.*

I *Jesus a Friend.*

2 Have we trials and temptations?
Is there trouble anywhere?
We should never be discouraged,
Take it to the Lord in prayer.
Can we find a friend so faithful,
Who will all our sorrows share?
Jesus knows our every weakness,
Take it to the Lord in prayer.

3 Are we weak and heavy laden,
Cumbered with a load of care?
Precious Saviour! still our refuge,—
Take it to the Lord in prayer.
Do thy friends despise, forsake thee?
Take it to the Lord in prayer;
In his arms He'll take and shield thee,
Thou wilt find a solace there.

GREENVILLE. 8, 7, D *Rosseau.*

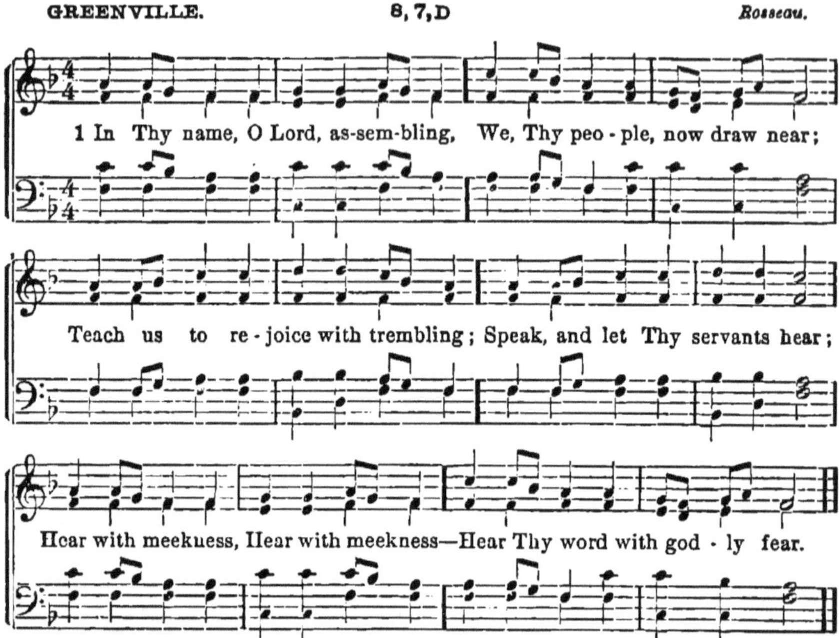

2 *Drawing Near.*

2 While our days on earth are lengthened,
May we give them, Lord, to thee;
Cheered by hope, and daily strengthened,
May we run, nor weary be,
Till Thy glory
Without cloud in heaven we see.

3 There, in worship purer, sweeter,
All Thy people shall adore;
Tasting of enjoyment greater
Than they could conceive before;
Full enjoyment,
Full and pure for evermore.

T. Kelly.

3 *Prayer for Blessing.*

1 Come, Thou soul-transforming Spirit,
Bless the sower and the seed;
Let each heart Thy grace inherit;
Raise the weak, the hungry feed:
From the gospel
Now supply Thy people's need.

2 Oh, may all enjoy the blessing
Which Thy word's designed to give;
Let us all, Thy love possessing,
Joyfully the truth receive,
And forever
To Thy praise and glory live.

4 *Dismission.*

1 Lord, dismiss us with Thy blessing;
Fill our hearts with joy and peace;
Let us each, Thy love possessing,
Triumph in redeeming grace:
Oh, refresh us,
Traveling through this wilderness.

2 Thanks we give, and adoration,
For Thy gospel's joyful sound;
May the fruits of Thy salvation
In our hearts and lives abound:
May Thy presence
With us evermore be found.

SWEET HOUR OF PRAYER. L. M. D. *Wm. B. Bradbury, by per.*

5 *Sweet Hour of Prayer.*

2 Sweet hour of prayer! sweet hour of prayer!
Thy wings shall my petition bear
To Him whose truth and faithfulness
Engage the waiting soul to bless.
And since He bids me seek His face,
Believe His word, and trust His grace,
I'll cast on Him my every care,
And wait for thee, sweet hour of prayer.

3 Sweet hour of prayer! sweet hour of prayer!
May I thy consolation share,
Till from Mount Pisgah's lofty height
I view my home and take my flight.
This robe of flesh I'll drop, and rise
To seize the everlasting prize,
And shout, while passing through the air,
Farewell, farewell, sweet hour of prayer.

Rev. W. W. Walford

WOODSTOCK. C. M. *Deodatus Dutton, Jr.*

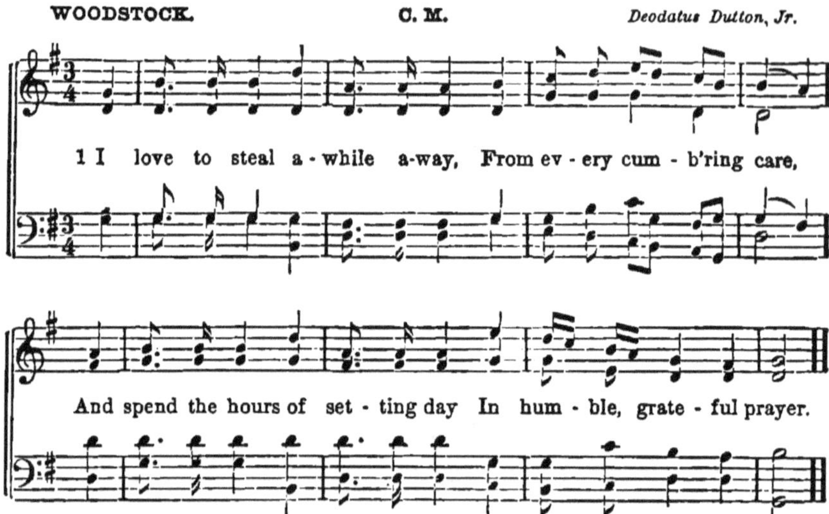

6

Setting Day.

2 I love, in solitude, to shed
The penitential tear;
And all His promises to plead
Where none but God can hear.

3 I love to think on mercies past,
And future good implore;
And all my cares and sorrows cast
On Him whom I adore.

4 I love, by faith, to take a view
Of brighter scenes in Heaven;
The prospect doth my strength renew,
While here by tempests driven.

5 Thus, when life's toilsome day is o'er,
May its departing ray
Be calm as this impressive hour,
And lead to endless day.

Mrs. P. H. Brown.

7

Power of Man in Prayer.

1 There is an eye that never sleeps
Beneath the wing of night;
There is an ear that never shuts,
When sink the beams of light.

2 There is an arm that never tires,
When human strength gives way;
There is a love that never fails,
When earthly loves decay.

3 And there's a power which man can wield
When mortal aid is vain,
That eye, that arm, that love to reach,
That listening ear to gain.

4 That power is prayer, which soars on high,
Through Jesus, to the throne;
And moves the hand which moves the world,
To bring salvation down!

8

"Far from the world."

1 Far from the world, O Lord, I flee,
From strife and tumult far;
From scenes where Satan wages still
His most successful war.

2 The calm retreat, the silent shade,
With prayer and praise agree,
And seem by Thy sweet bounty made
For those who follow Thee.

RETREAT. L. M. *Thomas Hastings.*

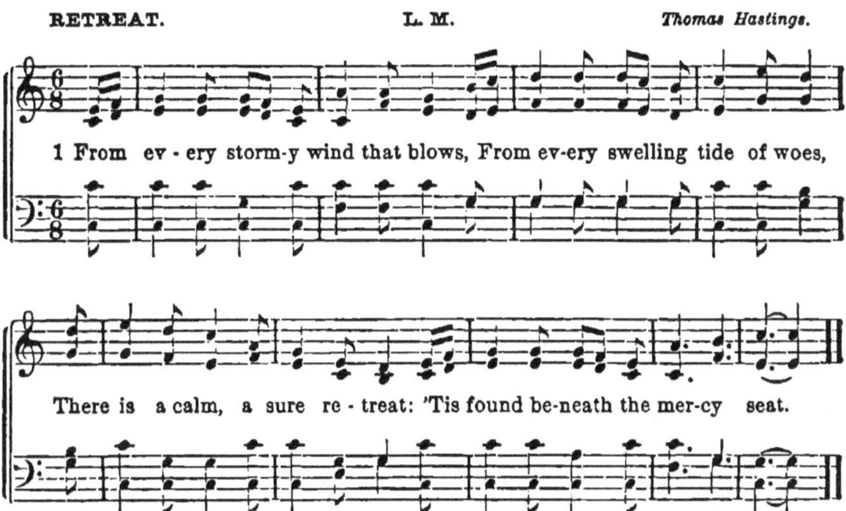

9 *The Mercy-Seat.*

2 There is a place where Jesus sheds
The oil of gladness on our heads;
A place than all besides more sweet:
It is the blood-bought mercy-seat.

3 There is a spot where spirits blend,
Where friend holds fellowship with friend;
Though sundered far, by faith they meet
Around one common mercy-seat.

4 There, there, on eagle wings we soar,
And time and sense seem all no more;
And Heaven comes down our souls to greet,
And glory crowns the mercy-seat.

5 Oh, may my hand forget her skill,
My tongue be silent, cold, and still,
This bounding heart forget to beat,
If I forget the mercy-seat.

Rev. Hugh Stowell.

10 THE LORD'S PRAYER. CHANT.

PLEYEL'S HYMN. 7. *Ignace Pleyel.*

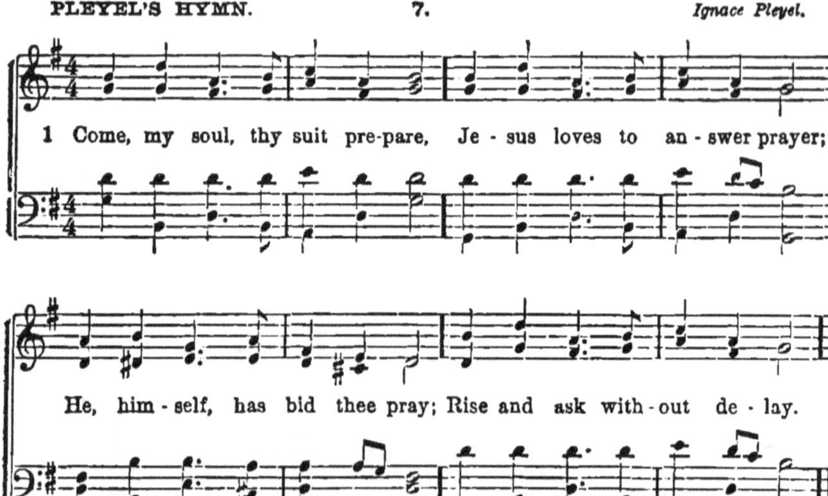

11 *"Only Believe."*

2 Thou art coming to a King,
Large petitions with thee bring;
For his grace and power are such,
None can ever ask too much.

3 With my burden I begin;
Lord, remove this load of sin:
Let Thy blood, for sinners spilt,
Set my conscience free from guilt.

4 Lord, I come to Thee for rest;
Take possession of my breast;
There Thy blood-bought right maintain,
And without a rival reign.

J. Newton.

12 *Morning, Noon, and Night.*

1 In the morning hear my voice,
Let me in Thy light rejoice;
God, my Sun, my strength renew,
Send Thy blessing down like dew.

2 Through the duties of the day,
Grant me grace to watch and pray;
Live as always seeing Thee,
Knowing—"Thou, God, seest me."

3 When the evening skies display
Richer pomp than noon's array,
Be the shades of death to me
Bright with immortality.

J. Montgomery.

13 *Evening Prayer.*

1 Softly now the light of day
Fades upon my sight away;
Free from care, from labor free,
Lord, I would commune with Thee.

2 Thou, whose all-pervading eye
Naught escapes, without, within,
Pardon each infirmity,
Open fault, and secret sin.

3 Soon, for me, the light of day
Shall forever pass away;
Then, from sin and sorrow free,
Take me, Lord, to dwell with Thee.

4 Thou who, sinless, yet hast known
All of man's infirmity,
Then, from Thine eternal throne,
Jesus, look with pitying eye.

G. W. Doane.

BOYLSTON. S. M. *Lowell Mason.*

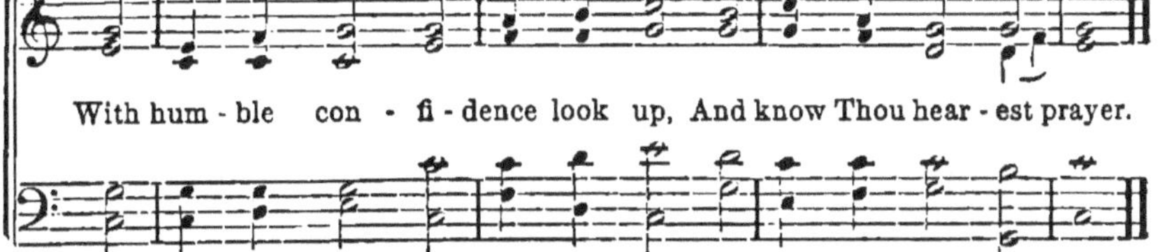

14 *"Watch unto Prayer."*

2 Oh, for a godly fear,
  A quick, discerning eye,
That looks to Thee when sin is near,
  And sees the tempter fly!

3 A spirit still prepared,
  And armed with jealous care,
Forever standing on its guard,
  And watching unto prayer!

4 A soul inured to pain,
  To hardship, grief, and loss;
Bold to take up, firm to sustain,
  My dear Redeemer's cross.

C. Wesley.

15 *"Arise, He Calleth Thee."*

1 Our Heavenly Father calls,
  And Christ invites us near;
With both, our friendship shall be sweet,
  And our communion dear.

2 Jesus, my living Head,
  We bless thy faithful care;
Mine Advocate before the throne,
  And my Forerunner there.

3 Here fix, my roving heart,
  Here wait my warmest love,,
Till the communion be complete,
  In nobler scenes above.

Rev. Philip Doddridge.

16 *"Still with Thee."*

1 Still with Thee, O my God,
  I would desire to be;
By day, by night, at home, abroad,
  I would be still with Thee:

2 With Thee, amid the crowd
  That throngs the busy mart,
To hear Thy voice, 'mid clamor loud,
  Speak softly to my heart:

3 With Thee, when darkness brings
  The signal of repose;
Calm in the shadow of Thy wings,
  Mine eyelids I would close:

4 With Thee, in Thee, by faith
  Abiding I would be;
By day, by night, in life, in death,
  I would be still with Thee.

Anon.

ROCKINGHAM. L. M. *Lowell Mason.*

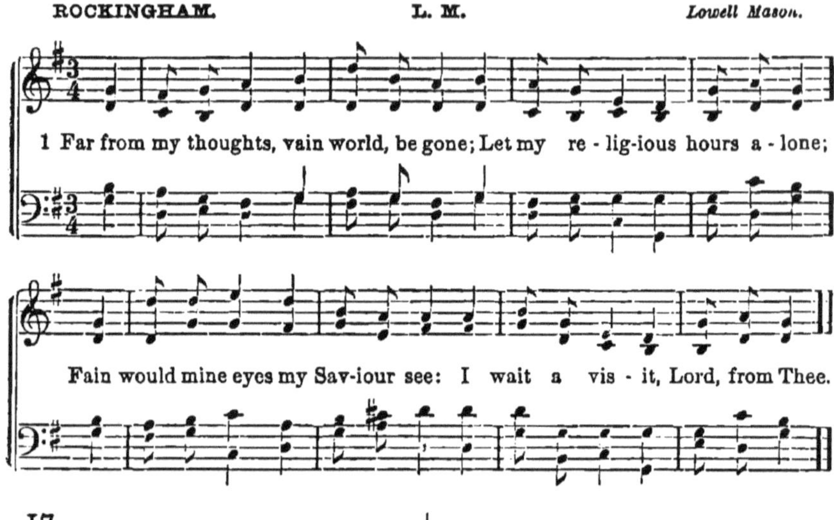

17 *Delight in Worship.*

2 My heart grows warm with holy fire,
And kindles with a pure desire;
Come, my dear Jesus, from above,
And feed my soul with heavenly love.

3 Blest Jesus, what delicious fare!
How sweet Thine entertainments are!
Never did angels taste above
Redeeming grace and dying love.

4 Hail, great Immanuel, all-divine,
In Thee Thy Father's glories shine:
Thou brightest, sweetest, fairest One
That eyes have seen or angels known!

Rev. Isaac Watts.

ALETTA. 7. *W. B. Bradbury.*

18 *"Ye Shall Seek Me, and Find Me.*

2 Lord, on Thee our souls depend,
In compassion now descend;
Fill our hearts with Thy rich grace,
Tune our lips to sing Thy praise.

3 In Thine own appointed way,
Now we seek Thee, here we stay;
Lord, we know not how to go,
Till a blessing Thou bestow.

4 Send some message from Thy word,
That may joy and peace afford;
Let thy spirit now impart
Full salvation to each heart.

5 Comfort those who weep and mourn,
Let the time of joy return;
Those that are cast down lift up,
Strong in faith, in love and hope.

Rev. William Hammond.

EVEN ME. 8, 7. *Arr. by Wm. B. Bradbury.*

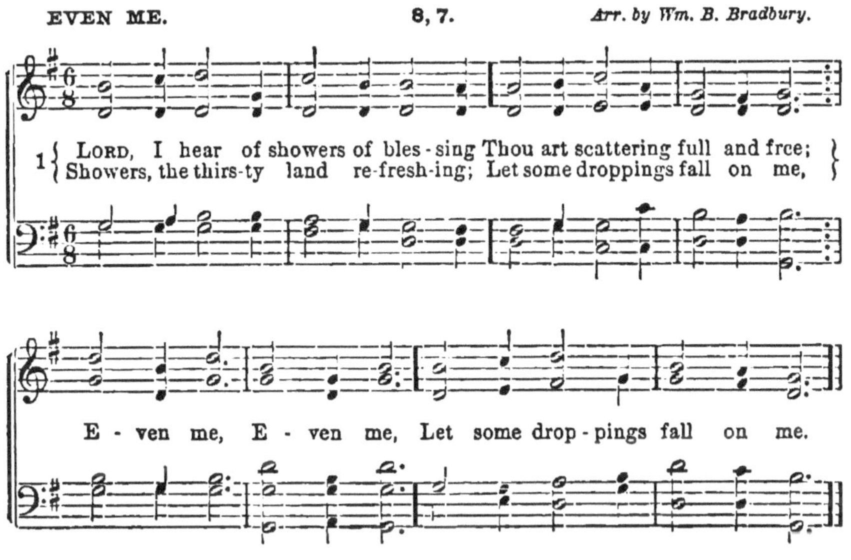

19 *"Bless Me, Even Me Also."*

2 Pass me not, O gracious Father,
Sinful though my heart may be;
Thou might'st leave me, but the rather
Let Thy mercy light on me,
Even me.

3 Pass me not, O tender Saviour,
Let me love and cling to Thee
I am longing for Thy favor;
When Thou comest, call for me,
Even me.

4 Pass me not, O mighty Spirit,
Thou canst make the blind to see;
Witnesser of Jesus' merit,
Speak the word of power to me,
Even me.

5 Love of God, so pure and changeless,
Blood of Christ, so rich and free,
Grace of God, so strong and boundless,
Magnify them all in me,
Even me.

Mrs. Elizabeth Codner.

STATE STREET. **S. M.** *J. C. Woodman.*

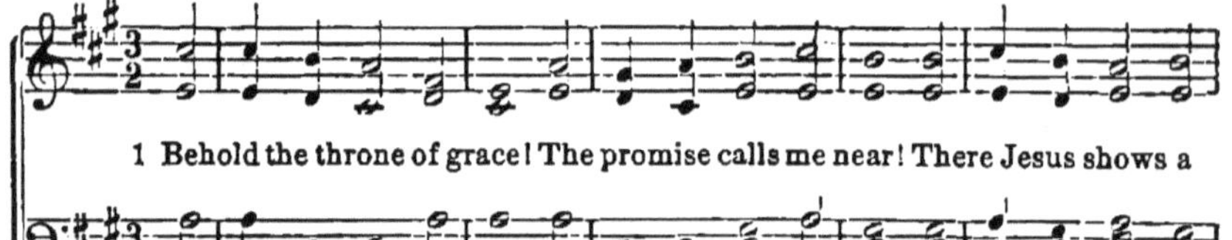

2 He bows His gracious ear,
We never plead in vain:
Then let us wait till He appear,
And pray, and pray again.

3 Jesus, the Lord, will hear
His chosen when they cry;
Yes; though He may awhile forbear,
He'll help them from on high.

4 Then let us earnest be,
And never faint in prayer;
He loves our importunity,
And makes our cause His care.
Rev. J. Newton.

20 *"The Throne of Grace."*

2 That rich atoning blood,
Which sprinkled round I see,
Provides for those who come to God
An all-prevailing plea.

3 My soul, ask what thou wilt;
Thou canst not be too bold:
Since his own blood for thee He spilt,
What else can he withhold?

4 Thine image, Lord, bestow,
Thy presence and Thy love;
I ask to serve Thee here below,
And reign with Thee above.

5 Teach me to live by faith;
Conform my will to thine:
Let me victorious be in death,
And then in glory shine.
Rev. J. Newton.

21 *Importunity in Prayer.*

1 Jesus, who knows full well
The heart of every saint,
Invites us all our griefs to tell,
To pray, and never faint.

22 *"Sweet is Thy Mercy."*

1 Sweet is Thy mercy, Lord;
Before Thy mercy-seat
My soul, adoring, pleads Thy word,
And owns Thy mercy sweet.

2 Wher'er Thy name is blest,
Wher'er Thy people meet,
There I delight in Thee to rest,
And find Thy mercy sweet.

3 Light Thou my weary way,
Place Thou my weary feet,
That while I stray on earth I may
Still find Thy mercy sweet.

4 Thus shall the heavenly host
Hear all my songs repeat
To Father, Son, and Holy Ghost,
My joy, thy mercy sweet.
Rev. J. S. B. Monsell.

HEBRON. **L. M.** *Lowell Mason.*

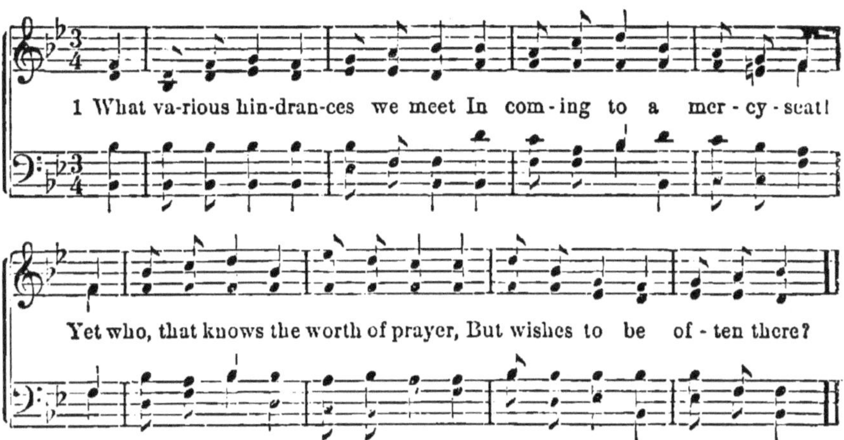

23 *The Mercy-Seat.*

2 Prayer makes the darkened cloud withdraw,
Prayer climbs the ladder Jacob saw;
Gives exercise to faith and love;
Brings every blessing from above.

3 Restraining prayer, we cease to fight;
Prayer makes the Christian's armor bright;
And Satan trembles when he sees
The weakest saint upon his knees.

4 Have you no words? ah! think again;
Words flow apace when you complain,
And fill your fellow-creature's ear
With the sad tale of all your care.

5 Were half the breath thus vainly spent,
To Heaven in supplication sent,
Your cheerful song would oftener be,
"Hear what the Lord has done for me."

William Cowper.

24 *"Where Two or Three."*

1 Where two or three, with sweet accord,
Obedient to their sovereign Lord,
Meet to recount His acts of grace,
And offer solemn prayer and praise:

2 There, says the Saviour, will I be,
Amid this little company;
To them unveil My smiling face,
And shed My glories round the place.

3 We meet at Thy command, dear Lord,
Relying on Thy faithful word:
Now send Thy Spirit from above,
Now fill our hearts with heavenly love.

Rev. Samuel Stennett.

25 *"Love One Another."*

1 O Lord, how joyful 'tis to see
The brethren join in love to Thee:
On Thee alone their heart relies;
Their only strength Thy grace supplies.

2 How sweet, within Thy holy place,
With one accord to sing Thy grace,
Besieging Thine attentive ear
With all the force of fervent prayer.

3 Lord, shower upon us from above
The sacred gift of mutual love;
Each other's wants may we supply,
And reign together in the sky.

Tr. by Rev. John Chandler.

ULEA. **H. M.** *Lowell Mason.*

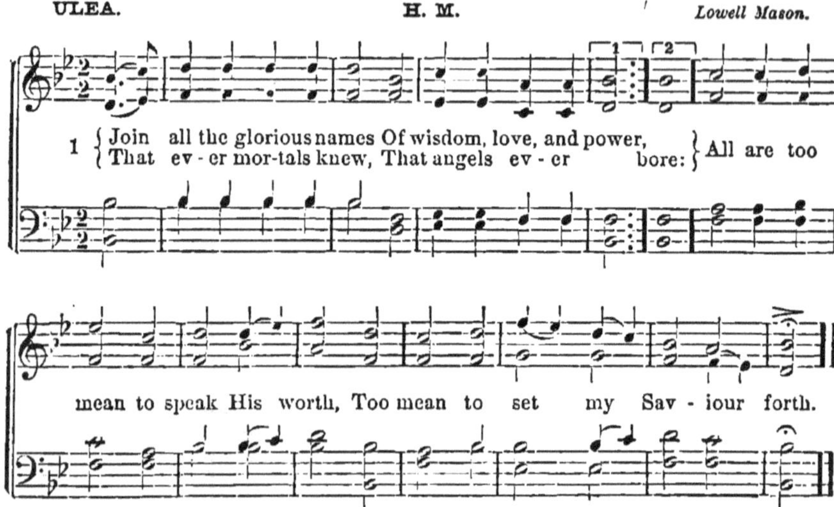

26

"Chosen of God, and Precious."

2 Great Prophet of our God!
My tongue would bless Thy name;
By Thee the joyful news
Of our salvation came:
The joyful news of sins forgiven,
Of hell subdued, and peace with Heav'n.

3 Jesus, our great High Priest,
Offered His blood, and died;
My guilty conscience seeks
No sacrifice beside:
His powerful blood did once atone,
And now it pleads before the throne.

4 O Thou Almighty Lord!
My Conqueror and my King!
Thy scepter and Thy sword,
Thy reigning grace I sing:
Thine is the power; behold, I sit,
In willing bonds, beneath Thy feet.

Isaac Watts.

27

Rev. 15:3, 4.

1 O holy, holy Lord,
Creation's sovereign King,
Thy majesty adored,
Let all Thy creatures sing:
Who wast, and art, and art to be;
Nor time shall see Thy sway depart.

2 Great are Thy works of praise,
O God of boundless might!
All just and true Thy ways,
Thou King of saints in light!
Let all above, and all below,
Conspire to show Thy power and love.

3 Who shall not fear Thee, Lord!
And magnify Thy name?
Thy judgments sent abroad,
Thy holiness proclaim:
Nations shall throng from every shore,
And Thee adore in holy song.

4 While all the powers on high
Their swelling chorus raise,
Let earth and man reply,
And echo back Thy praise:
Thy glory own, first, last, and best,
God ever blest, And God alone!

Anon.

NOEL. **C. M.** *Lowell Mason.*

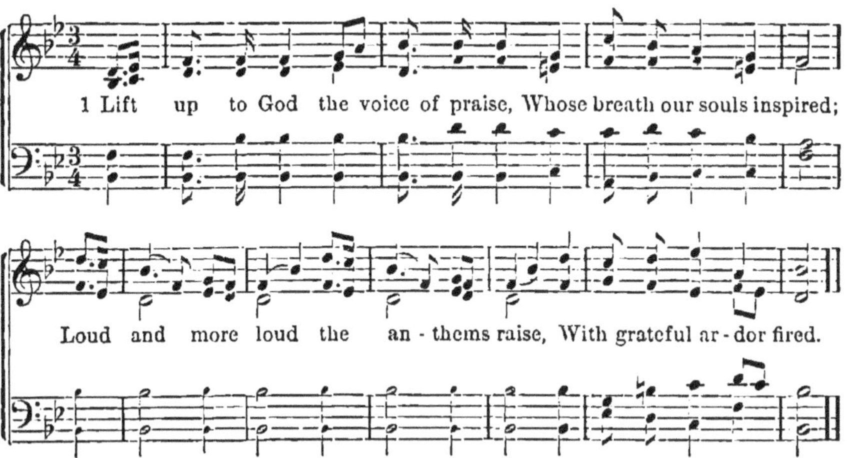

28 *"The Voice of Praise."*

2 Lift up to God the voice of praise,
Whose goodness, passing thought,
Loads every moment, as it flies,
With benefits unsought.

3 Lift up to God the voice of praise,
From whom salvation flows;
Who sent his Son our souls to save
From everlasting woes.

4 Lift up to God the voice of praise,
For hope's transporting ray,
Which lights through darkest shades of death,
To realms of endless day.

Wardlaw.

29 *Psalm* 136.

1 Oh, praise the Lord! for He is good;
In Him we rest obtain:
His mercy has through ages stood,
And ever shall remain.

2 Let all the people of the Lord
His praises spread around;
Let them His grace and love record,
Who have salvation found.

3 Now let the east in Him rejoice,
The west its tribute bring,
The north and south lift up their voice
In honor of their King.

Wrangham.

30 *"His tender mercies are over all His Works."*

1 Thy goodness, Lord, our souls confess;
Thy goodness we adore:
A spring whose blessings never fail;
A sea without a shore!

2 Thy bounty every season crowns
With all the bliss it yields;
With joyful clusters loads the vines,
With strengthening grain, the fields.

3 But chiefly Thy compassion, Lord,
Is in the gospel seen;
There, like a sun, Thy mercy shines,
Without a cloud between.

4 There pardon, peace, and holy joy,
Through Jesus' name are given;
He on the cross was lifted high,
That we might reign in Heaven.

Gibbons.

SILVER STREET. **S. M.** *Isaac Smith.*

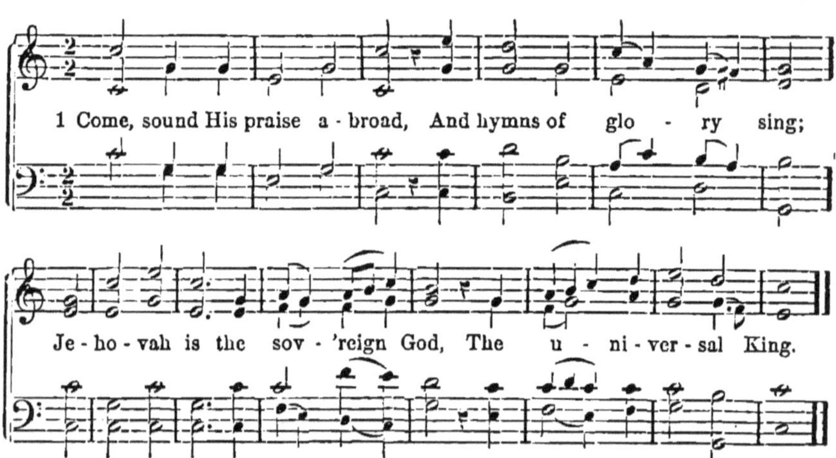

31 *Psalm 95.*

2 He formed the deeps unknown;
He gave the seas their bound;
The watery worlds are all His own,
And all the solid ground.

3 Come, worship at His throne;
Come, bow before the Lord;
We are His works, and not our own;
He formed us by His word.

4 To-day attend His voice,
Nor dare provoke His rod;
Come, like the people of His choice,
And own your gracious God.

Isaac Watts.

32 *Glory to the Lamb.*

1 Awake, and sing the song
Of glory to the Lamb!
Wake every heart and every tongue
To praise the Saviour's name.

2 Sing of His dying love,
Sing of His rising power;
Sing how He intercedes above,
For those whose sins He bore.

3 Sing on your heavenly way,
Ye sons of glory, sing;
Sing on rejoicing every day,
In Christ, th' eternal King!

4 Soon shall we hear Him say,
"Ye blessed children, come!"
Soon shall He call you hence away,
And take His wanderers home.

5 There shall our raptured tongue
His endless praise proclaim,
And sweeter voices swell the song
Of glory to the Lamb.

William Hammond.

33 *Close of Worship.*

1 Once more, before we part,
Oh, bless the Saviour's name;
Let every tongue and every heart
Adore and praise the same.

2 Lord, in Thy grace we came,
That blessing still impart;
We met in Jesus' sacred name,
In Jesus' name we part.

Joseph Hart

ERNAN. L. M. *Lowell Mason.*

34 *Praise for Salvation.*

2 Praises to Him, in grace who came,
To bear our woe, and sin, and shame;
Who lived to die, who died to rise,
The God accepted sacrifice.

3 Praises to Him the chain who broke,
Opened the prison, burst the yoke,
Sent forth its captives glad and free,
Heirs of an endless liberty.

4 Praises to Him who sheds abroad
Within our hearts the love of God
The Spirit of all truth and peace,
Fountain of joy and holiness!

5 To Father, Son, and Spirit now
The hands we lift, the knees we bow;
To Thee, Jehovah, thus we raise
The sinner's endless song of praise.

Rev. H. Bonar.

35 *God's Unspeakable Glory.*

1 Come, O my soul, in sacred lays
Attempt thy great Creator's praise;
But oh, what tongue can speak His fame?
What mortal verse can reach the theme?

2 Enthroned amid the radiant spheres,
He glory like a garment wears;
To form a robe of light divine,
Ten thousand suns around Him shine.

3 In all our Maker's grand designs,
Almighty power with wisdom shines;
His works, through all this wondrous frame,
Declare the glory of His name.

4 Raised on devotion's lofty wing,
Do thou, my soul, His glories sing;
And let His praise employ thy tongue,
Till listening worlds shall join the song

Rev. T. Blacklock.

36 *Brief Call to Praise Christ.*

1 Worthy the Lamb of boundless sway,
In earth and Heaven the Lord of all:
Let all the powers of earth obey,
And low before his footstool fall.

2 Higher, still higher, swell the strain;
Creation's voice the note prolong!
Jesus, the Lamb, shall ever reign:
Let hallelujahs crown the song!

Anon.

7. *Rev. Cæsar Malan.*

37

Psalm 136.

2 He, with all-commanding might,
Filled the new made world with light:
For His mercies shall endure,
Ever faithful, ever sure.

3 All things living He doth feed,
His full hand supplies their need:
For His mercies shall endure,
Ever faithful, ever sure.

4 Let us therefore warble forth
His high majesty and worth:
For His mercies shall endure,
Ever faithful, ever sure.

John Milton.

38

"Hallowed be Thy Name."

1 Holy, holy, holy Lord,
In the highest heavens adored,
Author of all nature's frame,—
Father, hallowed be Thy name.

2 Born anew, oh, may we feel
Filial love, the Spirit's seal!
Cleansed from guilt, redeemed from shame:
Father, hallowed be Thy name.

3 When in want, or when in wealth,
Joy or sorrow, pain or health,
Still our prayer shall be the same:
Father, hallowed be Thy name.

Conder.

39

Thanksgiving for a Revival.

1 Fount of everlasting love!
Rich Thy streams of mercy are—
Flowing purely from above,
Beauty marks their course afar.

2 Lo! Thy church, Thy garden, now
Blooms beneath the heavenly shower;
Sinners feel, and melt, and bow:
Mild, yet mighty, is Thy power.

3 God of grace, before Thy throne
Here our warmest thanks we bring;
Thine the glory, Thine alone:
Loudest praise to Thee we sing.

4 Hear, oh, hear our grateful song;
Let Thy Spirit still descend;
Roll the tide of grace along,
Widening, deepening to the end.

Palmer.

ALVAN. **8, 7, 4.**

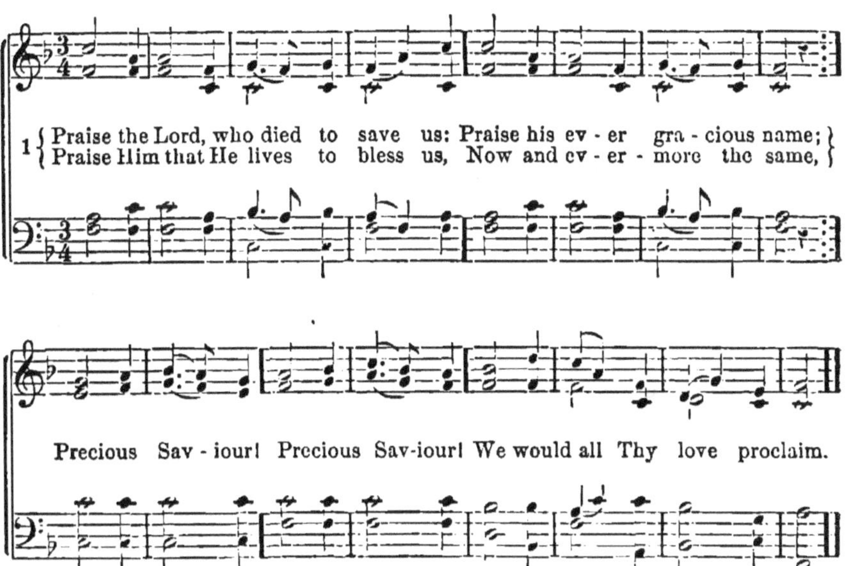

40 *"For by grace are ye saved."*

2 Grace it was, yea, grace abounding,
Brought Thee down to save the lost;
Ye above, His throne surrounding,
Praise Him, praise Him, all His host.
Saints, adore Him,
Ye are they who owe Him most.

3 We, of all His hand created,
Objects are of grace alone,
By eternal love elected,
Destined now to share His throne.
Sing with wonder,
Sing of what our Lord hath done.

4 Praise His name who died to save us;
'Tis by Him His people live;
And in Him the Father gave us
All that boundless love could give:
Life eternal
In our Saviour we receive.

Anon.

41 *"Honor and glory and blessing."*

1 Glory, glory everlasting
Be to Him who bore the cross!
Who redeemed our souls by tasting
Death—the death deserved by us:
Spread His glory,
Who redeemed His people thus!

2 His is love! 'tis love unbounded,
Without measure, without end:
Human thought is here confounded:
'Tis too vast to comprehend.
Praise the Saviour!
Magnify the sinner's Friend!

3 While we hear the wondrous story
Of the Saviour's cross and shame,
Sing we, "Everlasting glory
Be to God and to the Lamb!"
Hallelujah!
Give ye glory to His name!

Anon.

ITALIAN HYMN. 6, 4. *Giardini.*

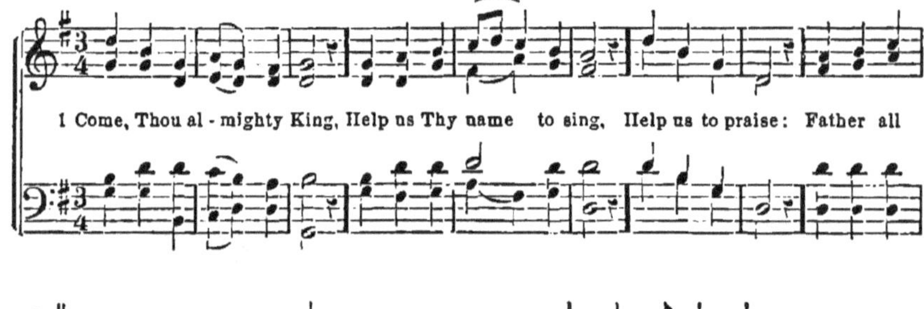

42 *The Trinity Invoked.*

2 Come, Thou Incarnate Word,
Gird on Thy mighty sword,
Our prayer attend:
Come, and Thy people bless,
And give Thy Word success;
Spirit of holiness,
On us descend.

3 Come, Holy Comforter,
Thy sacred witness bear
In this glad hour:
Thou who Almighty art,
Now rule in every heart,
And ne'er from us depart,
Spirit of power.

Rev. Charles Wesley.

43 *"At the name of Jesus every knee should bow."*

1 Let us awake our joys;
Strike up with cheerful voice;
Each creature sing:
Angels! begin the song;
Mortals! the strain prolong,
In accents sweet and strong,
"Jesus is King!"

2 Proclaim abroad His name;
Tell of His matchless fame;
What wonders done!
Above, beneath, around,
Let all the earth resound,
Till heaven's high arch rebound,
"Vict'ry is won!"

3 He vanquished sin and hell,
And our last foe will quell:
Mourners, rejoice!
His dying love adore;
Praise Him, now raised in power:
Praise Him for evermore,
With joyful voice.

4 All hail the glorious day,
When, through the heavenly way,
Lo, He shall come!
While they who pierced Him wail;
His promise shall not fail;
Saints, see your King prevail:
Great Saviour, come!

Kingsbury.

DORT. **6, 4.** *Lowell Mason.*

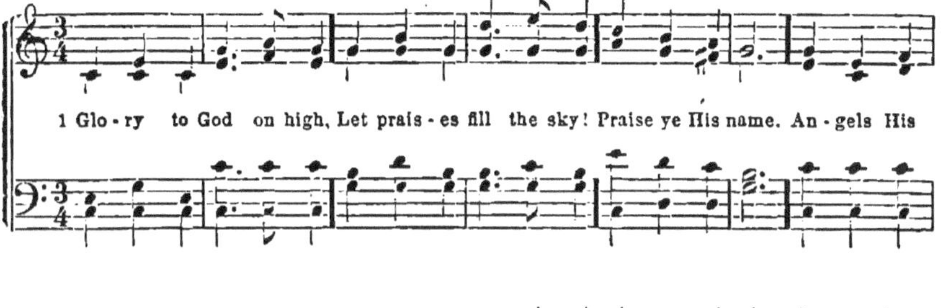

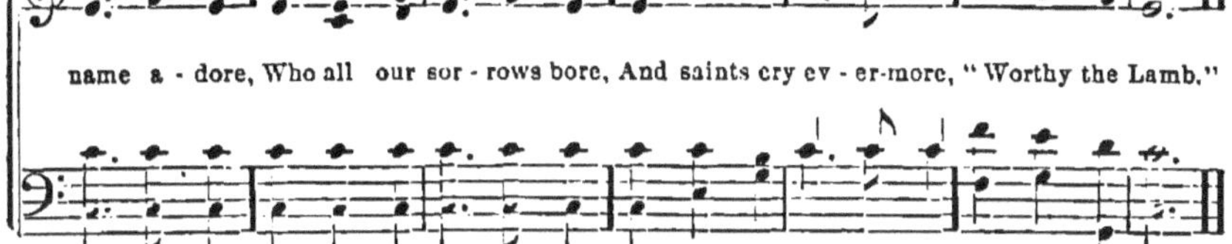

44 *"Worthy the Lamb."*

2 All they around the throne
Cheerfully join in one,
  Praising His name.
We who have felt His blood
Sealing our peace with God,
Spread His dear fame abroad:
  "Worthy the Lamb!"

3 To Him our hearts we raise;
None else shall have our praise·
  Praise ye His name!
Him, our exalted Lord,
By us below adored,
We praise with one accord,
  "Worthy the Lamb!"

4 Though we must change our place,
Our souls shall never cease
  Praising His name;
To Him we'll tribute bring,
Laud Him our gracious King,
And without ceasing sing,
  "Worthy the Lamb!"

Rev. James Allen.

45 *Praise to Jesus.*

1 Come, all ye saints of God,
Wide through the earth abroad
  Spread Jesus' fame;
Tell what His love has done;
Trust in His name alone;
Shout to His lofty throne,
  "Worthy the Lamb!"

2 Hence! gloomy doubts and fears;
Dry up your mournful tears;
  Join our glad theme;
Beauty for ashes bring;
Strike each melodious string;
Join heart and voice to sing,
  "Worthy the Lamb!"

3 Hark, how the choirs above,
Filled with the Saviour's love,
  Dwell on His name;
There, too, may we be found,
With light and glory crowned,
While all the heavens resound,
  "Worthy the Lamb."

Rev. James Boden.

SONG. 8, 5. *German Melody.*

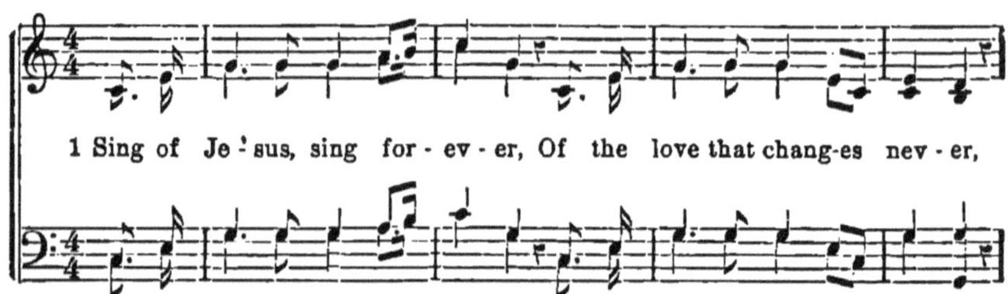

46 *"Sing unto the Lord."*

2 With His blood the Lord has bought them;
When they knew Him not, He sought them,
And from all their wanderings brought them;
His the praise alone.

3 Through the desert Jesus leads them,
With the bread of Heaven He feeds them,
And through all the way He speeds them
To their home above.

4 There they see the Lord who bought them,
Him who came from Heaven and sought them,
Him who by His Spirit taught them,
Him they serve and love.

Rev. T. Kelly.

47 *Heb. 12:15.*

1 Praise the Saviour, ye who know Him!
Who can tell how much we owe Him?
Gladly let us render to Him
All we have and are.

2 Jesus is the name that charms us,
He for conflict fits and arms us;
Nothing moves, and nothing harms us
When we trust in Him.

3 Trust in Him, ye saints, forever;
He is faithful, changing never;
Neither force nor guile can sever
Those He loves from Him.

4 Keep us, Lord, oh, keep us cleaving
To Thyself, and still believing,
Till the hour of our receiving
Promised joys in Heaven.

5 Then we shall be where we would be;
Then we shall be what we should be;
Things which are not now, nor could be,
Then shall be our own.

Anon.

MARLOW. C. M. *English Melody.*

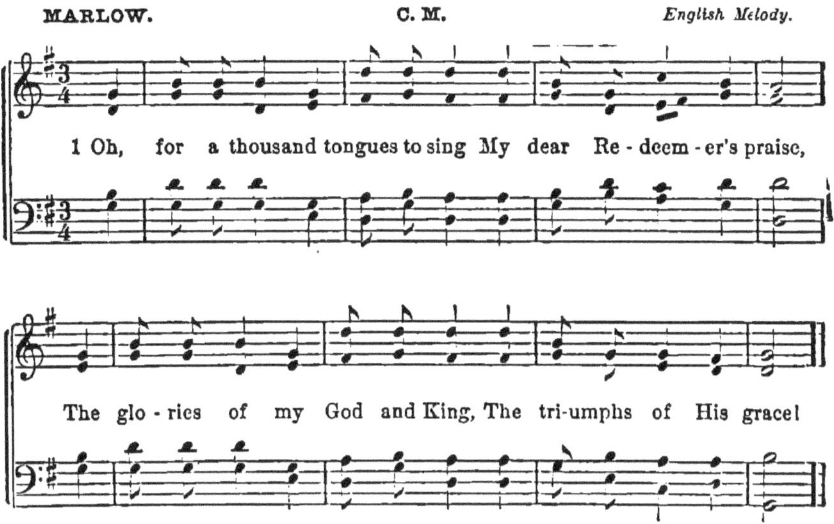

48 *"Thou shalt call His name Jesus.*

2 My gracious Master and my God,
Assist me to proclaim,
To spread through all the earth abroad
The honors of Thy name.

3 Jesus! the name that calms our fears,
That bids our sorrows cease—
'Tis music to my ravished ears,
'Tis life, and health, and peace.

4 He breaks the power of reigning sin,
He sets the prisoner free;
His blood can make the foulest clean,
His blood avails for me.

C. Wesley.

49 *"Under the shadow of The Almighty."*

1 Through all the changing scenes of life,
In trouble and in joy,
The praises of my God shall still
My heart and tongue employ.

2 The hosts of God encamp around
The dwellings of the just;
Deliverance he affords to all
Who on His succor trust.

3 Oh, make but trial of His love:
Experience will decide
How blest are they, and only they,
Who in His truth confide.

4 Fear Him, ye saints, and ye will then
Have nothing else to fear;
Make ye His service your delight,
He'll make your wants His care.

Tate and Brady.

50 *"Not to condemn, but save."*

1 Come, happy souls, approach your God,
With new, melodious songs;
Come, render to almighty grace
The tribute of your tongues.

2 So strange, so boundless was the love
That pitied dying men,
The Father sent his equal Son
To give them life again.

3 See, dearest Lord, our willing souls
Accept Thine offered grace;
We bless the great Redeemer's love,
And give the Father praise.

I. Watts.

NETTLETON. **8, 7. D.** *Rev. A. Nettleton.*

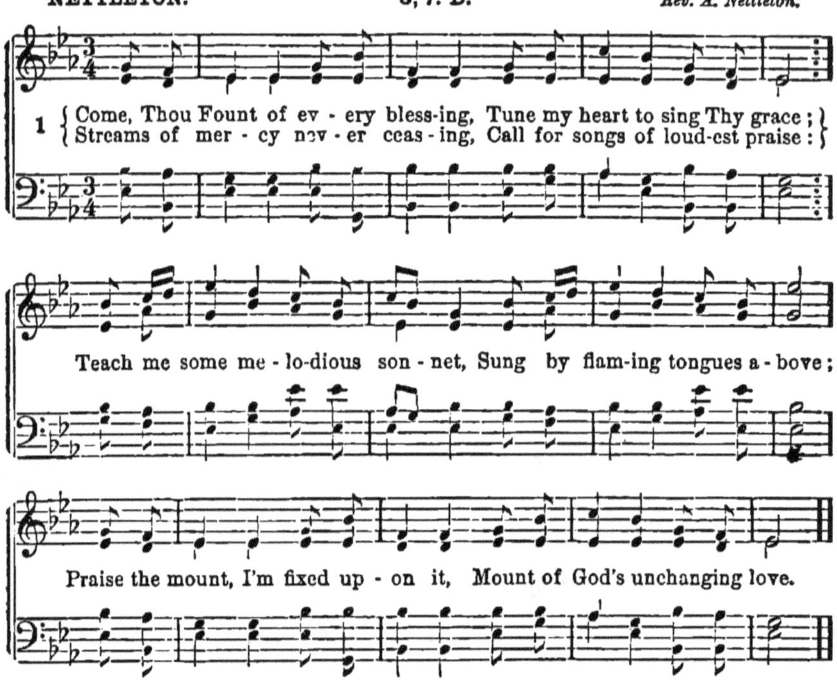

51 *Grateful Recollection.*

2 Here I raise my Ebenezer,
  Hither by Thy help I'm come ;
And I hope, by Thy good pleasure,
  Safely to arrive at home.
Jesus sought me, when a stranger,
  Wandering from the fold of God ;
He, to rescue me from danger,
  Interposed His precious blood.

3 Oh, to grace how great a debtor,
  Daily I'm constrained to be ;
Let Thy goodness, as a fetter,
  Bind my wandering heart to Thee.
Prone to wander, Lord, I feel it,
  Prone to leave the God I love ;
Here's my heart, oh, take and seal it,
  Seal it for Thy courts above.

Rev. R. Robinson.

52* *Ps. ciii.*

1 Praise, my soul, the King of Heaven ;
  To His feet thy tribute bring,
Ransomed, healed, restored, forgiven,
  Evermore His praises sing :
    Alleluia ! Alleluia !
  Praise the everlasting King.

2 Praise Him for His grace and favor
  To our fathers in distress ;
Praise Him still the same as ever,
  Slow to chide, and swift to bless :
    Alleluia ! Alleluia !
  Glorious in his faithfulness.

3 Father-like, He tends and spares us,
  Well our feeble frame He knows ;
In His hands He gently bears us,
  Rescues us from all our foes :
    Alleluia ! Alleluia !
  Praise with us the God of grace.

*Omit repeat. *Rev. H. F. Lyte.*

C. M. *A. Chapin.*

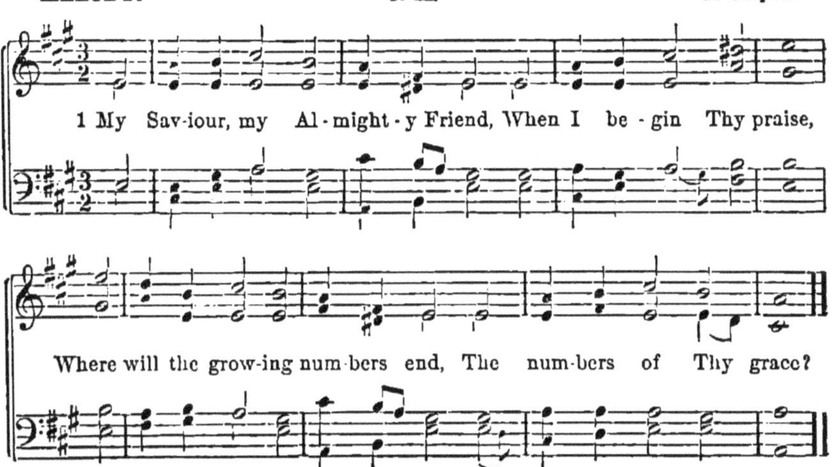

53 *Christ our Strength.*

2 Thou art my everlasting trust,
Thy goodness I adore;
And since I knew Thy graces first,
I speak Thy glories more.

3 When I am filled with sore distress
For some surprising sin,
I'll plead Thy perfect righteousness,
And mention none but Thine.

4 How will my lips rejoice to tell
The victories of my King!
My soul, redeemed from sin and hell,
Shall Thy salvation sing.

Isaac Watts.

54 *"Praise ye the Lord."*

1 "Praise ye the Lord," again, again,
The Spirit strikes the chord;
Nor toucheth He our hearts in vain;
We praise, we praise the Lord.

2 "Rejoice in Him," again, again,
The Spirit speaks the word;
And faith takes up the happy strain;
Our joy is in the Lord.

3 "Stand fast in Christ," ah! yet again,
He teaches all the band;
If human effort's all in vain,
In Christ it is we stand.

4 "Clean every whit;" Thou saidst it, Lord:
Shall one suspicion lurk?
Thine, surely is a faithful word,
And Thine a finished work.

5 Forever be the glory given
To Thee, O Lamb of God!
Our every joy on earth, in Heaven,
We owe it to Thy blood.

Anon.

55 *"Unto Him who hath redeemed us."*

1 Unto the Lamb that once was slain,
Be endless honors paid!
Salvation, glory, joy remain
Forever on Thy head!

2 Thou hast redeemed our souls with blood,
Hast set the prisoners free;
Hast made us kings and priests to God,
And we shall reign with Thee.

Anon

HARWELL. 8, 7, D. *Lowell Mason.*

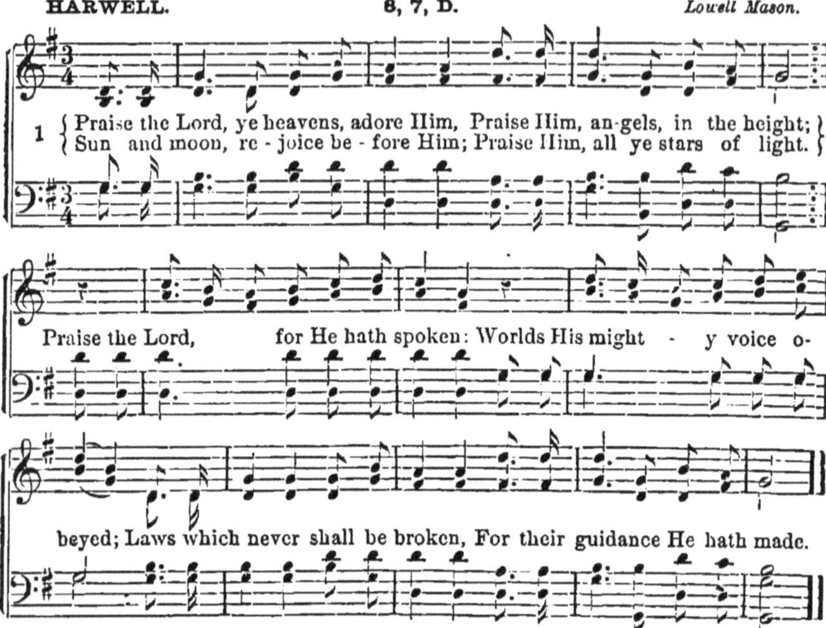

56 *Praise from the Whole Creation.*

2 Praise the Lord, for He is glorious;
Never shall His promise fail;
God hath made His saints victorious;
Sin and death shall not prevail.
Praise the God of our salvation;
Hosts on high, His power proclaim;
Heaven and earth, and all creation,
Laud and magnify His name.

3 Worship, honor, glory, blessing,
Lord, we offer unto Thee;
Young and old, Thy praise confessing,
In glad homage bend the knee.
As the saints in Heaven adore Thee,
We would bow before Thy throne;
As Thine angels serve before Thee,
So on earth Thy will be done.

Rev. John Kempthorne.

57 *Thrice Holy.*

1 Round the Lord in glory seated,
Cherubim and seraphim
Filled His temple, and repeated
Each to each th' alternate hymn:
"Lord, Thy glory fills the Heaven,
"Earth is with its fullness stored;
"Unto Thee be glory given,
"Holy, holy, holy Lord!"

2 Heaven is still with glory ringing;
Earth takes up the angels' cry,
"Holy, holy, holy singing,
"Lord of Hosts, the Lord Most High."
With His seraph train before Him,
With His holy Church below,
Thus conspire we to adore Him,
Bid we thus our anthem flow:

3 "Lord, Thy glory fills the Heaven,
Earth is with its fullness stored:
Unto Thee be glory given,
Holy, holy, holy Lord!"
Thus Thy glorious name confessing
We adopt the angels' cry,
Holy, holy, holy! blessing
Thee the Lord of Hosts Most High.

Richard Mant.

WILMOT. 8, 7. *Von Weber.*

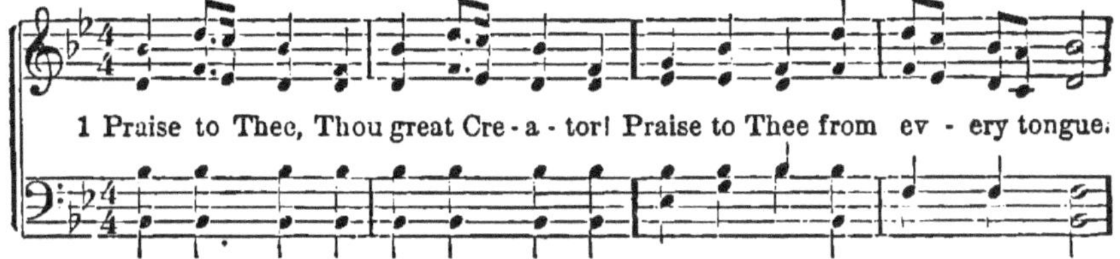

58 *Praise to Jehovah.*

2 Father, source of all compassion,
Pure, unbounded grace is Thine;
Hail the God of our salvation!
Praise Him for His love divine.

3 For ten thousand blessings given,
For the hope of future joy,
Sound His praise thro' earth and heaven,
Sound Jehovah's praise on high.

4 Joyfully on earth adore Him,
Till in Heaven our song we raise;
There, enraptured, fall before Him,
Lost in wonder, love, and praise.

Fawcett.

59 *Brief Ascription of Praise.*

1 Worship, honor, glory, blessing,
Lord, we offer to Thy name;
Young and old, their thanks expressing,
Join Thy goodness to proclaim.

2 As the hosts of Heaven adore Thee,
We, too, bow before Thy throne;
As the angels serve before Thee,
So on earth Thy will be done.

Anon.

60 *"Blessed be Thou."*

1 Blest be Thou, O God of Israel!
Thou, our Father and our Lord!
Majesty is Thine forever;
Ever be Thy name adored.

2 Riches come of Thee, and honor;
Power and might to Thee belong;
Thine it is to make us prosper,
Only Thine to make us strong.

3 Lord, our God, for these Thy bounties,
Hymns of gratitude we raise;
To Thy name, forever glorious,
Ever we address our praise.

Anon.

61 *Doxology.*

1 Praise the God of our salvation,
Praise the Father's boundless love;
Praise the Lamb, our expiation;
Praise the Spirit from above;

2 Praise the Fountain of salvation,
Him by whom our spirits live;
Undivided adoration
To the one Jehovah give!

THINE THE GLORY. *English Melody.*

62 *Thine the Glory.*

2 We praise Thee, O God! for Thy Spirit of light,
Who has shown us our Saviour, and scattered our night.

All glory and praise to the Lamb that was slain,
Who has borne all our sins, and has cleansed every stain.

4 All glory and praise to the God of all grace,
Who has bought us, and sought us, and guided our ways.

5 Revive us again; fill each heart with Thy love;
May each soul be rekindled with fire from above.

Rev. W. P. Mackay.

63 *Sound His Praises.*

1 Rejoice and be glad! The Redeemer has come!
Go look on His cradle, His cross, and His tomb!

CHORUS.

Sound His praises, tell the story of Him who was slain;
Sound His praises, tell with gladness, He liveth again.

2 Rejoice and be glad! it is sunshine at last!
The clouds have departed, the shadows are past.

3 Rejoice and be glad! for the blood hath been shed!
Redemption is finished, the price hath been paid.

4 Rejoice and be glad! now the pardon is free!
The Just for the unjust has died on the tree.

5 Rejoice and be glad! for the Lamb that was slain
O'er death is triumphant, and liveth again.

6 Rejoice and be glad! for our King is on high;
He pleadeth for us, on His throne in the sky.

7 Rejoice and be glad! for He cometh again;
He cometh in glory, the Lamb that was slain.

H. Bonar.

64 *Revive Us Again.*

1 My God, I have found the thrice blessed ground,
Where life, and where joy and true comfort abound.

CHORUS.
Hallelujah, Thine the glory, Hallelujah, Amen.
Hallelujah, Thine the glory, revive us again.

2 'Tis found in the blood of Him who once stood
My refuge and safety, my surety with God.

3 He bore on the tree the sentence for me,
And now both the Surety and sinner are free.

4 Accepted I am in the once-offered Lamb;
It was God who Himself had devised the plan.

5 And though here below, 'mid sorrow and woe,
My place is in Heaven with Jesus, I know.

6 And this I shall find, for such is His mind,
He'll not be in glory and leave me behind.

7 For soon He will come, and take me safe home,
And make me to sit with Himself on His throne.
Rowland Hill.

LOVING-KINDNESS. L. M. *Western Melody.*

65 *"The loving-kindness of the Lord."*

2 He saw me ruined in the fall,
Yet loved me notwithstanding all,
And saved me from my lost estate,
His loving-kindness is so great.

3 Through mighty hosts of cruel foes,
Where earth and hell my way oppose,
He safely leads my soul along,
His loving-kindness is so strong.
Rev. Samuel Medley.

OLD HUNDRED. L. M. *Guillaume Franc.*

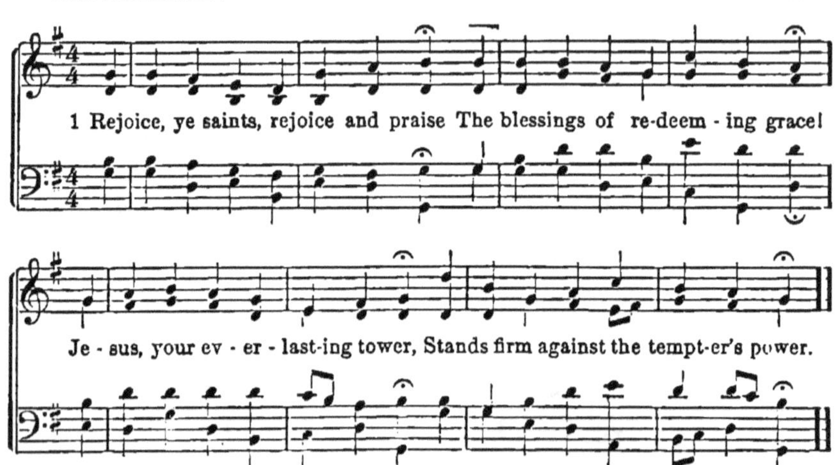

66 *"The Lord is our refuge."*

2 He is a refuge ever nigh;
His love endures as mountains high;
His name's a rock, which winds above,
And waves below, can never move.

3 Rejoice, ye saints, rejoice and praise
The blessings of this wondrous grace!
Jesus, your everlasting tower,
Can bear, unmov'd, the tempest's power.

4 For why? the Lord our God is good,
His mercy is forever sure;
His truth at all times firmly stood,
And shall from age to age endure.

W. Kethe.

67 *Psalm* 100.

1 All people that on earth do dwell,
Sing to the Lord with cheerful voice:
Him serve with mirth, his praise forth tell,
Come ye before Him and rejoice.

2 Know that the Lord is God indeed;
Without our aid He did us make:
We are his flock, He doth us feed,
And for His sheep He doth us take.

3 Oh, enter, then, His gates with praise,
Approach with joy His courts unto:
Praise, laud, and bless His name always,
For it is seemly so to do.

68 *Doxology.*

Praise God, from whom all blessings flow,
Praise Him, all creatures here below;
Praise Him above, ye heavenly host;
Praise Father, Son, and Holy Ghost.

T. Ken.

69 *Doxology.*

To God the Father, God the Son,
And God the Spirit, Three in One,
Be honor, praise, and glory given,
By all on earth, and all in Heaven.

I. Watts.

70 *Psalm* 117.

1 From all that dwell below the skies,
Let the Creator's praise arise;
Let the Redeemer's name be sung,
Through every land, by every tongue.

2 Eternal are Thy mercies, Lord!
Eternal truth attends Thy word;
Thy praise shall sound from shore to shore,
Till suns shall rise and set no more.

I. Watts.

UXBRIDGE. L. M. *Lowell Mason.*

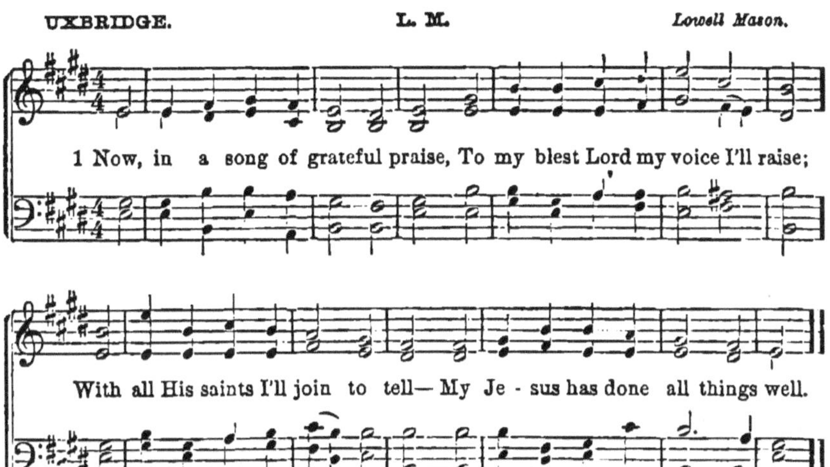

71 *"He doeth all things well."*

2 All worlds His glorious power confess,
His wisdom all His works express;
But, oh, His love what tongue can tell!
My Jesus has done all things well.

3 And since my soul has known His love,
What mercies has He made me prove!
Mercies which do all praise excel!
My Jesus has done all things well.

4 And when to that bright world I rise,
And join the anthems of the skies,
Above the rest this note shall swell—
My Jesus has done all things well.

Anon.

72 *The Atoning Priest.*

1 Now to the Lord, who makes us know
The wonders of His dying love,
Be humble honors paid below,
And strains of nobler praise above.

2 'Twas He who cleansed our foulest sins,
And washed us in His precious blood;
'Tis He who makes us priests and kings,
And brings us rebels near to God.

3 To Jesus, our atoning Priest,
To Jesus, our eternal King,
Be everlasting power confessed!
Let every tongue His glory sing.

I. Watts.

73 *"The Lord reigneth."*

1 The Lord is King: lift up thy voice
O earth, and all ye heavens rejoice;
From world to world the joy shall ring,
The Lord Omnipotent is King.

2 The Lord is King: who then shall dare
Resist His will, distrust His care,
Or murmur at His wise decrees,
Or doubt His royal promises?

3 The Lord is King: child of the dust,
The Judge of all the earth is just;
Holy and true are all His ways:
Let every creature speak His praise.

4 Oh, when His wisdom can mistake,
His might decay, His love forsake,
Then may His children cease to sing,
The Lord Omnipotent is King.

Josiah Conder.

OVIO. 8, 7. *Sab. Hymn & Tune Book.*

74 *"I would love Thee."*

2 I would love Thee! every blessing
Flows to me from out Thy throne:
I would love Thee—he who loves Thee
Never feels himself alone.

3 I would love Thee! look upon me,
Ever guide me with Thine eye:
I would love Thee! if not nourished
By Thy love, my soul would die.

4 I would love Thee! may Thy brightness
Dazzle my rejoicing eyes!
I would love Thee! may Thy goodness
Watch from Heaven o'er all I prize.

5 I would love Thee! I have vowed it;
On Thy love my heart is set:
While I love Thee I will never
My Redeemer's blood forget.

From the French.

75 *"God is love."* 1 John 4:8.

1 God is love; His mercy brightens
All the path in which we rove;
Bliss He wakes, and woe He lightens:
God is wisdom, God is love.

2 Chance and change are busy ever;
Man decays, and ages move:
But His mercy waneth never;
God is wisdom, God is love.

3 Ev'n the hour that darkest seemeth
Will His changeless goodness prove;
From the gloom His brightness streameth:
God is wisdom, God is love.

4 He, with earthly cares entwineth
Hope and comfort from above;
Everywhere His glory shineth:
God is wisdom, God is love.

Browning.

76 *A Parting Blessing.*

1 Lord, dismiss us with Thy blessing;
Bid us all depart in peace;
Still on gospel manna feeding,
Pure seraphic joys increase.

2 Fill our hearts with consolation;
Unto Thee our voices raise;
When we reach that blissful station,
We will give Thee nobler praise.

Edward Smyth.

FLEET STREET. **H. M.** *Sab. Hymn & Tune Book.*

hearts and voices bring: Sound, sound thro' all the earth abroad, The love, th' e-ter - nal love of God.

77 *"God so loved the world."*

2 Unnumbered myriads stand,
  Of seraphs bright and fair;
Or bow at His right hand,
  And pay their homage there:
But strive in vain, with loudest chord,
To sound the wondrous love of God.

3 Though earth and hell assail,
  And doubts and fears arise,
The weakest shall prevail,
  And grasp the heavenly prize;
And through an endless age record
The love, th' unchanging love of God.

J. Young.

78 *God our Preserver.*

1 Upward I lift mine eyes,
  From God is all my aid;
The God that built the skies,
  And earth and nature made:
God is the tower to which I fly:
His grace is nigh in every hour.

2 My feet shall never slide,
  And fall in fatal snares,
Since God, my guard and guide,
  Defends me from my fears:
Those wakeful eyes that never sleep,
Shall Israel keep when dangers rise.

3 No burning heats by day,
  Nor blasts of evening air,
Shall take my health away,
  If God be with me there:
Thou art my sun, and Thou my shade,
To guard my head by night o[illegible]on.

4 Hast Thou not given Thy word
  To save my soul from death?
And I can trust my Lord
  To keep my mortal breath:
I'll go and come, nor fear to die,
Till from on high Thou call me home.

Isaac Watts.

TYNG. 7, 6. *Sab. Hymn and Tune Book.*

79 *Everlasting.*

2 Our years are like the shadows
On sunny hills that lie,
Or grasses in the meadows
That blossom but to die:
A sleep, a dream, a story,
By strangers quickly told,
An unremaining glory
Of things that soon are old.

3 O Thou who canst not slumber,
Whose light grows never pale,
Teach us aright to number
Our years before they fail!
On us Thy mercy lighten,
On us Thy goodness rest,
And let Thy Spirit brighten
The hearts Thyself hast blessed!

F. Bickersteth.

80 *"The Lord is my salvation."*

1 God is my strong salvation;
What foe have I to fear?
In darkness and temptation,
My Light, my Help is near.

2 Though hosts encamp around me,
Firm in the fight I stand;
What terror can confound me,
With God at my right hand?

3 Place on the Lord reliance;
My soul, with courage wait;
His truth be thine affiance,
When faint and desolate.

4 His might thy heart shall strengthen,
His love thy joy increase;
Mercy thy days shall lengthen;
The Lord will give thee peace!

Montgomery.

HORTON. 7. *Xavier Schnyder Von Wartensee.*

81 *"Holy, holy, holy is the Lord of hosts."*

2 Though unworthy, Lord, Thine ear
Deigns our humble songs to hear;
Purer praise we hope to bring,
When around Thy throne we sing.

3 While on earth ordained to stay,
Guide our footsteps in Thy way,
Till we come to dwell with Thee,
Till we all Thy glory see.

4 Then with angel-harps again
We will wake a nobler strain;
There, in joyful songs of praise,
Our triumphant voices raise.

Anon.

82 *"My times are in Thy hand."*

1 Sovereign Ruler of the skies,
Ever gracious, ever wise!
All my times are in Thy hand;
All events at Thy command.

2 Times of sickness, times of health,
Times of penury and wealth,—
All must come, and last, and end
As shall please my heavenly Friend.

3 O Thou gracious, wise and just!
In Thy hands my life I trust;
Have I somewhat dearer still?—
I resign it to Thy will.

4 Thee at all times will I bless;
Having Thee, I all possess:
Ne'er can I bereaved be,
While I do not part with Thee.

Ryland.

83 *"Sing unto the Lord, who prepareth rain for the earth."*

1 Praise on Thee, in Zion's gates,
Daily, O Jehovah, waits;
Unto Thee, O God, belong
Grateful words and holy song.

2 Thou dost visit earth, and rain
Blessings on the thirsty plain,
From the copious founts on high,
From the rivers of the sky.

3 Thus the clouds Thy power confess,
And Thy paths drop fruitfulness,
And the voice of song and mirth
Rises from the tribes of earth!

Conder.

NICAEA. *Rev. John B. Dykes.*

1 Ho - ly, ho - ly, ho - ly, Lord God Al - might-y! Ear - ly in the morn - ing our song shall rise to Thee; Ho - ly, ho - ly, ho - ly! Mer-ci - ful and Might - y! God in Three Per-sons, Bless-ed Trin - i - ty!

84

"Which was, and is, and is to come."

2 Holy, holy, holy! all the saints adore Thee,
Casting down their golden crowns around the glassy sea;
Cherubim and seraphim falling down before Thee,
Which wert, and art, and evermore shalt be.

3 Holy, holy, holy! though the darkness hide Thee,
Though the eye of sinful man Thy glory may not see,
Only Thou art holy, there is none beside Thee,
Perfect in power, in love and purity.

4 Holy, holy, holy! Lord God Almighty!
All Thy works shall praise Thy name, in earth, and sky, and sea;
Holy, holy, holy! Lord God Almighty!
God in Three Persons, Blessed Trinity!

Bp. Reginald Heber.

L. M. *Arr. by Lowell Mason.*

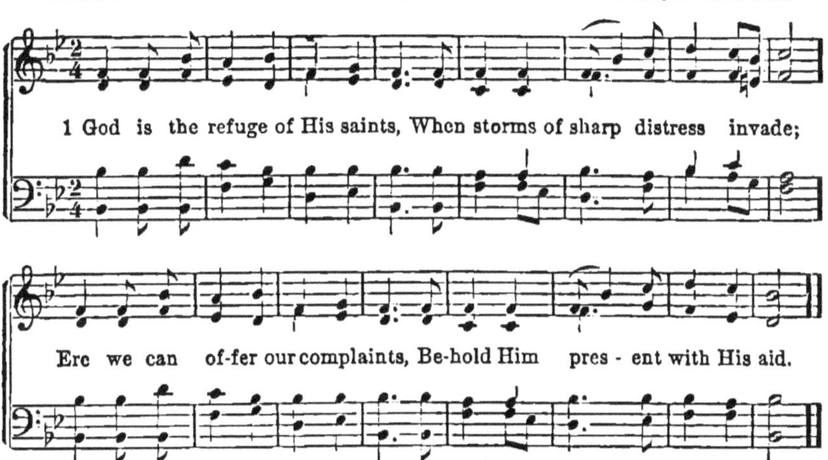

85 *Safety and Triumph of God's People.*

2 Let mountains from their seats be hurled
Down to the deep, and buried there,
Convulsions shake the solid world;
Our faith shall never yield to fear.

3 Loud may the troubled ocean roar;
In sacred peace our souls abide,
While every nation, every shore,
Trembles, and dreads the swelling tide.

4 There is a stream, whose gentle flow
Supplies the city of our God,
Life, love, and joy still gliding through,
And watering our divine abode.

5 That sacred stream, Thine holy word,
Our grief allays, our fear controls;
Sweet peace Thy promises afford,
And give new strength to fainting souls.

6 Zion enjoys her Monarch's love,
Secure against a threatening hour;
Nor can her firm foundations move,
Built on His truth, and armed with power.

I. Watts.

86 *New Year.*

1 Our Helper, God! we bless Thy name,
The same Thy power, Thy grace the same;
The tokens of Thy loving care
Open and crown and close the year.

2 Amid ten thousand snares we stand,
Supported by Thy guardian hand;
And see, when we survey our ways,
Ten thousand monuments of praise.

3 Thus far Thine arm hath led us on;
Thus far we make Thy mercy known;
And while we tread this desert land,
New mercies shall new songs demand

Doddridge.

87 *Doxology.*

Eternal Father! throned above,
Thou Fountain of redeeming love!
Eternal Word! who left Thy throne
For man's rebellion to atone;
Eternal Spirit, who dost give
That grace whereby our spirits live:
Thou God of our salvation, be
Eternal praises paid to Thee!

MENDON. **L. M.** *German Melody.*

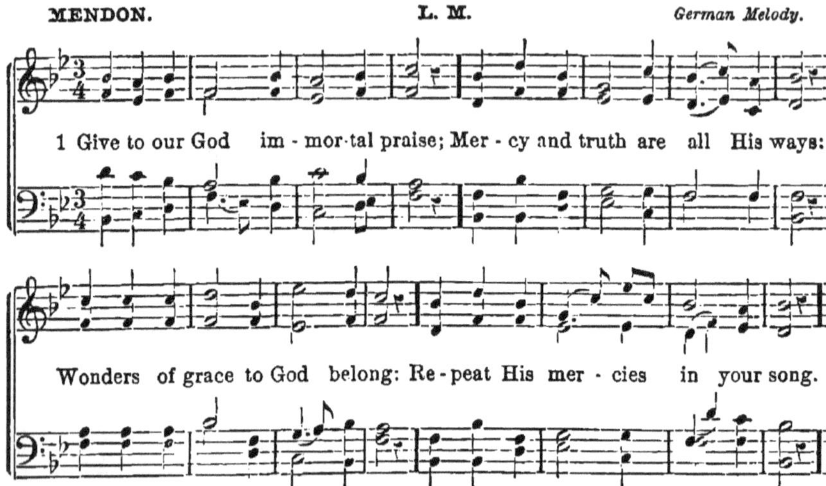

88 *"His mercy endureth forever."*

2 He built the earth, He spread the sky,
And fixed the starry lights on high:
Wonders of grace to God belong;
Repeat His mercies in your song.

3 He fills the sun with morning light,
He bids the moon direct the night:
His mercies ever shall endure,
When suns and moons shall shine no more.

4 He sent His Son with power to save
From guilt, and darkness, and the grave:
Wonders of grace to God belong;
Repeat His mercies in your song.

5 Through this vain world He guides our feet,
And leads us to His heavenly seat·
His mercies ever shall endure,
When this vain world shall be no more.

I. Watts.

89 *"Be still, and know that I am God."*

1 Wait, O my soul, thy Maker's will!
Tumultuous passions, all be still;
Nor let a murm'ring thought arise:
His ways are just, His counsels wise.

2 He in the thickest darkness dwells,
Performs His work, the cause conceals;
And, tho' His footsteps are unknown,
Judgment and truth support His throne

3 In heaven, and earth, and air, and seas,
He executes His firm decrees;
And by His saints it stands confessed,
That what He does is ever best.

Rev. Benjamin Beddome.

90 *"Bless the Lord, O my soul."*

1 Bless, O my soul, the living God;
Call home thy tho'ts that rove abroad:
Let all the powers within me join
In work and worship so divine.

2 Bless, O my soul, the God of grace,
His favors claim Thy highest praise;
Why should the wonders He hath wrought
Be lost in silence, and forgot?

3 'Tis He, my soul, that sent His Son
To die for crimes which thou hast done;
He owns the ransom, and forgives
The hourly follies of our lives.

Anon.

91 *Providence.*

2 In each event of life how clear
Thy ruling hand I see!
Each blessing to my soul more dear
Because conferred by Thee.
In every joy that crowns my days,
In every pain I bear,
My heart shall find delight in praise,
Or seek relief in prayer.

3 When gladness wings my favored hour,
Thy love my thoughts shall fill;
Resigned, when storms of sorrow lower,
My soul shall meet Thy will.
My lifted eye, without a tear,
The gathering storm shall see;
My steadfast heart shall know no fear;
That heart will rest on Thee.

H. M. Williams.

92 *Psalm 116.*

1 What shall I render to my God,
For all His kindness shown?
My feet shall visit Thine abode,
My songs address Thy throne.

2 Among the saints that fill Thine house,
My offering shall be paid;
There shall my zeal perform the vows
My soul in anguish made.

3 How much is mercy Thy delight,
Thou ever blessed God!
How dear Thy servants in Thy sight!
How precious is their blood!

4 How happy all Thy servants are!
How great Thy grace to me!
My life, which Thou hast made Thy care,
Lord, I devote to Thee.

I. Watts

CAROL. **C. M. D.** *R. S. Willis.*

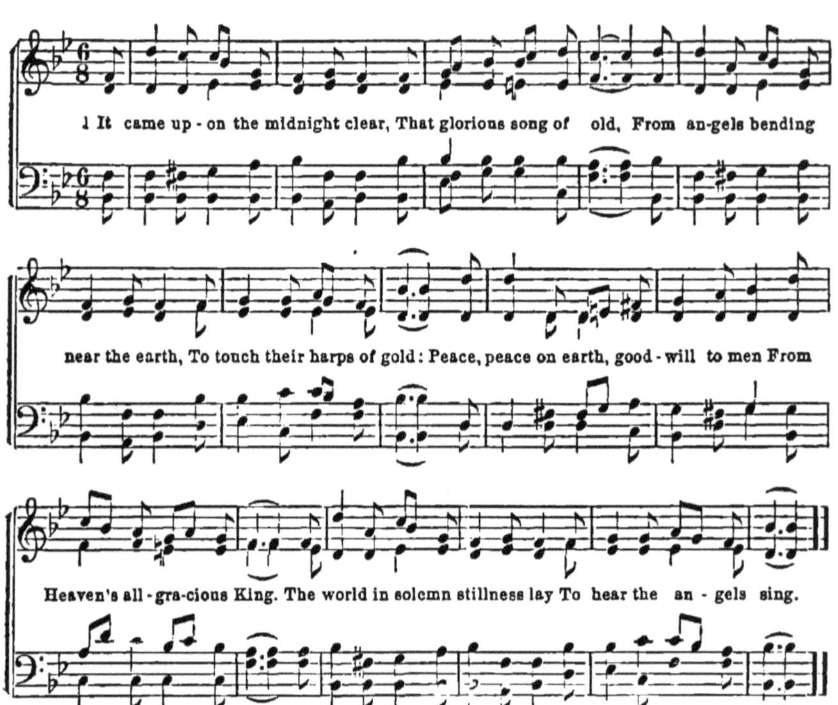

93 *Christmas Carol.*

2 Still thro' the cloven skies they come,
With peaceful wings unfurled;
And still their heavenly music floats
O'er all the weary world:
Above its sad and lowly plains
They bend on hovering wing,
And ever o'er its Babel sounds
The blessed angels sing.

3 But with the woes of sin and strife
The world has suffered long;
Beneath the angel-strain have rolled
Two thousand years of wrong;
And man, at war with man, hears not
The love-song which they bring:
Oh, hush the noise, ye men of strife,
And hear the angels sing.

4 And ye, beneath life's crushing load
Whose forms are bending low,
Who toil along the climbing way,
With painful steps and slow,—
Look now; for glad and golden hours
Come swiftly on the wing:
Oh, rest beside the weary road,
And hear the angels sing.

5 For lo, the days are hastening on
By prophet bards foretold,
When with the ever circling years
Comes round the age of gold:
When Peace shall over all the earth
Its ancient splendors fling,
And the whole world give back the song
Which now the angels sing.

Rev. E. H. Sears

HIDING IN THEE. *Ira D. Sankey.*

94 *Hiding in the Rock of Ages.*

2 In the calm of the noontide, in sorrow's lone hour,
In times when temptation casts o'er me its power;
In the tempests of life, on its wide, heaving sea,
Thou blest "Rock of Ages," I'm hiding in Thee.

3 How oft in the conflict, when pressed by the foe,
I have fled to my Refuge and breathed out my woe;
How often when trials like sea-billows roll,
Have I hidden in Thee, O Thou Rock of my soul.

Rev. Wm. O. Cushing

DENFIELD. C. M. *C. G. Glaser.*

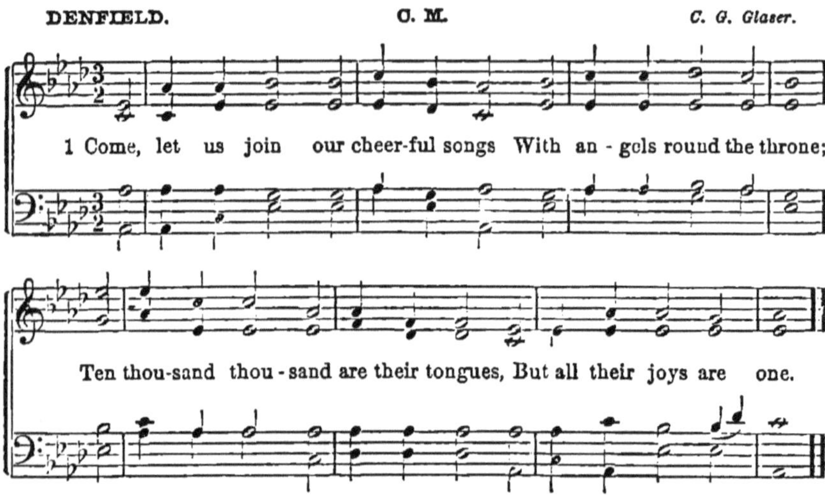

95 *"Worthy the Lamb!"*

2 "Worthy the Lamb that died," they cry,
"To be exalted thus!"
"Worthy the Lamb!" our lips reply,
"For He was slain for us."

3 Jesus is worthy to receive
Honor and power divine;
And blessings, more than we can give,
Be, Lord, forever Thine!

4 Let all that dwell above the sky,
And air, and earth, and seas,
Conspire to lift Thy glories high,
And speak Thine endless praise.

5 The whole creation join in one,
To bless the sacred name
Of Him who sits upon the throne,
And to adore the Lamb!

I. Watts.

96 *Reconciliation.*

1 Come, let us lift our joyful eyes,
Up to the courts above,
And smile to see our Father there,
Upon a throne of love.

2 Now we may bow before His feet,
And venture near the Lord:
No fiery cherub guards His seat,
Nor double flaming sword.

3 To Thee ten thousand thanks we bring,
Great Advocate on high,
And glory to the eternal King,
Who lays His anger by.

I. Watts.

97 *"With full assurance of faith."*

1 Oh, see how Jesus trusts Himself
Unto our childish love!
As though by His free ways with us
Our earnestness to prove.

2 The light of love is round His feet,
His paths are never dim;
And He comes nigh to us when we
Dare not come nigh to Him.

3 Let us be simple with Him then,
Not backward, stiff, nor cold,
As though our Bethlehem could be
What Sinai was of old

F. W. Faber.

VARINA. **C. M. D.** *George F. Root.*

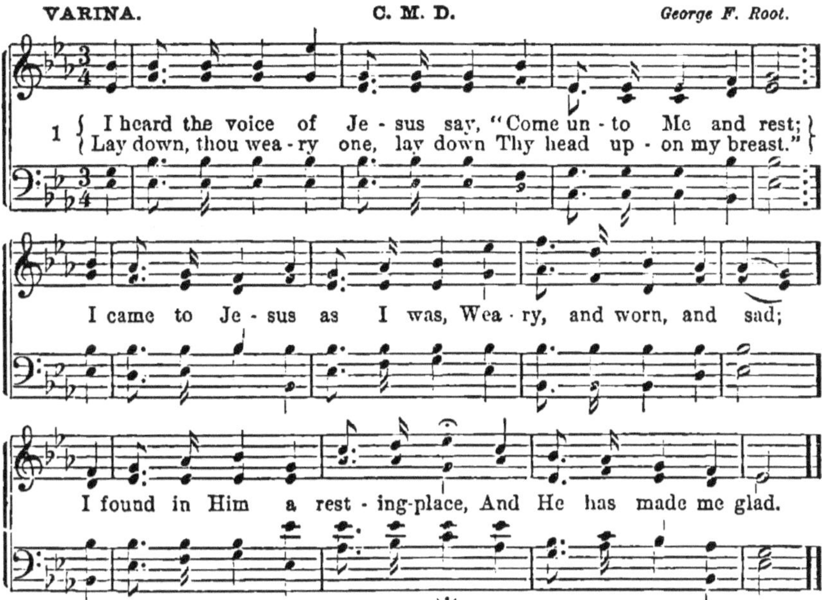

98 *The Voice of Jesus.*

2 I heard the voice of Jesus say,
"Behold, I freely give
The living water—thirsty one,
Stoop down, and drink, and live."
I came to Jesus, and I drank
Of that life-giving stream;
My thirst was quench'd, my soul reviv'd,
And now I live in Him.

3 I heard the voice of Jesus say,
"I am this dark world's Light;
Look unto Me, thy morn shall rise,
And all thy day be bright."
I looked to Jesus, and I found
In Him my Star, my Sun;
And in that light of life I'll walk
Till trav'ling days are done.

H. Bonar.

99 *Union to Christ.*

1 Lord Jesus, are we one with Thee?
Oh, height! oh, depth of love!
With Thee we died upon the tree,
In thee we live above.
Such was Thy grace, that for our sake
Thou didst from Heaven come down,
Thou didst of flesh and blood partake,
In all our sorrows one.

2 Our sins, our guilt, in love divine,
Confessed and borne by Thee;
The gall, the curse, the wrath, were Thine,
To set Thy members free.
Ascended now, in glory bright,
Still one with us Thou art;
Nor life, nor death, nor depth, nor height,
Thy saints and Thee can part.

3 Oh, teach us, Lord, to know and own
This wondrous mystery,
That Thou with us art truly one,
And we are one with Thee!
Soon, soon shall come that glorious day,
When, seated on Thy throne,
Thou shalt to wondering worlds display,
That Thou with us art one.

J. G. Deck.

ORTONVILLE. **C. M.** *Thomas Hastings.*

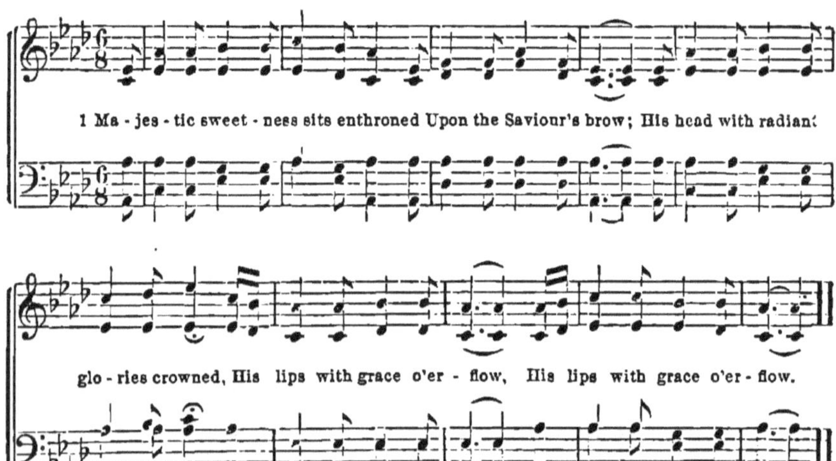

100 *"Majestic Sweetness."*

2 No mortal can with Him compare
Among the sons of men;
Fairer is He than all the fair
That fill the heavenly train.

3 He saw me plunged in deep distress,
He flew to my relief;
For me He bore the shameful cross
And carried all my grief.

4 To Him I owe my life and breath,
And all the joys I have;
He makes me triumph over death,
He saves me from the grave.

5 To Heaven, the place of His abode,
He brings my weary feet,
Shows me the glories of my God,
And makes my joy complete.

6 Since from His bounty I receive
Such proofs of love divine,
Had I a thousand hearts to give,
Lord, they should all be Thine.

Rev. Samuel Stennett.

101 *Christ Precious.*

1 Jesus, I love Thy charming name,
'Tis music to mine ear:
Fain would I sound it out so loud
That earth and Heaven should hear.

2 Yes, Thou art precious to my soul,
My Transport and my Trust;
Jewels to Thee are gaudy toys,
And gold is sordid dust.

3 All my capacious powers can wish,
In Thee doth richly meet;
Not to mine eyes is light so dear,
Nor friendship half so sweet.

4 Thy grace still dwells upon my heart,
And sheds its fragrance there;
The noblest balm of all its wounds,
The cordial of its care.

5 I'll speak the honors of Thy name
With my last laboring breath;
Then, speechless, clasp Thee in mine arms,
The antidote of death.

Rev. Philip Doddridge.

102 *Christ our Light.*

1 O Jesus, Light of all below,
Thou Fount of life and fire,
Surpassing all the joys we know,
All that we can desire;

2 May every heart confess Thy name,
And ever Thee adore;
And seeking Thee, itself inflame
To seek Thee more and more.

3 Thee may our tongues forever bless;
Thee may we love alone;
And ever in our lives express
The image of Thine own.

Bernard of Clairvaux.

103 *Christ our only Joy.*

1 Jesus, the very thought of Thee
With sweetness fills my breast;
But sweeter far Thy face to see,
And in Thy presence rest.

2 Nor voice can sing, nor heart can frame,
Nor can the memory find
A sweeter sound than Thy blest name,
O Saviour of mankind!

3 O Hope of every contrite heart,
O Joy of all the meek,
To those who fall, how kind Thou art!
How good to those who seek!

4 Jesus, our only Joy be Thou,
As Thou our Prize wilt be;
Jesus, be Thou our Glory now,
And through eternity.

Bernard of Clairvaux.

104 *"Altogether lovely."*

1 Oh, teach me more of Thy blest ways,
Thou Holy Lamb of God!
And fix and root me in Thy grace,
As one redeem'd by blood.

2 Oh, tell me often of Thy love,
Of all Thy grief and pain;
And let my heart with joy confess
That thence comes all my gain.

3 For this, oh, may I freely count
Whate'er I have but loss;
The dearest object of my love,
Compared with Thee, but dross.

4 Engrave this deeply on my heart
With an eternal pen,
That I may, in some small degree,
Return Thy love again.

Anon.

105 *"The unsearchable riches of Christ."*

1 To our Redeemer's glorious name,
Awake the sacred song;
Oh, may His love (immortal flame!)
Tune every heart and tongue.

2 He left His radiant throne on high—
Left the bright realms of bliss,
And came to earth to bleed and die:
Was ever love like this?

3 Dear Lord, while we adoring pay
Our humble thanks to Thee,
May every heart with rapture say,
"The Saviour died for me."

4 Oh, may the sweet, the blissful theme,
Fill every heart and tongue,
Till strangers love Thy charming name,
And join the sacred song!

Mrs. Steele.

106 *King Most Wonderful.*

1 O Jesus, King most wonderful,
Thou Conqueror renowned,
Thou sweetness most ineffable,
In whom all joys are found;

2 When once Thou visitest the heart,
Then truth begins to shine,
Then earthly vanities depart,
Then kindles love divine.

Anon.

BOYLSTON. **S. M.** *Lowell Mason.*

107 *"None other name."*

2 But Christ the heavenly Lamb
Takes all our sins away,
A sacrifice of nobler name
And richer blood than they.

3 My faith would lay her hand
On that dear head of Thine,
While like a penitent I stand,
And there confess my sin.

4 My soul looks back to see
The burdens Thou didst bear,
When hanging on the cursed tree,
And hopes her guilt was there.

5 Believing, we rejoice
To see the curse remove;
We bless the Lamb with cheerful voice,
And sing His dying love.

I. Watts.

108 *Safety in God.*

1 My spirit, on Thy care,
Blest Saviour, I recline:
Thou wilt not leave me to despair,
For Thou art Love Divine.

2 In Thee I place my trust,
On Thee I calmly rest;
I know Thee good, I know Thee just,
And count Thy choice the best.

3 Whate'er events betide,
Thy will they all perform;
Safe in Thy breast my head I hide,
Nor fear the coming storm.

4 Let good or ill befall,
It must be good for me;
Secure of having Thee in all,
Of having all in Thee.

Rev. H. F. Lyte.

109 *"I will fear no evil, for Thou art with me."*

1 While my Redeemer's near,
My Shepherd and my Guide,
I bid farewell to anxious fear:
My wants are all supplied.

2 To ever-fragrant meads,
Where rich abundance grows,
His gracious hand indulgent leads,
And guards my sweet repose.

3 Dear Shepherd, if I stray,
My wandering feet restore;
To Thy fair pastures guide my way,
And let me rove no more.

Kelly.

THE GREAT PHYSICIAN. *Rev. J. H. Stockton.*

110 *"Thy sins are forgiven."*

2 Your many sins are all forgiven,
Oh! hear the voice of Jesus.
Go on your way in peace to Heaven,
And wear a crown with Jesus.

3 All glory to the dying Lamb,
I now believe in Jesus:
I love the blessed Saviour's name,
I love the name of Jesus.

4 His name dispels my guilt—and fear,
No other name but Jesus:
Oh! how my soul delights to hear
The charming name of Jesus.

Anon.

CORONATION. **C. M.** *Oliver Holden.*

III "*Lord of all.*"

2 Crown Him, ye morning stars of light,
Who fixed this floating ball;
Now hail the strength of Israel's might,
And crown Him Lord of all.

3 Sinners, whose love can ne'er forget
The wormwood and the gall,
Go, spread your trophies at His feet,
And crown Him Lord of all.

4 Let every kindred, every tribe,
On this terrestrial ball,
To Him all majesty ascribe,
And crown Him Lord of all.

Rev. Edward Perronet.

112 *Christ, our Priest.*

1 Come, let us join our songs of praise
To our ascended Priest;
He entered Heaven with all our names
Engraven on His breast.

2 Clothed with our nature still, He knows
The weakness of our frame,
And how to shield us from the foes
Which He Himself o'ercame.

3 Nor time, nor distance, e'er shall quench
The fervor of His love;
For us He died in kindness here,
For us He lives above.

A. Pirrie.

113 "*Hosanna to the Son of David.*"

1 Hosanna! be our cheerful song
To Christ our Saviour King;
His praise, to whom we all belong,
Let all unite to sing.

2 Hosanna! here in joyful bands,
Let old and young proclaim;
And hail, with voices, hearts, and hands,
The Son of David's name.

3 Hosanna! sound from hill to hill,
And spread from plain to plain;
While louder, sweeter, clearer still,
Woods echo to the strain.

4 Hosanna! on the wings of light,
O'er earth and ocean fly,
Till morn to eve, and noon to night,
And heaven to earth reply.

Anon.

ANTIOCH. C. M. *Lowell Mason, arr.*

114 *"Joy to the world."*

2 Joy to the earth, the Saviour reigns:
Let men their songs employ;
While fields and floods, rocks, hills, and plains,
Repeat the sounding joy.

3 No more let sins and sorrows grow,
Nor thorns infest the ground:
He comes to make His blessings flow
Far as the curse is found.

4 He rules the world with truth and grace,
And makes the nations prove
The glories of His righteousness,
And wonders of His love.

I. Watts.

115 *Christ's Coming.*

1 Sing to the Lord, ye distant lands,
Ye tribes of every tongue:
His new discovered grace demands
A new and nobler song.

2 Say to the nations, Jesus reigns,
God's own almighty Son;
His power the sinking world sustains,
And grace surrounds His throne.

3 Behold He comes, He comes to bless
The nations as their God;
To show the world His righteousness,
And send His truth abroad.

I. Watts.

116 *The Promised Lord.*

1 Hark, the glad sound! the Saviour comes,
The Saviour promised long;
Let every heart prepare a throne,
And every voice a song.

2 He comes, the prisoner to release,
In Satan's bondage held;
The gates of brass before Him burst,
The iron fetters yield.

3 He comes, the broken heart to bind,
The bleeding soul to cure,
And with the treasures of His grace,
Enrich the humble poor.

4 Our glad hosannas, Prince of Peace,
Thy welcome shall proclaim,
And Heaven's eternal arches ring
With Thy beloved name.

P. Doddridge.

ABBOTT. **C. M.** *From Louis Spohr.*

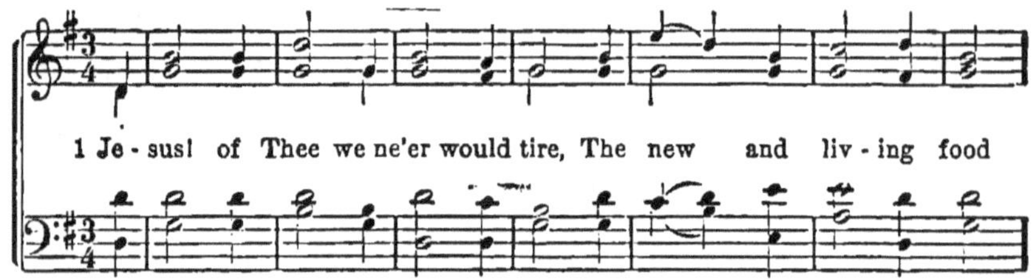

117 *"I am the bread of life."*

2 If such the happy midnight song
Our prisoned spirits raise,
What are the joys that cause ere long
Eternal bursts of praise?

3 To look within and see no stain—
Abroad no curse to trace;
To shed no tears, to feel no pain,
But see Thee face to face:

4 To find each hope of glory gained—
Fulfilled each precious word;
And fully all to have attained
The image of our Lord.

5 For this we're pressing onward still,
And in this hope would be
More subject to the Father's will,
E'en now much more like Thee.

Anon.

118 *"If we suffer with Him, we shall also reign."*

1 The head that once was crowned with thorns,
Is crowned with glory now;
A royal diadem adorns
The mighty victor's brow.

2 Delight of all who dwell above!
The joy of saints below!
To us still manifest Thy love,
That we its depths may know.

3 To us Thy cross, with all its shame—
With all its grace, be given!
Though earth disowns Thy lowly name,
All worship it in Heaven.

4 Who suffer with Thee, Lord, below,
Will reign with Thee above;
Then let it be our joy to know
The way of peace and love.

5 To us Thy cross is life and health,
Though shame and death to Thee!
Our present glory, joy, and wealth,
Our everlasting stay!

Rev. Thos. Kelly.

DENFIELD. C. M. *C. G. Glaser.*

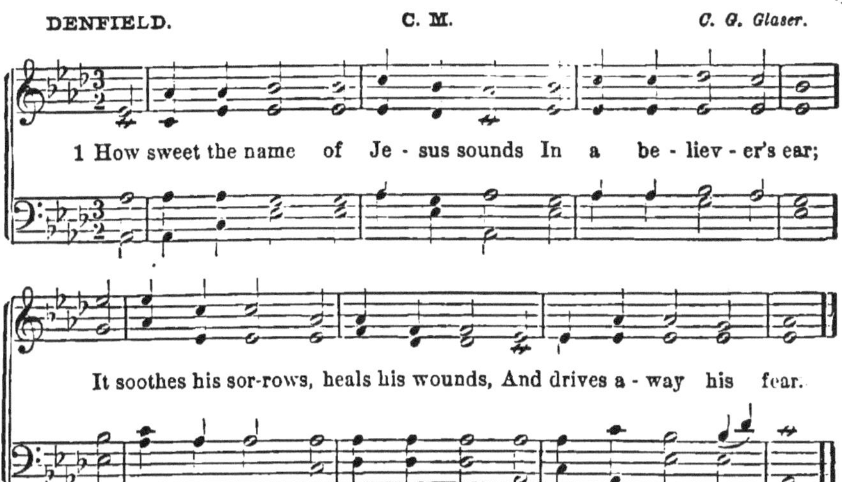

119 *The Sweet Name.*

2 It makes the wounded spirit whole,
And calms the troubled breast;
'Tis manna to the hungry soul,
And to the weary, rest.

3 Dear Name! the rock on which I build,
My shield and hiding-place,
My never-failing treasury, filled
With boundless stores of grace.

4 Weak is the effort of my heart,
And cold my warmest thought;
But when I see Thee as Thou art,
I'll praise Thee as I ought.

Rev. John Newton.

120 *The Dearest Name.*

1 There is a name I love to hear,
I love to sing its worth;
It sounds like music in mine ear,
The sweetest name on earth.

2 It tells me of a Saviour's love,
Who died to set me free;
It tells me of His precious blood,
The sinner's perfect plea.

3 It tells of One, whose loving heart
Can feel my deepest woe,
Who in each sorrow bears a part
That none can bear below.

4 Jesus, the name I love so well,
The name I love to hear,
No saint on earth its worth can tell—
No heart conceive how dear.

Frederick Whitfield.

121 *"Every tongue should confess that Jesus Christ is Lord."*

1 Jesus! exalted far on high,
To whom a name is given—
A name surpassing every name
That's known in earth or Heaven!

2 Before Thy throne shall every knee
Bow down with one accord;
Before Thy throne shall every tongue
Confess that Thou art Lord.

3 Oh, may that mind in us be formed,
Which shone so bright in Thee—
An humble, meek, and lowly mind,
From pride and envy free!

4 To others we would stoop, and learn
To emulate Thy love;
So shall we bear Thine image here,
And share Thy throne above.

Anon.

L. M. *From Haydn.*

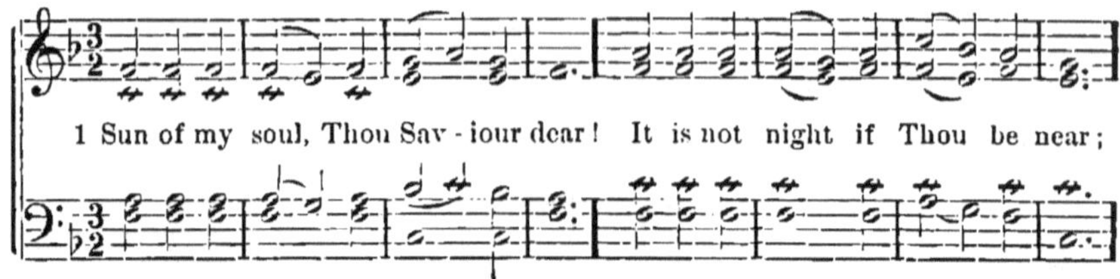

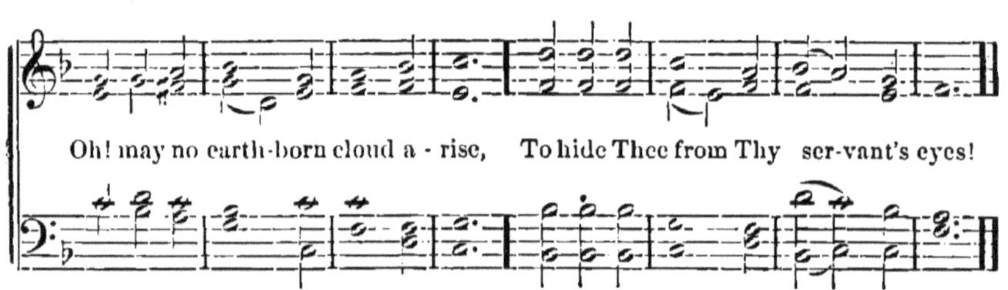

122 *Evening Hymn.*

2 When the soft dews of kindly sleep
My wearied c elids gently steep,
Be my last thought, How sweet to rest
Forever on my Saviour's breast!

3 Abide with me from morn till eve,
For without Thee I cannot live;
Abide with me when night is nigh,
For without Thee I dare not die.

4 If some poor wandering child of Thine
Have spurned to-day the voice divine,
Now, Lord, the gracious work begin;
Let him no more lie down in sin.

5 Watch by the sick; enrich the poor
With blessings from Thy boundless store;
Be every mourner's sleep to-night,
Like infant's slumbers, pure and light!

6 Come near and bless us when we wake,
Ere through the world our way we take;
Till, in the ocean of Thy love,
We lose ourselves in Heaven above.

John Keble.

123 *The Meekness of Christ.*

1 How beauteous were the marks divine,
That in Thy meekness used to shine,
That lit Thy lonely pathway, trod
In wondrous love, O Son of God.

2 Oh, who like Thee, so calm, so bright,
So pure, so made to live in light?
Oh, who like thee did ever go
So patient, through a world of woe?

3 Oh, who like Thee, so humbly bore
The scorn, the scoffs of men, before?
So meek, forgiving, godlike, high,
So glorious in humility?

4 And death, that sets the prisoner free,
Was pang, and scoff, and scorn to Thee;
Yet love thro' all Thy torture glowed,
And mercy with Thy life-blood flowed.

5 Oh, in Thy light be mine to go,
Illuming all my way of woe;
And give me ever, on the road,
To trace Thy footsteps, O my God.

Bp. A. C. Coxe.

124 "*Over all, God blessed forever.*"

2 Lo! Jehovah, we adore Thee;
Thee, our Saviour; Thee, our God!
From His throne His beams of glory
Shine through all the world abroad.

3 Jesus, Thee our Saviour hailing,
Thee, our God, in praise we own;
Highest honors, never failing,
Rise eternal round Thy throne.

4 Now, ye saints, His power confessing,
In your grateful strains adore;
For His mercy, never ceasing,
Flows, and flows for evermore.

Anon.

125 *Worship of the Living Christ.*

1 Jesus, hail! enthroned in glory,
There forever to abide;
All the heavenly hosts adore Thee,
Seated at Thy Father's side.

2 There for sinners Thou art pleading,
There Thou dost our place prepare;
Ever for us interceding,
Till in glory we appear.

3 Worship, honor, power, and blessing,
Thou art worthy to receive;
Loudest praises, without ceasing,
Meet it is for us to give.

Bakewell.

126 "*Being the brightness of His glory.*"

1 Brightness of the Father's glory,
Shall Thy praise unuttered lie?
Break, my tongue, such guilty silence;
Sing the Lord who came to die.

2 Did archangels sing Thy coming?
Did the shepherds learn their lays?
Shame would cover me, ungrateful,
Should my tongue refuse to praise.

3 From the highest throne in glory
To the cross of deepest woe,
All to ransom guilty captives!
Flow, my praise, forever flow.

4 Re-ascend, immortal Saviour!
Leave Thy footstool, take Thy throne:
Thence return, and reign forever;
Be the kingdom all Thine own.

Robinson.

WILMOT. 8, 7. *C. M. von Weber.*

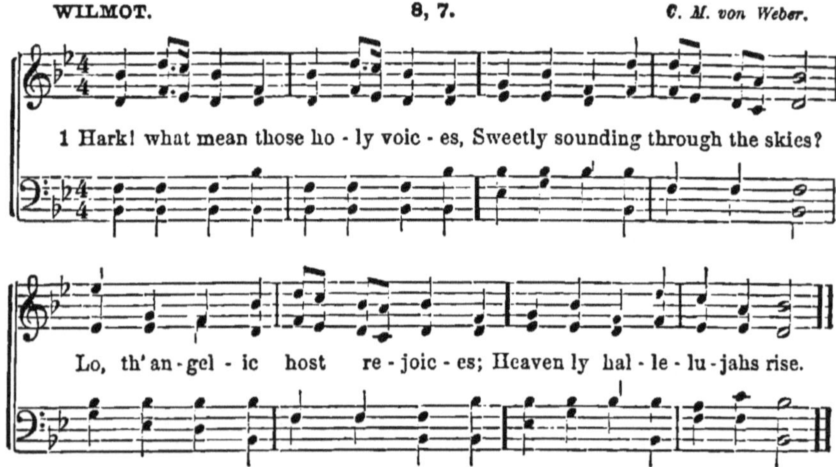

127 *The Holy Voices.*

2 Listen to the wondrous story,
Which they chant in hymns of joy:
"Glory in the highest, glory,
Glory be to God Most High.

3 "Peace on earth, good-will from Heaven,
Reaching far as man is found;
Souls redeemed, and sins forgiven,
Loud our golden harps shall sound.

4 "Christ is born, the great Anointed;
Heaven and earth His glory sing:
Glad receive whom God appointed
For your Prophet, Priest, and King.

5 "Hasten, mortals, to adore Him;
Learn His name and taste His joy:
Till in Heaven you sing before Him,
'Glory be to God Most High.'"

Rev. John Cawood.

128 *Desire of all Nations.*

1 Come, Thou long-expected Jesus,
Born to set Thy people free:
From our fears and sins release us,
Let us find our rest in Thee.

2 Israel's Strength and Consolation,
Hope of all the earth Thou art;
Dear Desire of every nation,
Joy of every longing heart.

3 Born Thy people to deliver,
Born a child, and yet a King,
Born to reign in us forever,
Now Thy gracious kingdom bring.

4 By Thine own eternal Spirit,
Rule in all our hearts alone;
By Thine all-sufficient merit,
Raise us to Thy glorious throne.

Rev. Charles Wesley.

129 *Apostolic Benediction.*

1 May the grace of Christ the Saviour,
And the Father's boundless love,
With the Holy Spirit's favor,
Rest upon us from above.

2 Thus may we abide in union
With each other and the Lord,
And possess, in sweet communion,
Joys which earth cannot afford.

Anon.

DE FLEURY. 8, D. *Lewis Edson.*

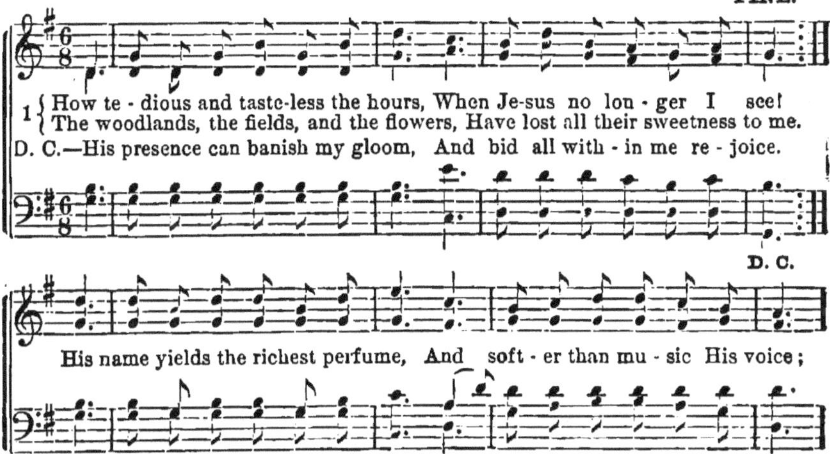

130 *"Whom have I but Thee?"*

2 Dear Lord! if indeed I am Thine,
And Thou art my light and my song;
Say, why do I languish and pine,
And why are my winters so long?
Oh, drive these dark clouds from the sky,
Thy soul-cheering presence restore;
Or bid me soar upward on high,
Where winters and storms are no more.

J. Newton.

131 *"Altogether lovely."*

1 My gracious Redeemer I love,
His praises aloud I'll proclaim:
And join with the armies above,
To shout His adorable name.
To gaze on His glories divine
Shall be my eternal employ;
To see them incessantly shine,
My boundless, ineffable joy.

2 He freely redeemed with His blood
My soul from the confines of hell,
To live on the smiles of my God,
And in His sweet presence to dwell:—
To shine with the angels in light,
With saints and with seraphs to sing,
To view, with eternal delight,
My Jesus, my Saviour, my King!

B. Francis.

132 *"Having a desire to depart."*

1 To Jesus, the crown of my hope,
My soul is in haste to be gone;
Oh, bear me, ye cherubim, up,
And waft me away to His throne.

2 My Saviour, whom absent I love;
Whom, not having seen, I adore;
Whose name is exalted above
All glory, dominion and power.

3 Dissolve Thou these bands that detain
My soul from her portion in Thee,
Ah! strike off this adamant chain,
And make me eternally free.

4 Oh, then shall the vail be removed!
And round me Thy brightness be poured;
I shall meet Him whom absent I loved,
I shall see whom unseen I adored.

5 And then, nevermore shall the fears,
The trials, temptations, and woes,
Which darken this valley of tears,
Intrude on my blissful repose.

Anon.

PRECIOUS NAME. *W. H. Doane.*

133 *The Name of Jesus.*

2 Take the name of Jesus ever,
As a shield from every snare;
If temptations 'round you gather,
Breathe that holy name in prayer.

3 Oh! the precious name of Jesus;
How it thrills our souls with joy,
When His loving arms receive us,
And His songs our tongues employ!

4 At the name of Jesus bowing,
Falling prostrate at His feet,
King of kings in Heaven we'll crown
Him,
When our journey is complete.

Mrs. Lydia Baxter.

ARLINGTON. C. M. *Dr. T. Arne.*

134 *"The Way, the Truth, the Life."*

2 Thou art the Truth: Thy word alone
True wisdom can impart;
Thou only canst inform the mind,
And purify the heart.

3 Thou art the Life: the rending tomb
Proclaims Thy conquering arm,
And those who put their trust in Thee,
Nor death nor hell shall harm.

4 Thou art the Way, the Truth, the Life;
Grant us that Way to know,
That Truth to keep, that Life to win,
Whose joys eternal flow.

Bp. George W. Doane.

135 *"Thou dear Redeemer, dying Lamb."*

1 Thou dear Redeemer, dying Lamb,
I love to hear of Thee;
No music's like Thy charming name,
Nor half so sweet can be.

2 Oh, may I ever hear Thy voice
In mercy to me speak;
In Thee, my Priest, will I rejoice,
And Thy salvation seek.

3 My Jesus shall be still my theme,
While on this earth I stay;
I'll sing my Jesus' lovely name,
When all things else decay.

4 When I appear in yonder cloud,
With all His favored throng,
Then will I sing more sweet, more loud,
And Christ shall be my song.

Cennick.

136 *The name "Jesus."*

1 The Saviour! oh, what endless charms
Dwell in the blissful sound!
Its influence every fear disarms,
And spreads sweet comfort round.

2 Th' almighty Former of the skies
Stooped to our vile abode;
While angels viewed with wondering eyes
And hailed th' incarnate God.

3 Oh, the rich depths of love divine!
Of bliss a boundless store!
Dear Saviour, let me call Thee mine;
I cannot wish for more.

4 On Thee alone my hope relies,
Beneath Thy cross I fall;
My Lord, my Life, my Sacrifice,
My Saviour, and my All!

A. Steele.

LENOX. 6, 8. *J. Edson.*

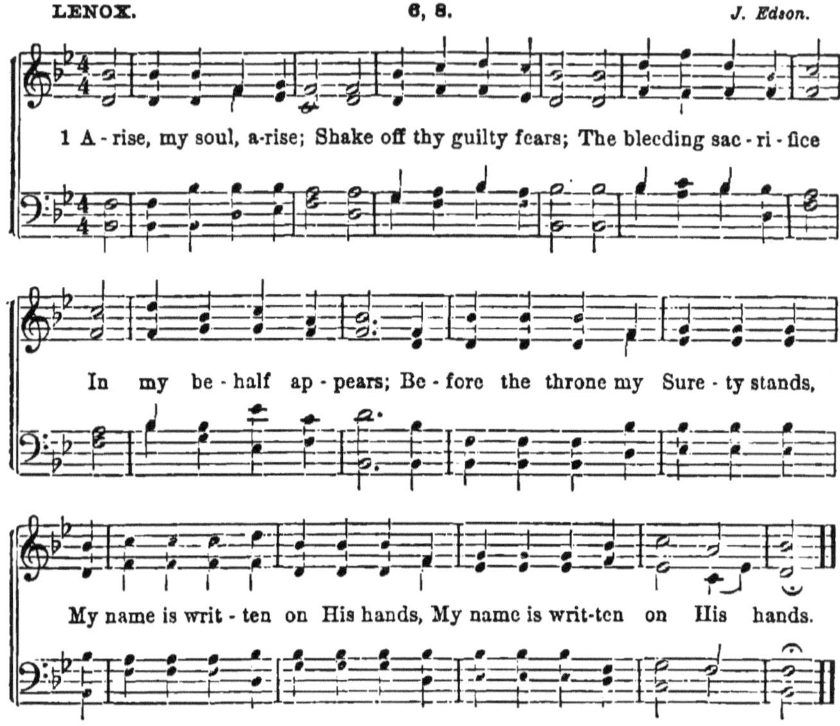

137 *Our Surety.*

2 He ever lives above,
For me to intercede,
His all-redeeming love,
His precious blood to plead;
His blood atoned for all our race,
And sprinkles now the throne of grace.

3 My God is reconciled;
His pardoning voice I hear;
He owns me for His child;
I can no longer fear;
With confidence I now draw nigh,
And Father, Abba, Father, cry.

C. Wesley.

138 *Year of Jubilee.*

1 Blow ye the trumpet blow;—
The gladly solemn sound;—
Let all the nations know,
To earth's remotest bound,
The year of jubilee is come:
Return, ye ransomed sinners, home.

2 Jesus, our great High Priest,
Hath full atonement made;
Ye weary spirits, rest;
Ye mournful souls, be glad:
The year of jubilee is come;
Return, ye ransomed sinners, home.

3 Extol the Lamb of God,
The all-atoning Lamb:
Redemption in His blood
Throughout the world proclaim:
The year of jubilee is come;
Return, ye ransomed sinners, home.

C. Wesley.

ROCK OF AGES. 7, 6 L. *Thos. Hastings.*

139 *The Rock of Ages.*

2 Should my tears forever flow,
Should my zeal no languor know,
This for sin could not atone,
Thou must save and Thou alone:
In my hand no price I bring;
Simply to Thy cross I cling.

3 While I draw this fleeting breath,
When mine eyelids close in death,
When I rise to worlds unknown,
And behold Thee on Thy throne,
Rock of Ages, cleft for me!
Let me hide myself in Thee.

A. H. Toplady.

140 *"Only Thee."*

1 Once again beside the cross,
All my gain I count but loss;
Earthly pleasures fade away,
Clouds they are that hide my day:
Hence, vain shadows! let me see
Jesus crucified for me.

2 From beneath that thorny crown
Trickle drops of cleansing down;
Pardon from Thy pierced hand
Now I take, while here I stand:
Only then I live to Thee,
When Thy wounded side I see.

3 Blessed Saviour, Thine am I,
Thine to live, and Thine to die;
Height or depth, or earthly power
Ne'er shall hide my Saviour more:
Ever shall my glory be,
Only, only, only Thee!

Rev. George Duffield

I NEED THEE EVERY HOUR. *Rev. Robert Lowry.*

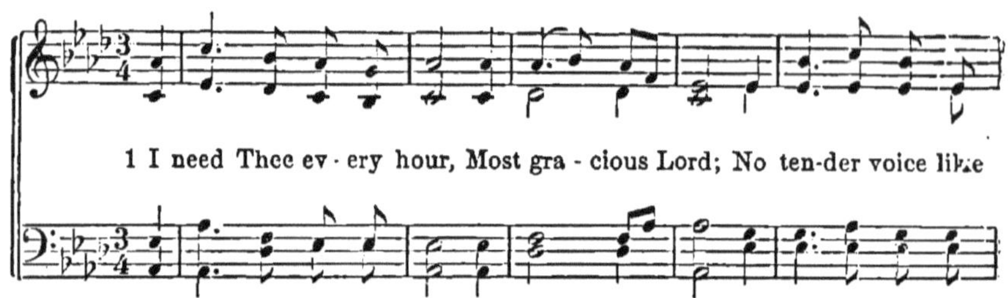

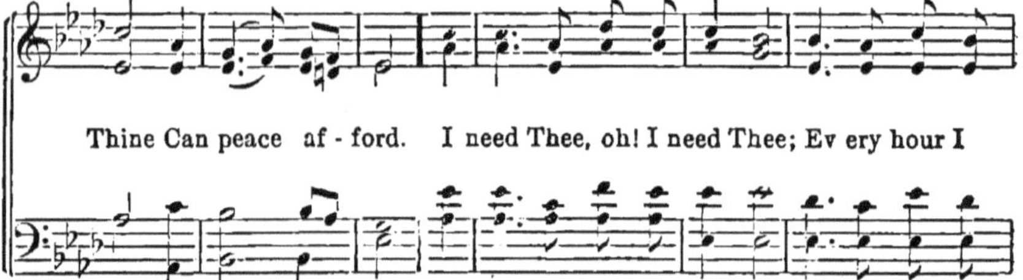

141 *I Need Thee.*

2 I need Thee every hour;
Stay Thou near by;
Temptations lose their power
When Thou art nigh.

3 I need Thee every hour,
In joy or pain;
Come quickly and abide,
Or life is vain.

4 I need Thee every hour;
Teach me Thy will;
And Thy rich promises
In me fulfill.

5 I need Thee every hour,
Most Holy One;
Oh, make me Thine indeed,
Thou blessed Son.

Mrs. Annie S. Hawks.

L. M. *Geo. Kingsley.*

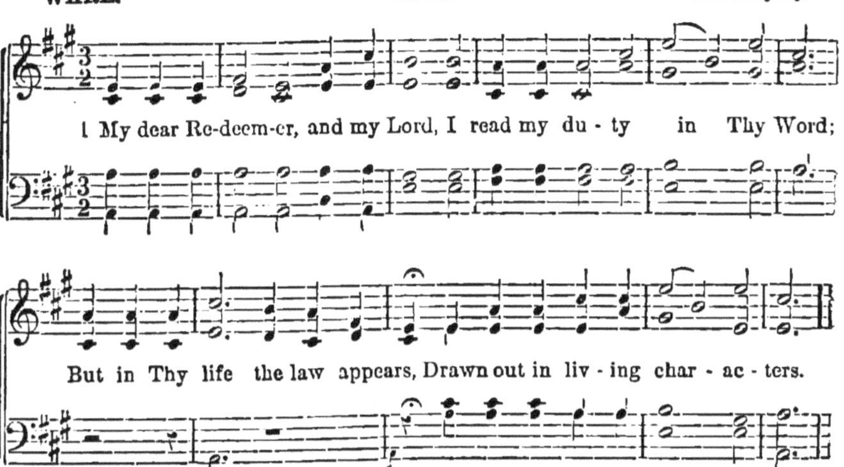

142 *Christ's Example.*

2 Such was Thy truth, and such Thy zeal,
Such deference to Thy Father's will,
Such love, and meekness so divine,
I would transcribe and make them mine.

3 Cold mountains and the midnight air
Witnessed the fervor of Thy prayer;
The desert Thy temptations knew,
Thy conflict and Thy victory too.

4 Be Thou my pattern; make me bear
More of Thy gracious image here;
Then God, the Judge, shall own my name
Amongst the followers of the Lamb.

I. Watts.

143 *The Song of Songs.*

1 Come, let us sing the song of songs—
The saints in Heaven began the strain,
The homage which to Christ belongs:
"Worthy the Lamb, for He was slain!"

2 Slain to redeem us by His blood,
To cleanse from every sinful stain,
And make us kings and priests to God—
"Worthy the Lamb, for He was slain!"

3 To Him, enthroned by filial right,
All power in Heaven and earth proclaim,
Honor, and majesty, and might:
"Worthy the Lamb, for He was slain!"

4 Long as we live, and when we die,
And while in Heaven with Him we reign,
This song our song of songs shall be:
"Worthy the Lamb, for He was slain!"

Montgomery.

144 *"A name which is above every name."*

1 There is none other name than Thine,
Jehovah Jesus! Name divine!
On which to rest for sins forgiven—
For peace with God, for hope of Heav'n.

2 There is none other name than Thine,
When cares, and fears, and griefs are mine,
That, with a gracious power can heal
Each care, and fear, and grief I feel.

3 Name, above every name! Thy praise
Shall fill the remnant of my days:
Jehovah Jesus! Name divine,
Ro k of salvation! Thou art mine.

Anon.

FEDERAL STREET. **L. M.** *H. K. Oliver.*

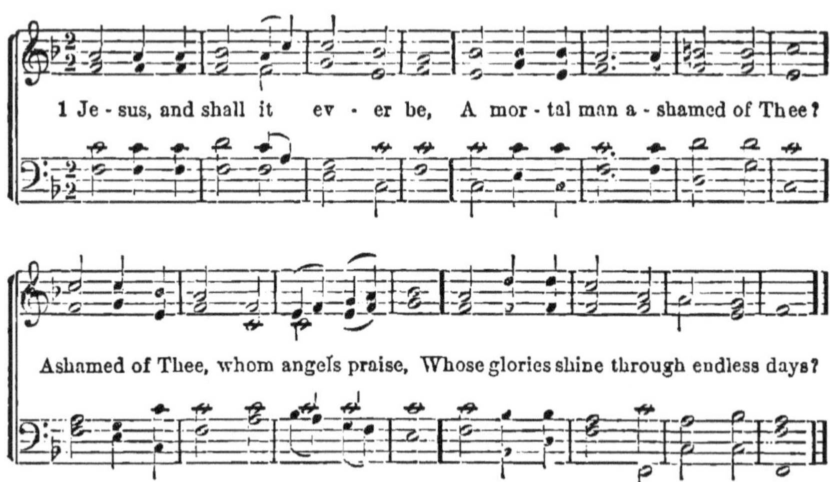

145 *Not Ashamed of Jesus.*

2 Ashamed of Jesus, that dear Friend
On whom my hopes of Heaven depend!
No; when I blush, be this my shame,
That I no more revere His name.

3 Ashamed of Jesus! yes, I may,
When I've no guilt to wash away,
No tear to wipe, no good to crave,
No fear to quell, no soul to save.

4 Till then, nor is my boasting vain,
Till then I boast a Saviour slain;
And oh, may this my glory be,
That Christ is not ashamed of me.

Rev. Joseph Grigg.

146 *Bearing the Cross for Christ.*

1 My precious Lord, for Thy dear name
I bear the cross, despise the shame;
Nor do I faint, while Thou art near;
I lean on Thee; how can I fear?

2 No other name but Thine is given
To cheer my soul in earth or Heaven;
No other wealth will I require;
No other friend can I desire.

3 Yea, into nothing would I fall
For Thee alone, my All in all;
To feel Thy love, my only joy,
To tell Thy love, my sole employ.

Moravian Collection.

147 *All in all.*

1 In Christ I've all my soul's desire;
His spirit does my heart inspire
With boundless wishes large and high;
And Christ will all my wants supply.

2 Christ is my Hope, my Strength, and Guide;
For me He bled, and groaned, and died;
He is my Sun, to give me light,
He is my soul's supreme Delight.

3 Christ is the source of all my bliss;
My wisdom and my righteousness;
My Saviour, Brother, and my Friend;
On Him alone I now depend.

4 Christ is my King, to rule and bless,
And all my troubles to redress;
He's my Salvation and my All,
Whate'er on earth shall me befall.

John Dobell's Collection.

6, 4. *Lowell Mason.*

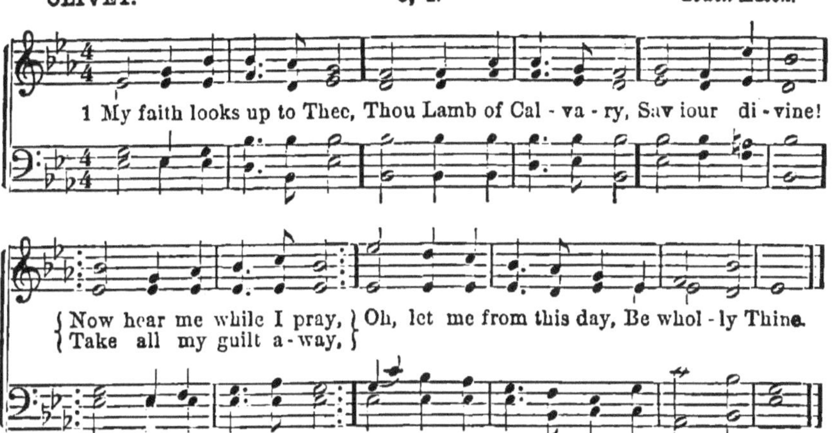

148 *Looking to Jesus.*

2 May Thy rich grace impart
Strength to my fainting heart;
My zeal inspire;
As Thou hast died for me,
Oh, may my love to Thee
Pure, warm, and changeless be,
A living fire!

3 While life's dark maze I tread,
And griefs around me spread,
Be Thou my Guide;
Bid darkness turn to day,
Wipe sorrow's tears away,
Nor let me ever stray
From Thee aside.

4 When ends life's transient dream,
When death's cold, sullen stream
Shall o'er me roll,
Blest Saviour! then, in love,
Fear and distrust remove;
Oh, bear me safe above,
A ransomed soul!

Ray Palmer.

149 *Jesus, All in All.*

1 Jesus! Thy name I love,
All other names above,
Jesus, my Lord!
Oh, Thou art all to me;
Nothing to please I see,
Nothing apart from Thee,
Jesus, my Lord!

2 Thou blessed Son of God!
Hast bought me with Thy blood,
Jesus, my Lord!
Oh, how great is Thy love,
All other loves above,—
Love that I daily prove,
Jesus, my Lord!

3 When unto Thee I flee,
Thou wilt my Refuge be,
Jesus, my Lord!
What need I now to fear?
What earthly grief or care?
Since Thou art ever near,
Jesus, my Lord!

4 Soon Thou wilt come again;
I shall be happy then,
Jesus, my Lord!
Then Thine own face I'll see,
Then I shall like Thee be,
Then evermore with Thee,
Jesus, my Lord!

Anon.

ALL TO CHRIST I OWE. 6. *John Thomas Grape.*

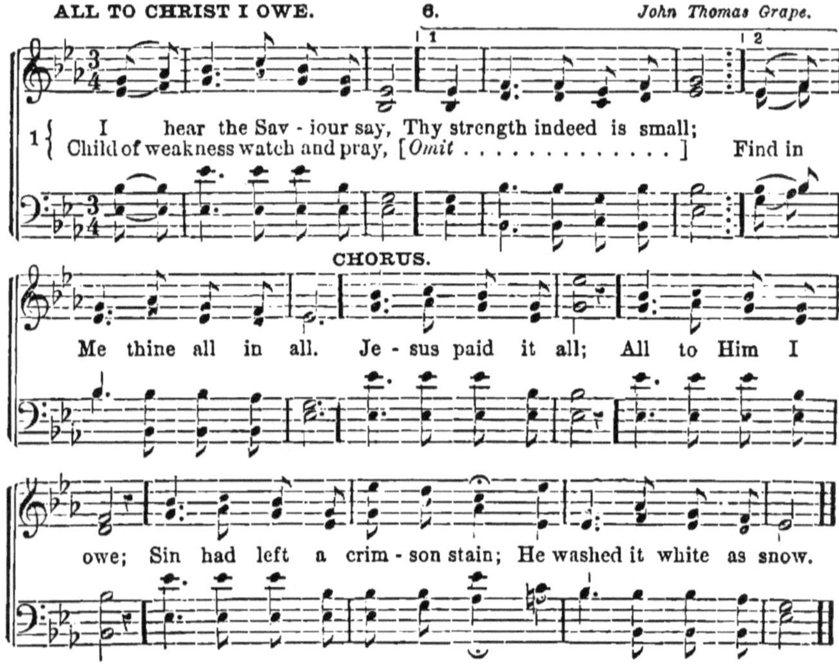

150 *"Jesus paid it all."*

2 Lord, now indeed I find
Thy faith, and Thine alone,
Can change the leper's spots,
And melt the heart of stone.

3 For nothing good have I
Whereby Thy grace to claim;
I'll wash my garment white
In the blood of Calv'ry's Lamb.

4 When from my dying bed
My ransomed soul shall rise,
Then "Jesus paid it all,"
Shall rend the vaulted skies.

5 And when before the throne
I stand, in Him complete,
I'll lay my trophies down,
All down at Jesus' feet.

Mrs. E. M. Hall.

151 *Wounded for Us.*

1 Thy tears, not mine, O Christ,
Have wept my guilt away;
And turned this night of mine
Into a blessed day.

2 Thy wounds, not mine, O Christ,
Can heal my bruised soul;
Thy stripes, not mine, contain
The balm that makes me whole.

3 Thy cross, not mine, O Christ,
Has borne the awful load
Of sins that none could bear
But the incarnate God.

4 Thy death, not mine, O Christ,
Has paid the ransom due;
Ten thousand deaths like mine
Would have been all too few.

H. Bonar.

ARIEL. C. P. M. *Lowell Mason, arr.*

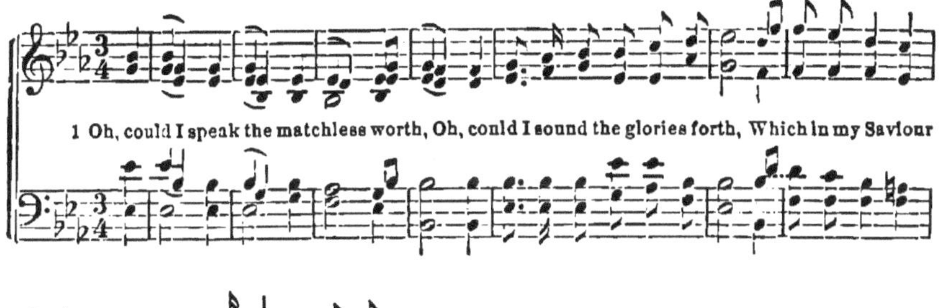

152 *"He is precious."*

2 I'd sing the precious blood He spilt,
My ransom from the dreadful guilt,
Of sin and wrath divine!
I'd sing His glorious righteousness,
In which all-perfect heavenly dress
My soul shall ever shine.

3 I'd sing the characters He bears,
And all the forms of love He wears,
Exalted on His throne:
In loftiest songs of sweetest praise,
I would to everlasting days
Make all His glories known.

4 Well, the delightful day will come,
When my dear Lord will bring me home,
And I shall see His face:
Then with my Saviour, Brother, Friend,
A blest eternity I'll spend,
Triumphant in His grace.

S. Medley.

153 *The Fullness of Christ's Love.*

1 O love divine, how sweet thou art!
When shall I find my willing heart
All taken up by thee?
I thirst, I faint, I die to prove
The greatness of redeeming love,—
The love of Christ to me.

2 Stronger His love than death or hell,—
No mortal can its riches tell,
Nor first-born sons of light:
In vain they long its depths to see;
They cannot reach the mystery,—
The length, the breadth, the height.

3 God only knows the love of God;
Oh that it now were shed abroad
In this poor, stony heart!
For love I sigh, for love I pine;
This only portion, Lord, be mine—
Be mine this better part.

4 Oh that I could forever sit
In transport at my Saviour's feet!
Be this my happy choice;
My only care, delight, and bliss,
My joy, my heaven on earth be this,
To hear my Saviour's voice.

C. Wesley.

UXBRIDGE. L. M. *Lowell Mason.*

1 Come, gracious Spir-it, heavenly Dove, With light and comfort from a - bove:

Be Thou our guardian, Thou our guide, O'er every thought and step pre - side.

154 *Prayer for the Guidance of the Spirit.*

2 The light of truth to us display,
And make us know and choose Thy way;
Plant holy fear in every heart,
That we from God may ne'er depart.

3 Lead us to holiness—the road
Which we must take to dwell with God;
Lead us to Christ, the living way,
Nor let us from His pastures stray.

4 Lead us to God, our final rest,
To be with Him forever blest;
Lead us to Heaven, its bliss to share—
Fullness of joy forever there!

Browne.

155 *"Veni Creator!"*

1 Come, O Creator Spirit blest!
And in our souls take up Thy rest:
Come, with Thy grace, and heavenly aid,
To fill the hearts which Thou hast made.

2 Great Comforter! to Thee we cry;
O highest gift of God Most High!
O fount of life! O fire of love!
Send sweet anointing from above!

3 Kindle our senses from above,
And make our hearts o'erflow with love;
With patience firm, and virtue high,
The weakness of our flesh supply.

4 Far from us drive the foe we dread,
And grant us Thy true peace instead;
So shall we not, with Thee for guide,
Turn from the path of life aside.

E. Caswall.

156 *Spirit of grace.*

1 Come, sacred Spirit, from above,
And fill the coldest heart with love:
Oh, turn to flesh the flinty stone,
And let Thy sovereign power be known.

2 Speak Thou, and from the haughtiest eyes
Shall floods of contrite sorrow rise;
While all their glowing souls are borne
To seek that grace which now they scorn.

3 Oh, let a holy flock await
In crowds around Thy temple-gate!
Each pressing on with zeal to be
A living sacrifice to thee.

P. Doddridge.

BALERMA. C. M. *Spanish Melody.*

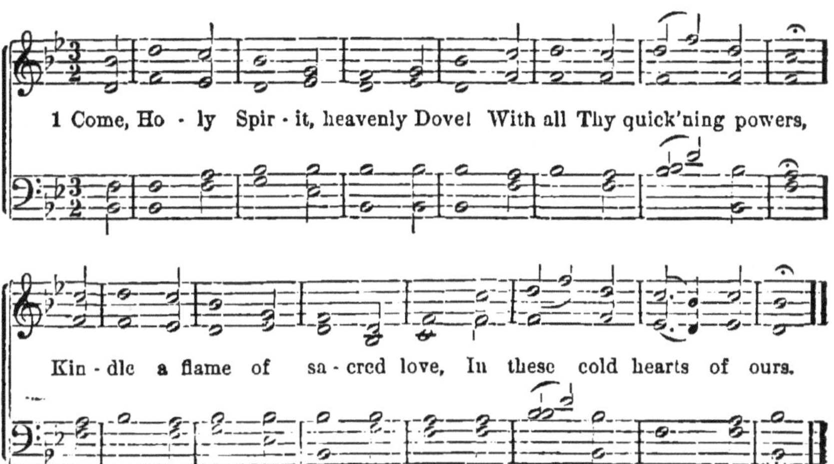

157 *Come, Holy Spirit.*

2 Look—how we grovel here below,
Fond of these trifling toys!
Our souls can neither fly nor go,
To reach eternal joys.

3 In vain we tune our formal songs,
In vain we strive to rise;
Hosannas languish on our tongues,
And our devotion dies.

4 Dear Lord! and shall we ever live
At this poor dying rate?
Our love so faint, so cold to Thee,
And Thine to us so great?

5 Come, Holy Spirit, heavenly Dove!
With all Thy quick'ning powers;
Come, shed abroad a Saviour's love,
And that shall kindle ours.

I. Watts.

158 *Descent of the Spirit.*

1 Spirit Divine! attend our prayers,
And make this house Thy home;
Descend with all Thy gracious powers,
Oh! come, great Spirit! come.

2 Come as the fire; and purge our hearts,
Like sacrificial flame;
Let our whole soul an offering be
To our Redeemer's name.

3 Come as the dove; and spread Thy wings,
The wings of peaceful love;
And let Thy church on earth become
Bless'd as the church above.

Andrew Reed.

159 *Eternal Spirit.*

1 Eternal Spirit! God of truth!
Our contrite hearts inspire;
Kindle the flame of heavenly love,
And feed the pure desire.

2 'Tis Thine to soothe the sorrowing soul,
With guilt and fear oppressed;
'Tis Thine to bid the dying live,
And give the weary rest.

3 Subdue the power of every sin,
Whate'er that sin may be;
That we, in singleness of heart,
May worship only Thee.

Thomas Cotterill.

GUIDE. **7, D.** *M. M. Wells, by per.*

160 *The Holy Spirit our Guide.*

2 Ever present, truest Friend,
Ever near Thine aid to lend,
Leave us not to doubt and fear,
Groping on in darkness drear.
When the storms are raging sore,
Hearts grow faint, and hopes give o'er—
Whisper softly, Wanderer, come!
Follow Me, I'll guide thee home.

3 When our days of toil shall cease,
Waiting still for sweet release,
Nothing left but Heaven and prayer,
Wondering if our names are there;
Wading deep the dismal flood,
Pleading naught but Jesus' blood—
Whisper softly, Wanderer, come!
Follow Me, I'll guide thee home.

Anon.

161 *Prayer for the Spirit.*

1 Holy Spirit, from on high,
Bend o'er us a pitying eye;
Now refresh the drooping heart;
Bid the power of sin depart.
Light up every dark recess
Of our hearts' ungodliness;
Show us every devious way
Where our steps have gone astray.

2 Teach us with repentant grief,
Humbly to implore relief;
Then the Saviour's blood reveal,
And our broken spirits heal.
May we daily grow in grace,
And pursue the heavenly race,
Trained in wisdom, led by love,
Till we reach our rest above.

Rev. W. H. Bathurst.

NEW HAVEN. **6, 4.** *Thomas Hastings.*

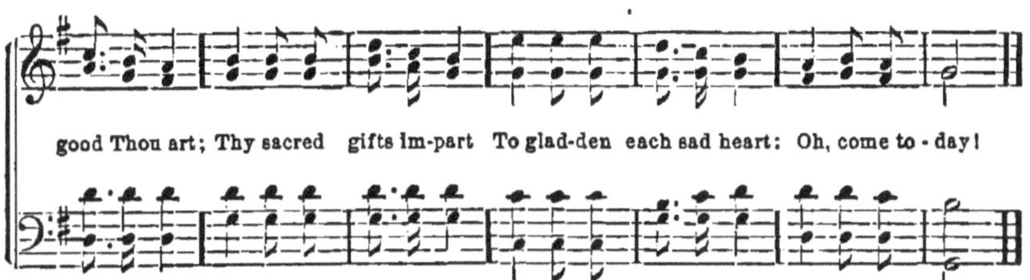

162 *"Veni, Sancte Spiritus."*

2 Come, tenderest Friend, and best,
Our most delightful guest,
With soothing power:
Rest, which the weary know,
Shade, 'mid the noontide glow,
Peace, when deep griefs o'erflow,
Cheer us, this hour!

3 Come, Light serene, and still
Our inmost bosoms fill;
Dwell in each breast;
We know no dawn but Thine;
Send forth Thy beams divine,
On our dark souls to shine,
And make us blest!

4 Come, all the faithful bless;
Let all who Christ confess,
His praise employ:
Give virtue's rich reward;
Victorious death accord,
And, with our glorious Lord,
Eternal joy!

Anon.

163 *Evening Prayer.*

1 Father of love and power,
Guard Thou our evening hour,
Shield with Thy might:
For all Thy care this day
Our grateful thanks we pay,
And to our Father pray,
Bless us to-night.

2 Jesus Immanuel,
Come in Thy love to dwell
In hearts contrite:
For many sins we grieve,
But we Thy grace receive,
And in Thy word believe;
Bless us to-night.

3 Spirit of truth and love,
Life-giving, Holy Dove,
Shed forth Thy light:
Heal every sinner's smart,
Still every throbbing heart,
And Thine own peace impart;
Bless us to-night.

George Rawson.

HORTON. 7. *Xavier Schnyder von Wartensee.*

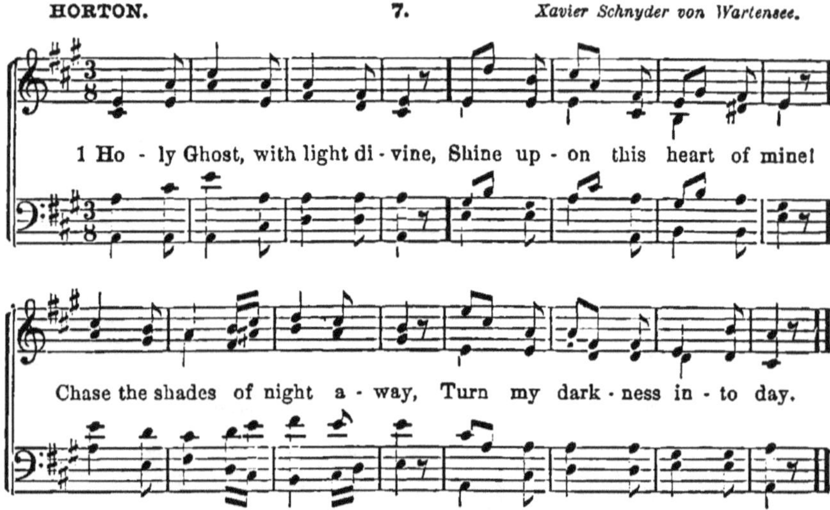

164 *"Holy Spirit, all Divine."*

2 Holy Ghost, with power divine,
Cleanse this guilty heart of mine;
Long hath sin, without control,
Held dominion o'er my soul.

3 Holy Ghost, with joy divine,
Cheer this saddened heart of mine;
Bid my many woes depart,
Heal my wounded, bleeding heart!

4 Holy Spirit, all divine!
Dwell within this heart of mine;
Cast down every idol-throne;
Reign supreme, and reign alone!
A. Reed.

165 *"It is God that worketh in you."*

1 Holy Ghost, Thou source of light!
We invoke Thy kindling ray:
Dawn upon our spirits' night,
Turn our darkness into day.

2 To the anxious soul impart
Hope, all other hopes above;
Stir the dull and hardened heart
With a longing and a love.

3 Work in all, in all renew,
Day by day, the life divine;
All our wills to Thee subdue,
All our hearts to Thee incline.
Cotterill.

166 *Keep me, Lord."*

1 Gracious Spirit, Love divine!
Let Thy light within me shine;
All my guilty fears remove,
Fill me with Thy heavenly love.

2 Speak Thy pardoning grace to me,
Set the burdened sinner free;
Lead me to the Lamb of God;
Wash me in His precious blood.

3 Life and peace to me impart,
Seal salvation on my heart;
Breathe Thyself into my breast,—
Earnest of immortal rest.

4 Let me never from Thee stray,
Keep me in the narrow way;
Fill my soul with joy divine,
Keep me, Lord, forever Thine.
J. Stocker.

167 *Near the Cross.*

2 Near the cross, a trembling soul
Love and mercy found me;
There the bright and morning star
Shed its beams around me.

3 Near the cross! O Lamb of God,
Bring its scenes before me;
Help me walk from day to day
With its shadow o'er me.

4 Near the cross I'll watch and wait,
Hoping, trusting ever,
Till I reach the golden strand,
Just beyond the river.

Anon.

168 *Trusting in Christ.*

1 I am coming to the cross:
I am poor, and weak, and blind;
I am counting all but dross;
I shall full salvation find.

2 Here I give my all to Thee,—
Friends, and time, and earthly store;
Soul and body Thine to be—
Wholly Thine—for evermore.

3 In the promises I trust;
Now I feel the blood applied;
I am prostrate in the dust;
I with Christ am crucified.

4 Jesus comes! He fills my soul!
Perfected in love I am;
I am every whit made whole;
Glory, glory to the Lamb!

Anon.

MAITLAND. C. M. *Aaron Chapin.*

169 *No Cross, no Crown.*

2 How happy are the saints above,
Who once went sorrowing here!
But now they taste unmingled love,
And joy without a tear.

3 The consecrated cross I'll bear,
Till death shall set me free;
And then go home my crown to wear,
For there's a crown for me.

4 Upon the crystal pavement, down
At Jesus' pierced feet,
Joyful I'll cast my golden crown,
And His dear name repeat.

5 And palms shall wave, and harps shall ring,
Beneath heaven's arches high;
The Lord that lives, the ransomed sing,
That lives, no more to die.

6 O precious cross! O glorious crown!
O resurrection day!
Ye angels, from the stars come down,
And bear my soul away.

G. N. Allen.

170 *"I am not ashamed."*

1 I'm not ashamed to own my Lord,
Or to defend His cause,
Maintain the honor of His word,
The glory of His cross.

2 Jesus, my God! I know His name,
His name is all my trust;
Nor will He put my soul to shame,
Nor let my hope be lost.

3 Firm as His throne His promise stands,
And He can well secure
What I've committed to His hands,
Till the decisive hour.

4 Then will He own my worthless name
Before His Father's face,
And in the New Jerusalem
Appoint my soul a place.

I. Watts.

LIFE FOR A LOOK. *Rev. E. G. Taylor, by per.*

171 *Life for a Look.*

2 Oh, why was He there as a bearer of sin,
If on Jesus thy guilt was not laid?
Oh, why from His side flowed the sin-cleansing blood,
If His dying thy debt has not paid?

3 It is not thy tears of repentance, and prayers,
But the Blood, that atones for the soul;
On Him, then, who shed it, thou mayest at once
Thy weight of iniquities roll.

4 Then doubt not thy welcome, since God has declared
There remaineth no more to be done;
That once in the end of the world He appeared,
And completed the work He begun.

5 Then take with rejoicing from Jesus at once
The life everlasting He gives;
And know with assurance thou never canst die,
Since Jesus, thy righteousness, lives.

Amelia M. Hull.

HAMBURG. **L. M.** *Lowell Mason.*

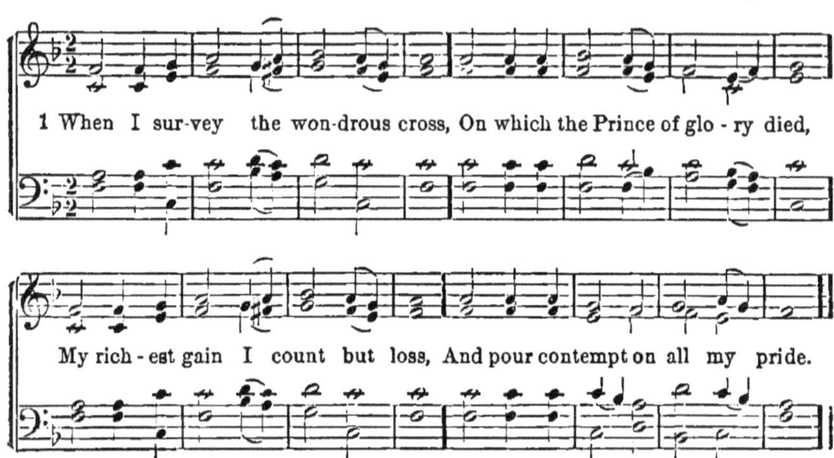

172 *Crucified to the World.*

2 Forbid it, Lord! that I should boast,
Save in the death of Christ, my God;
All the vain things that charm me most,
I sacrifice them to His blood.

3 See! from His head, His hands, His feet,
Sorrow and love flow mingled down;
Did e'er such love and sorrow meet?
Or thorns compose so rich a crown?

4 His dying crimson, like a robe,
Spreads o'er His body on the tree;
Then am I dead to all the globe,
And all the globe is dead to me.

5 Were the whole realm of nature mine,
That were a present far too small;
Love so amazing, so divine,
Demands my soul, my life, my all.

I. Watts.

173 *The Wonders of the Cross.*

1 Nature, with open volume, stands
To spread her Maker's praise abroad;
And every labor of His hands
Shows something worthy of a God.

2 But, in the grace that rescued man,
His brightest form of glory shines;
Here, on the cross, 'tis fairest drawn
In precious blood, and crimson lines.

3 Oh! the sweet wonders of that cross
Where God, the Saviour, loved and died!
Her noblest life my spirit draws
From His dear wounds and bleeding side.

I. Watts.

174 *"It is finished."*

1 "'Tis finished!"—so the Saviour cried,
And meekly bowed His head and died;
"Tis finished!"—yes, the race is run,
The battle fought, the vict'ry won.

2 "Tis finished!"—Heaven is reconciled,
And all the powers of darkness spoiled:
Peace, love, and happiness, again
Return, and dwell with sinful men.

3 "Tis finished!"—let the joyful sound
Be heard through all the nations round:
"'Tis finished!"—let the echo fly
Thro' heaven and hell, thro' earth and sky.

Samuel Stennett.

THERE IS A GREEN HILL FAR AWAY. *Geo. C. Stebbins, by per.*

175 *He Died for Us.*

2 We may not know, we cannot tell
What pains He had to bear;
But we believe it was for us
He hung and suffered there.

3 He died that we might be forgiven,
He died to make us good,
That we might go at last to Heaven,
Saved by His precious blood.

4 There was no other good enough
To pay the price of sin;
He only could unlock the gate
Of Heaven and let us in.

Mrs. C. F. Alexander.

RATHBUN. **8, 7.** *Ithamar Conkey.*

176 *"God forbid that I should glory, save in the cross of our Lord Jesus Christ."*

2 When the woes of life o'ertake me,
Hopes deceive, and fears annoy,
Never shall the cross forsake me:
Lo! it glows with peace and joy.

3 When the sun of bliss is beaming
Light and love upon my way,
From the cross the radiance streaming
Adds new lustre to the day.

4 Bane and blessing, pain and pleasure,
By the cross are sanctified;
Peace is there, that knows no measure,
Joys that through all time abide.

5 In the cross of Christ I glory,
Towering o'er the wrecks of time;
All the light of sacred story
Gathers round its head sublime.

John Bowring.

177 *Contemplating the Cross.*

1 Sweet the moments, rich in blessing,
Which before the cross we spend;
Life and health and peace possessing,
From the sinner's dying Friend!

2 Here we rest, in wonder viewing
All our sins on Jesus laid;
Here we see redemption flowing
From the sacrifice He made.

3 Truly blessed is the station,
Low before the cross to lie;
And behold the great salvation
To rebellious man brought nigh.

4 Here we find the dawn of Heaven,
While upon the cross we gaze;
See our trespasses forgiven,
And our songs of triumph raise.

5 Oh, that near the cross abiding,
We may to the Saviour cleave!
Nought with Him our hearts dividing,
All for Him content to leave.

6 May we still, the cross discerning,
There alone for comfort go;
And new wonders daily learning,
More of Jesus' fullness know.

James Allen.

STEPHENS. C. M. *Wm. Jones*

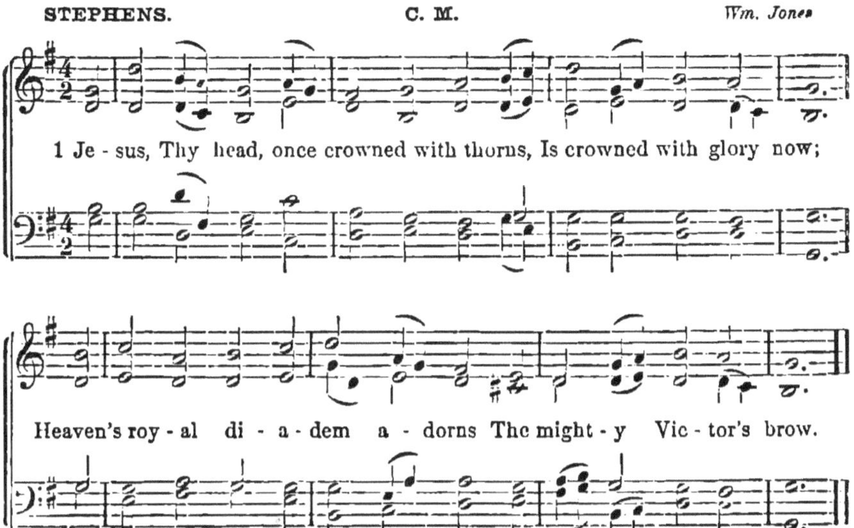

178 *"We shall also reign with Him."*

2 Delight of all who dwell above,
The joy of saints below;
To us still manifest Thy love,
That we its depths may know.

3 To us Thy cross, with all its shame,
With all its grace be given;
Though earth disowns Thy lowly name,
All worship it in Heaven.

4 Who suffer with Thee, Lord, below,
Will reign with Thee above;
Then let it be our joy to know
This way of peace and love.

5 To us Thy cross is life and health,
Though shame and death to Thee;
On earth it is our joy and wealth,
In Heaven, our crown shall be.

Anon.

179 *"The Lord hath laid on Him the iniquity of us all."*

1 O Christ, our ever-blessed Lord,
For man's transgression slain,
We Thy redeeming love record
In songs of thankful strain.

2 We upward lift our longing eyes,
And muse on Calvary;
On Thy mysterious sacrifice,
Thy shame and agony.

3 We all like erring sheep had strayed
From God the Father's care;
The guilt of all on Thee was laid,
Our burden Thou didst bear.

4 O Christ, be Thou our present joy,
Our future great reward;
Our only glory may it be,
To glory in the Lord!

5 Oh, may we through Thy cross and pain,
With all who Thee adore,
A blessed resurrection gain,
And life for evermore!

Anon.

180 *Doxology.*

To Father, Son, and Holy Ghost,
One God, whom we adore,
Be glory as it was, is now,
And shall be evermore!

AVON. **C. M.** *Hugh Wilson.*

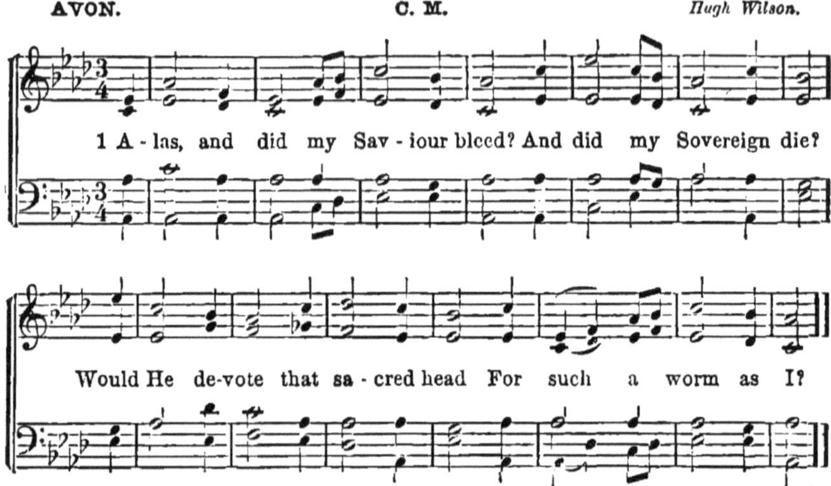

181 *Godly Sorrow in View of Christ's Sufferings.*

2 Was it for crimes that I had done
He groaned upon the tree?
Amazing pity! grace unknown!
And love beyond degree!

3 Well might the sun in darkness hide,
And shut His glories in,
When Christ, the mighty Maker, died
For man the creature's sin.

4 Thus might I hide my blushing face,
While His dear cross appears:
Dissolve, my heart, in thankfulness,
And melt, mine eyes, to tears.

5 But drops of grief can ne'er repay
The debt of love I owe:
Here, Lord, I give myself away;
'Tis all that I can do.

I. Watts.

182 *Kneeling at the Cross.*

1 O Jesus, sweet the tears I shed,
While at Thy cross I kneel,
Gaze on Thy wounded, fainting head,
And all Thy sorrows feel.

2 My heart dissolves to see Thee bleed,
This heart so hard before;
I hear Thee for the guilty plead,
And grief o'erflows the more.

3 'Twas for the sinful Thou didst die,
And I a sinner stand:
What love speaks from Thy dying eye,
And from each pierced hand!

4 I know this cleansing blood of Thine
Was shed, dear Lord, for me:
For me, for all, O grace divine!
Who look by faith on Thee.

5 O Christ of God, O spotless Lamb,
By love my soul is drawn;
Henceforth, forever, Thine I am;
Here life and peace are born

6 In patient hope, the cross I'll bear,
Thine arm shall be my stay;
And Thou, enthroned, my soul shalt spare,
On Thy great judgment day.

Rev. Ray Palmer.

HAMDEN. **8, 7, 4.** *Lowell Mason.*

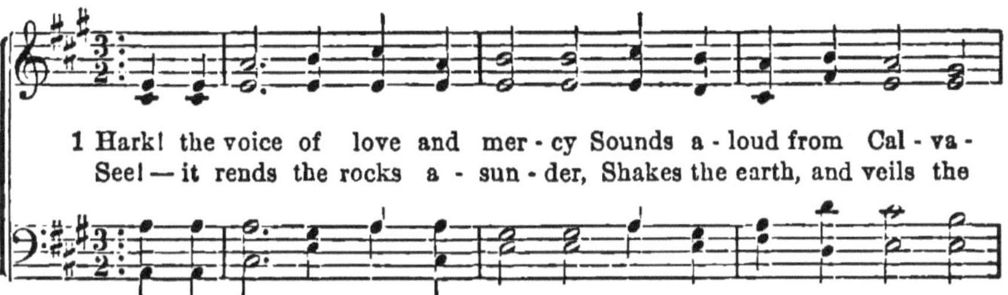

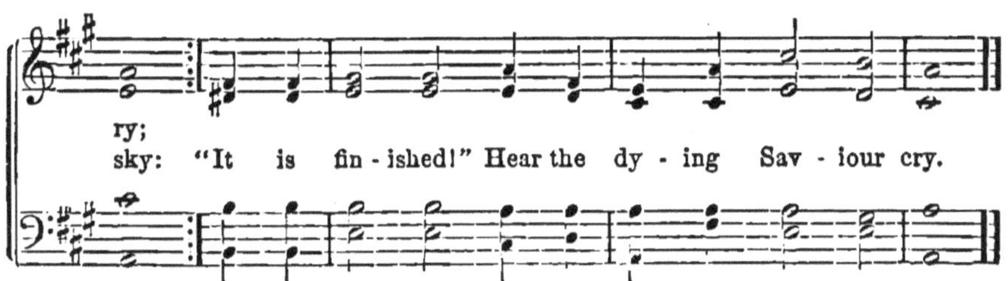

183 *The Finished Redemption.*

2 "It is finished!"—Oh! what pleasure
Do these charming words afford!
Heavenly blessings, without measure,
Flow to us from Christ the Lord:
"It is finished!"
Saints, the dying words record.

3 Finished all the types and shadows
Of the ceremonial law!
Finished all that God had promised;
Death and hell no more shall awe:
"It is finished!"
Saints, from hence your comfort draw.

4 Tune your harps anew, ye seraphs!
Join to sing the pleasing theme;
All on earth, and all in Heaven,
Join to praise Immanuel's name:
Hallelujah!
Glory to the bleeding Lamb!

Jonathan Evans.

184 *Welcome to the Saviour.*

1 Come, ye souls, by sin afflicted!
Bowed with fruitless sorrow down,
By the perfect law convicted,
Through the cross, behold the crown,
Look to Jesus;
Mercy flows through Him alone.

2 Take His easy yoke, and wear it;
Love will make obedience sweet;
Christ will give you strength to bear it,
While His wisdom guides your feet
Safe to glory,
Where His ransomed captives meet.

3 Sweet, as home to pilgrims weary,
Light to newly-opened eyes,
Or full springs in deserts dreary,
Is the rest the cross supplies;
All who taste it,
Shall to rest immortal rise.

Joseph Swain.

ROSEFIELD. 7, 6 L. *Rev. C. H. A. Malan.*

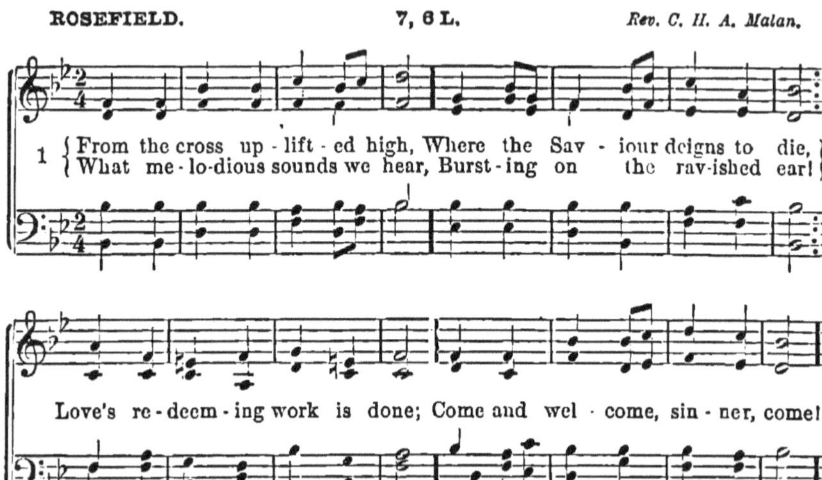

185 *Welcome!*

2 "Spread for Thee, the festal board
See with richest dainties stored;
To thy Father's bosom pressed,
Yet again a child confessed,
Never from His house to roam:
Come and welcome, sinner, come!

3 "Soon the days of life shall end;
Lo, I come, your Saviour, Friend!
Safe your spirits to convey
To the realms of endless day,
Up to my eternal home:
Come and welcome, sinner, come!"

Hawels.

186 *Pleading with Sinners.*

1 Heart of stone, relent, relent!
Break, by Jesus' cross subdued;
See His body mangled, rent,
Covered with His flowing blood:
Sinful soul, what hast thou done!
Crucified th' incarnate Son!

2 Yes; thy sins have done the deed,
Driven the nails that fixed Him there:
Crowned with thorns His sacred head,
Pierced Him with the cruel spear,
Made His soul a sacrifice,
While for sinful man He dies.

3 Wilt thou let Him bleed in vain?
Still to death thy Lord pursue?
Open all His wounds again,
And the shameful cross renew?
No; with all my sins I'll part:
Break, oh, break, my bleeding heart!

C. Wesley.

187 *"My flesh is meat indeed."*

1 Bread of Heaven! on Thee I feed,
For Thy flesh is meat indeed;
Ever may my soul be fed
With this true and living Bread;
Day by day with strength supplied
Through the life of Him who died.

2 Vine of Heaven! Thy blood supplies
This blest cup of sacrifice;
'Tis Thy wounds my healing give;
To Thy cross I look, and live;
Thou, my Life, oh, let me be
Rooted, grafted, built on Thee!

Conder.

C. M. *From G. Rossini.*

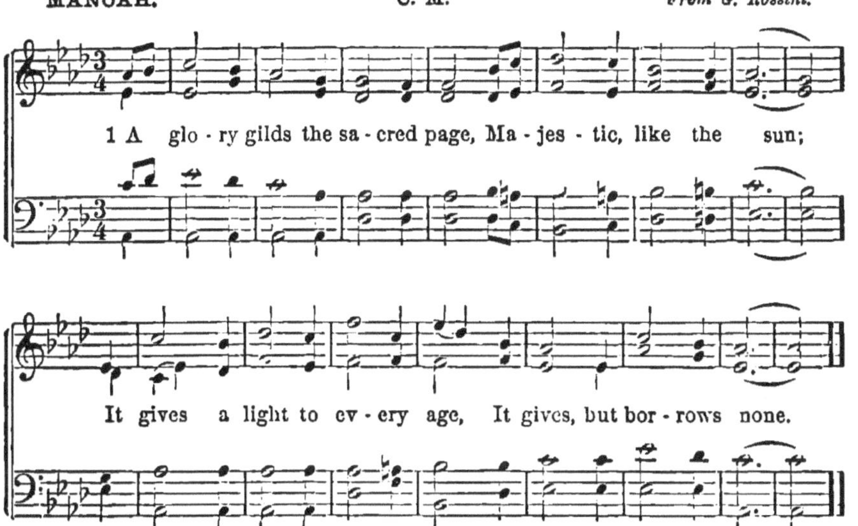

188 *The Light and Glory of the Word.*

2 The hand that gave it still supplies
The gracious light and heat;
Its truths upon the nations rise,
They rise, but never set.

3 Let everlasting thanks be Thine,
For such a bright display,
As makes a world of darkness shine
With beams of heavenly day.

4 My soul rejoices to pursue
The steps of Him I love,
Till glory breaks upon my view,
In brighter worlds above.

William Cowper.

189 *A Lamp, and a Light.*

1 How precious is the book divine,
By inspiration given:
Bright as a lamp its doctrines shine,
To guide our souls to Heaven.

2 Its light, descending from above,
Our gloomy world to cheer,
Displays a Saviour's boundless love,
And brings His glories near.

3 It shows to man his wandering ways,
And where his feet have trod;
And brings to view the matchless grace
Of a forgiving God.

4 It sweetly cheers our drooping hearts,
In this dark vale of tears;
Life, light, and joy it still imparts,
And quells our rising fears.

5 This lamp, thro' all the tedious night
Of life, shall guide our way,
Till we behold the clearer light
Of an eternal day.

Rev. John Fawcett.

190 *Doxology.*

1 Let God the Father, and the Son,
And Spirit, be adored,
Where there are works to make Him known,
Or saints to love the Lord!

Anon.

DUKE STREET. **L. M.** *John Hatton.*

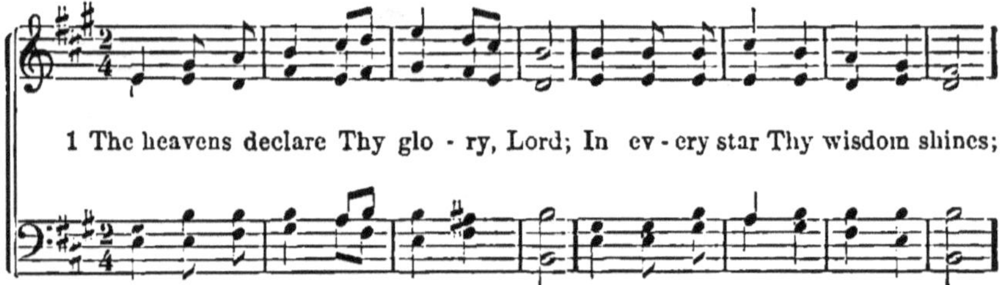

But when our eyes be - hold Thy word, We read Thy name in fair - er lines.

191 *The two Revelations.*

2 The rolling sun, the changing light,
And nights and days, Thy power confess,
But the blest volume Thou hast writ,
Reveals Thy justice and Thy grace.

3 Sun, moon, and stars convey Thy praise
Round the whole earth, and never stand;
So when Thy truth began its race,
It touched and glanced on every land.

4 Nor shall Thy spreading gospel rest,
Till thro' the world Thy truth has run;
Till Christ has all the nations blessed
That see the light, and feel the sun.

5 Great Sun of Righteousness, arise,
Bless the dark world with heav'nly light;
Thy gospel makes the simple wise,
Thy laws are pure, Thy judgments right.

I. Watts.

192 *God's Word our Guide.*

1 God in the gospel of His Son,
Makes His eternal counsels known:
Where love in all its glory shines,
And truth is drawn in fairest lines.

2 Here sinners, of an humble frame,
May taste His grace, and learn His name;
May read, in characters of blood,
The wisdom, power, and grace of God.

3 Here faith reveals to mortal eyes
A brighter world beyond the skies;
Here shines the light which guides our way
From earth to realms of endless day.

4 O grant us grace, Almighty Lord,
To read and mark Thy holy word;
Its truth with meekness to receive,
And by its holy precepts live.

Rev. Benjamin Beddome.

DEDHAM. C. M. *William Gardiner.*

193 *"Endless Glory."*

2 Here, the fair tree of knowledge grows,
And yields a free repast;
Sublimer sweets than nature knows
Invite the longing taste.

3 Here, the Redeemer's welcome voice
Spreads heavenly peace around;
And life and everlasting joys
Attend the blissful sound.

4 Divine Instructor, gracious Lord!
Be Thou forever near;
Teach me to love Thy sacred word,
And view my Saviour there.

A. Steele.

194 *Psalm 119.*

1 The Spirit breathes upon the word,
And brings the truth to sight;
Precepts and promises afford
A sanctifying light.

2 A glory gilds the sacred page,
Majestic, like the sun;
It gives a light to every age;—
It gives, but borrows none.

3 The hand that gave it still supplies
The gracious light and heat;
Its truths upon the nations rise,—
They rise, but never set.

4 Let everlasting thanks be Thine,
For such a bright display,
As makes a world of darkness shine
With beams of heavenly day.

5 My soul rejoices to pursue
The steps of Him I love,
Till glory breaks upon my view,
In brighter worlds above.

W. Cowper.

195 *Dull of Heart.*

1 Laden with guilt, and full of fears,
I fly to Thee, my Lord,
And not a glimpse of hope appears,
But in Thy written word.

2 Oh, may Thy counsels, mighty God!
My roving feet command;
Nor I forsake the happy road
That leads to Thy right hand.

I. Watts.

BROWN. C. M. *W. B. Bradbury.*

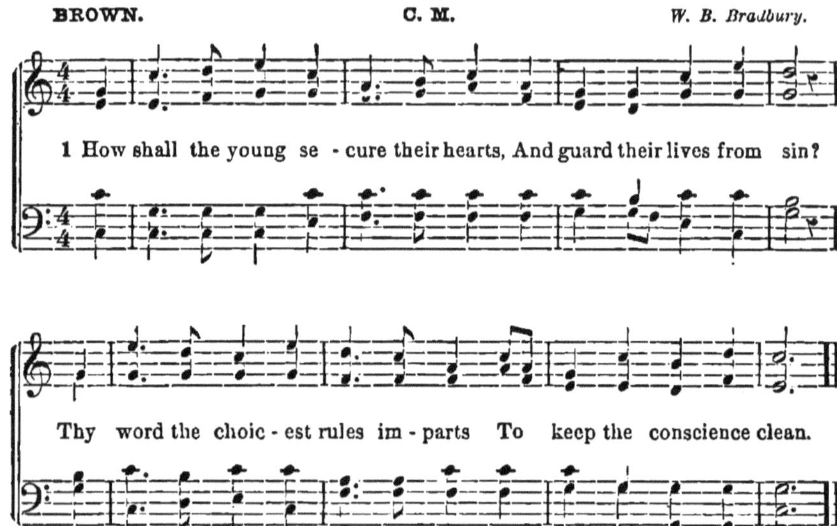

196

Psalm 119.

2 When once it enters to the mind,
It spreads such light abroad,
The meanest souls instruction find,
And raise their thoughts to God.

3 'Tis like the sun, a heavenly light,
That guides us all the day;
And, through the dangers of the night,
A lamp to lead our way.

4 Thy word is everlasting truth;
How pure is every page!
That holy book shall guide our youth,
And well support our age.

I. Watts.

197

"Lamp of our Feet."

1 Lamp of our feet, whereby we trace
Our path when wont to stray;
Stream from the Fount of heav'nly grace,
Brook by the traveler's way;

2 Bread of our souls, whereon we feed,
True manna from on high;
Our guide and chart, wherein we read
Of realms beyond the sky;

3 Word of the Everlasting God,
Will of His glorious Son;
Without Thee how could earth be trod,
Or Heaven itself be won?

4 Lord, grant us all aright to learn
The wisdom it imparts;
And to its heavenly teaching turn,
With simple, childlike hearts.

Bernard Barton.

198

Hail, Sacred Truth.

1 Hail, sacred truth, whose piercing rays
Dispel the shades of night;
Diffusing, o'er the mental world,
The healing beams of light.

2 Jesus, Thy word, with friendly aid,
Restores our wandering feet;
Converts the sorrows of the mind
To joys divinely sweet.

3 Oh, send Thy light and truth abroad
In all their radiant blaze;
And bid th' admiring world adore
The glories of Thy grace.

John Buttress.

OLMUTZ. **S. M.** *Adapted by Lowell Mason.*

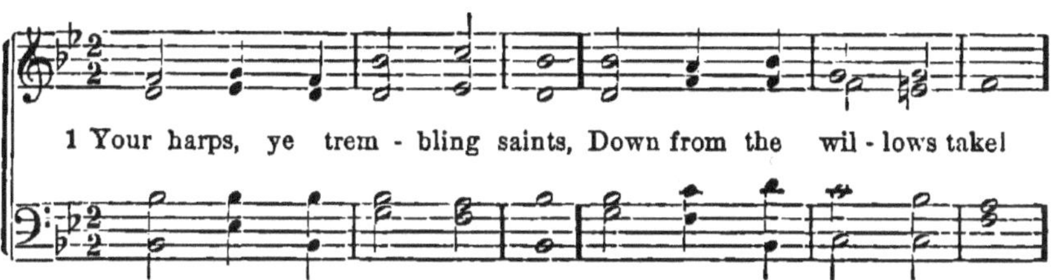

199 *Trusting in God.*

2 Though in a foreign land,
We are not far from home;
And, nearer to our house above,
We every moment come.

3 His grace will, to the end,
Stronger and brighter shine;
Nor present things, nor things to come,
Shall quench the spark divine.

4 When we in darkness walk,
Nor feel the heavenly flame,
Then is the time to trust our God,
And rest upon His name.

5 Soon shall our doubts and fears
Subside at His control;
His loving-kindness shall break through
The midnight of the soul.

6 Blest is the man, O God,
That stays himself on Thee:—
Who wait for Thy salvation, Lord,
Shall Thy salvation see.

Toplady.

200 *One with Christ.*

1 My Saviour! I am Thine
By everlasting bands;
My name, my heart, I would resign,
My soul is in Thy hands.

2 To Thee I still would cleave,
With ever-growing zeal;
Let millions tempt me Christ to leave,
They never shall prevail.

3 His Spirit shall unite
My soul, to Him, my Head;
Shall form me to His image bright,
And teach His path to tread.

4 Death may my soul divide
From this abode of clay;
But love shall keep me near His side,
Through all the gloomy way.

5 Since Christ and we are one,
What should remain to fear?
If He in Heaven hath fixed His throne,
He'll fix His members there.

Philip Doddridge.

THE LORD WILL PROVIDE. *Philip Phillips, by per.*

201 *The Lord will Provide.*

2 At some time or other the Lord will provide;
It may not be *my* time,
It may not be *thy* time;
And yet, in His *own* time,
"The Lord will provide."

3 Despond then no longer: the Lord will provide;
And this be the token—
No word He hath spoken
Was ever yet broken:
"The Lord will provide."

4 March on then right boldly; the sea shall divide;
The pathway made glorious,
With shoutings victorious,
We'll join in the chorus,
"The Lord will provide."

Mrs. M. A. W. Cook.

MERIBAH. C. P. M. *Lowell Mason.*

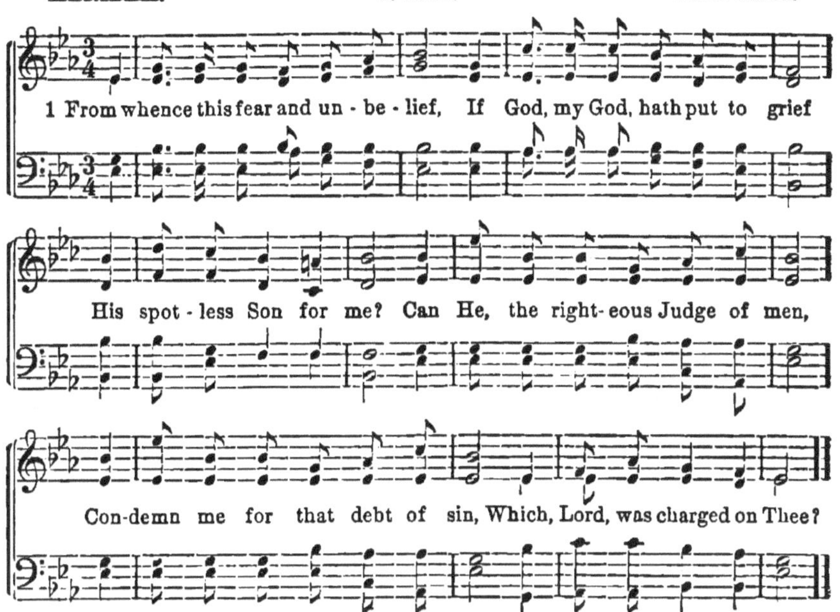

202 *The Debt is Paid.*

2 Complete atonement Thou hast made,
And to the utmost farthing paid
Whate'er Thy people owed;
How then can wrath on me take place,
Now standing in God's righteousness,
And sprinkled by Thy blood?

3 If Thou hast my discharge procured,
And freely in my place endured
The whole of wrath Divine,
Payment God will not twice demand,
First at my bleeding Surety's hand,
And then again at mine.

4 Turn then, my soul, unto thy rest;
The merits of thy great High Priest
Speak peace and liberty;
Trust in His efficacious blood,
Nor fear thy banishment from God,
Since Jesus died for thee.

Anon.

203 *"Fear not, little flock."*

1 Fear not, O little flock, the foe
Who madly seeks your overthrow,
Dread not his rage and power:
What though your courage sometimes faints,
His seeming triumph o'er God's saints
Lasts but a little hour.

2 As true as God's own word is true,
Not earth or hell with all their crew
Against us shall prevail.
A jest and byword are they grown:
God is with us; we are His own;
Our victory cannot fail.

3 Amen, Lord Jesus, grant our prayer!
Great Captain, now Thine arm make bare;
Fight for us once again!
So shall Thy saints and martyrs raise
A mighty chorus to Thy praise,
World without end. Amen.

Rev. Jacob Fabricus.

MIGDOL. L. M. *Lowell Mason.*

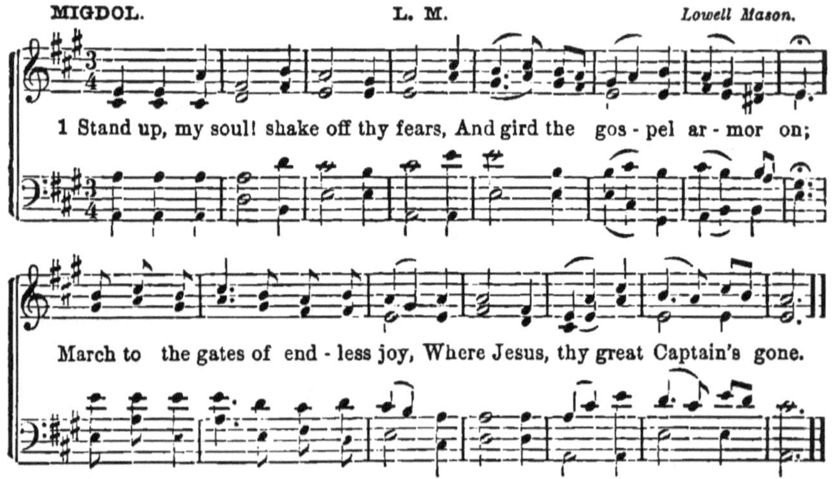

204 *The Christian Warfare.*

2 Hell and thy sins resist thy course,
But hell and sin are vanquished foes,
Thy Jesus nailed them to the cross,
And sung the triumph when He rose.

3 Then let my soul march boldly on,
Press forward to the heavenly gate,
There peace and joy eternal reign,
And glittering robes for conquerors wait.

4 There shall I wear a starry crown,
And triumph in almighty grace,
While all the armies of the skies
Join in my glorious Leader's praise.
I. Watts.

205 *Security of the Saints.*

1 Who shall the Lord's elect condemn?—
'Tis God, that justifies their souls;
And mercy, like a mighty stream,
O'er all their sins divinely rolls.

2 Who shall adjudge the saints to hell!
'Tis Christ that suffered in their stead,
And, the salvation to fulfill,
Behold Him, rising from the dead!

3 He lives, He lives, and sits above,
Forever interceding there;
Who shall divide us from His love?
Or what shall tempt us to despair?

4 Shall persecution or distress,
Famine, or sword, or nakedness!
He, that hath loved us, bears us through,
And makes us more than conquerors too.

5 Not all that men on earth can do,
Nor powers on high, nor powers below,
Shall cause His mercy to remove,
Or wean our hearts from Christ our love.
I. Watts.

206 *"When I am weak, then am I strong."*

1 Let me but hear my Saviour say,
"Strength shall be equal to thy day;"
Then I rejoice in deep distress,
Leaning on all-sufficient grace.

2 I can do all things—or can bear
All suffering, if my Lord be there;
Sweet pleasures mingle with the pains,
While He my sinking head sustains.

3 I glory in infirmity,
That Christ's own power may rest on me;
When I am weak, then am I strong;
Grace is my shield, and Christ my song.
I. Watts.

PORTUGUESE HYMN. **11.** *John Reading.*

"Exceeding great and precious Promises."

207

2 "Fear not, I am with thee, oh, be not dismayed,
For I am thy God, and will still give thee aid;
I'll strengthen thee, help thee, and cause thee to stand,
Upheld by My righteous, omnipotent hand.

3 "When through the deep waters I call thee to go,
The rivers of woe shall not thee overflow;
For I will be with thee thy trouble to bless,
And sanctify to thee thy deepest distress.

4 "E'en down to old age, all My people shall prove
My sovereign, eternal, unchangeable love;
And when hoary hairs shall their temples adorn,
Like lambs they shall still in My bosom be borne.

5 "The soul that on Jesus hath leaned for repose
I will not, I will not desert to his foes;
That soul, though all hell should endeavor to shake,
I'll never, no never, no never forsake."

George Keith.

STOCKWELL. 8, 7. *D. E. Jones.*

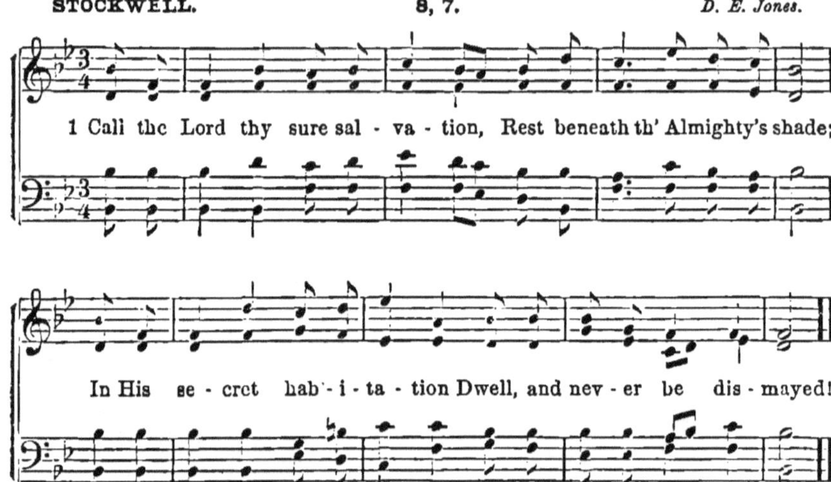

208 *"Under His wings shalt thou trust."*

2 There no tumult can alarm thee,
Thou shalt dread no hidden snare;
Guile nor violence can harm thee,
In eternal safeguard there.

3 Thee, tho' winds and waves are swelling,
God, thy Hope, shall bear through all;
Plague shall not come nigh thy dwelling,
Thee no evil shall befall.

4 He shall charge His angel legions
Watch and ward o'er thee to keep,
Though thou walk thro' hostile regions,
Though in desert wilds thou sleep.

5 Since, with firm and pure affection,
Thou on God hast set thy love,
With the wings of His protection
He shall shield thee from above.

Montgomery.

209 *"From grace to glory."*

1 Know, my soul, thy full salvation;
Rise o'er sin, and fear, and care;
Joy to find in every station
Something still to do or bear.

2 Think what Spirit dwells within thee;
Think what Father's smiles are thine;
Think that Jesus died to win thee:
Child of Heaven, canst thou repine?

3 Haste thee on from grace to glory,
Armed by faith, and winged by prayer;
Heaven's eternal day before thee—
God's own hand shall guide thee there.

4 Soon shall close thine earthly mission,
Soon shall pass thy pilgrim days;
Hope shall change to glad fruition,
Faith to sight, and prayer to praise.

Miss Grant.

210 *Psalm 127.*

1 Vainly through night's weary hours,
Keep we watch lest foes alarm;
Vain our bulwarks and our towers,
But for God's protecting arm.

2 Seek we then the Lord's Anointed;
He shall grant us peace and rest:
Ne'er was suppliant disappointed
Who to Christ his prayer addressed.

Lyte.

ST. ANN'S. C. M. *Dr. Wm. Croft.*

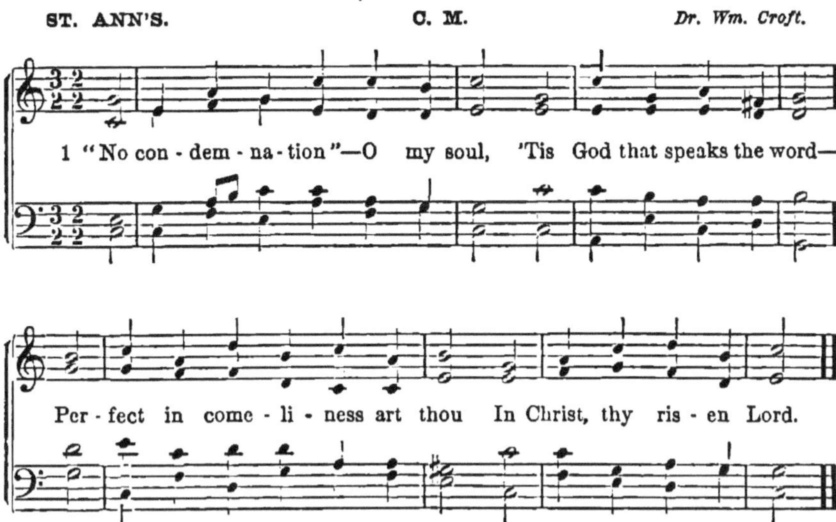

211 *"No Condemnation."*

2 In Heaven His blood forever speaks
In God the Father's ear:
His Church, the jewels, on His heart
Jesus will ever bear.

3 "No condemnation!"—precious word—
Consider it, my soul:
Thy sins were all on Jesus laid,
His stripes have made thee whole.

4 Teach us, O God, to fix our eyes
On Christ, the spotless Lamb;
So shall we love Thy gracious will,
And glorify Thy name.

Anon.

212 *"Made nigh by the blood of Christ."*

1 A mind at "perfect peace" with God:
Oh, what a word is this!
A sinner reconciled through blood:
This, this indeed is peace!

2 By nature and by practice far—
How very far from God!
Yet now by grace brought near to Him,
Through faith in Jesus' blood.

3 So near, so very near to God,
I cannot nearer be;
For in the person of His Son,
I am as near as He.

4 So dear, so very dear to God,
More dear I cannot be;
The love wherewith He loves the Son—
Such is His love to me.

Anon.

213 *"I know that my Redeemer liveth."*

1 I know that my Redeemer lives,
And ever prays for me:
A token of His love He gives,
A pledge of liberty.

2 I find Him lifting up my head;
He brings salvation near:
His presence makes me free indeed,
And he will soon appear.

3 When God is mine, and I am His,
Of paradise possessed,
I taste unutterable bliss,
And everlasting rest.

C. Wesley.

A. Chapin.

214 *"If God be for us, who can be against us?"*

2 In me He ever dwells;
O'er all my mind He reigns;
All care and sadness He dispels,
And soothes away my pains.

3 At cost of all I have,—
At cost of life and limb,
I cling to God, who yet shall save;
I will not turn from Him.

4 The world may fail and flee;
Thou, God, my Father art;
Not fire, nor sword, nor plague, from Thee
My trusting soul shall part.

5 No joys that angels know,
No throne nor wide-spread fame,
No love nor loss, nor fear nor woe,
No grief of heart or shame—

6 Man cannot aught conceive,
Of pleasure or of harm,
That e'er shall tempt my soul to leave
Her refuge in Thine arm.

From Paul Gerhardt.

215 *"That we should be called the sons of God."*

1 Behold, what wondrous grace
The Father has bestowed
On sinners of a mortal race,
To call them sons of God!

2 Nor doth it yet appear
How great we must be made;
But when we see our Saviour here,
We shall be like our Head.

3 A hope so much divine
May trials well endure;
May purify our souls from sin,
As Christ, the Lord, is pure.

4 If in my Father's love
I share a filial part,
Send down Thy Spirit, like a dove,
To rest upon my heart.

5 We would no longer lie
Like slaves beneath the throne;
Our faith shall "Abba, Father," cry,
And Thou the kindred own.

I. Watts.

LYONS. 10, 11. *Haydn.*

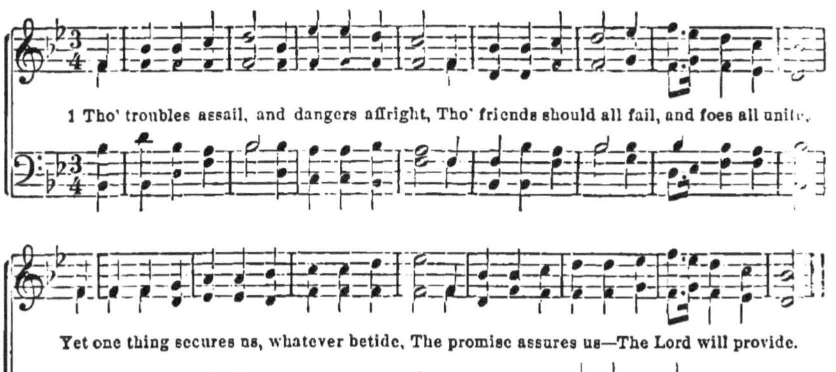

216 *The Lord will Provide.*

2 The birds, without barn or storehouse, are fed;
From them let us learn to trust for our bread;
His saints what is fitting shall ne'er be denied,
So long as 'tis written,—The Lord will provide.

3 When Satan appears to stop up our path,
And fills us with fears, we triumph by faith;
He cannot take from us (though oft he has tried)
The heart-cheering promise,—The Lord will provide.

4 He tells us we're weak,—our hope is in vain;
The good that we seek we ne'er shall obtain:
But when such suggestions our graces have tried,
This answers all questions,—The Lord will provide.

Newton.

217 "*Who is like unto the Lord our God?*"

1 Oh, worship the King, all-glorious above;
Oh, gratefully sing His power and His love!
Our Shield and Defender, the Ancient of Days,
Pavilioned in splendor, and girded with praise.

2 Oh, tell of His might, oh, sing of His grace,
Whose robe is the light, whose canopy, space!
His chariots of wrath the deep thunder-clouds form,
And dark is His path on the wings of the storm.

3 Thy bountiful care what tongue can recite?
It breathes in the air, it shines in the light,
It streams from the hills, it descends to the plains,
And sweetly distills in the dew and the rains.

4 Frail children of dust, and feeble as frail,
In Thee do we trust, nor find Thee to fail;
Thy mercies how tender! how firm to the end!
Our Maker, Defender, Redeemer, and Friend.

R. Grant.

WARWICK. C. M. *S. Stanley.*

218 *Benevolence of God's Decrees.*

2 Good, when He gives, supremely good;
Nor less when He denies;
Ev'n crosses from His sovereign hand,
Are blessings in disguise.

3 Why should we doubt a Father's love,
So constant and so kind!
To His unerring, gracious will
Be every wish resigned.

4 In Thy fair book of life divine,
My God, inscribe my name;
There let it fill some humble place
Beneath my Lord the Lamb!

Hervey.

219 *"Let me know my Father reigns."*

1 My God, my Father, blissful name!
Oh, may I call Thee mine?
May I with sweet assurance claim
A portion so divine?

2 Whate'er Thy providence denies
I calmly would resign;
For Thou art good, and just, and wise;
Oh, bend my will to Thine!

3 Whate'er Thy sacred will ordains,
Oh, give me strength to bear!
And let me know my Father reigns,
And trust His tender care.

4 Thy sovereign ways are all unknown
To my weak, erring sight;
Yet let my soul adoring own
That all Thy ways are right.

Mrs. Steele.

220 *"Lord, increase our faith."*

1 Oh for a faith that will not shrink
Though pressed by every foe;
That will not tremble on the brink
Of any earthly woe!—

2 That will not murmur nor complain
Beneath the chastening rod,
But in the hour of grief or pain,
Will lean upon its God;—

3 A faith that shines more bright and clear
When tempests rage without;
That, when in danger, knows no fear,
In darkness, feels no doubt;—

4 Lord, give us such a faith as this,
And then, whate'er may come,
We'll taste, ev'n here, the hallowed bliss
Of an eternal home.

Anon.

DOVER. S. M. *English Melody.*

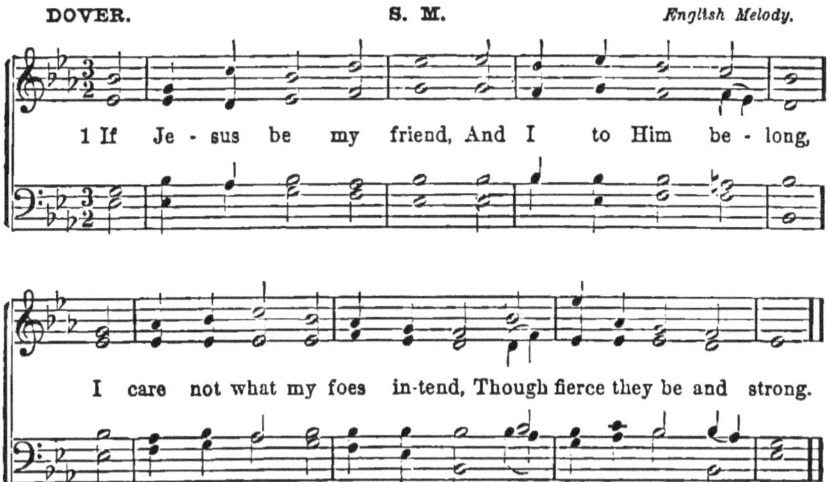

221 *"There is laid up for me a crown."*

2 I rest upon the ground
Of Jesus and His blood;
For I in Him alone have found
The true, eternal good.

3 He whispers in my breast
Sweet words of holy cheer,
How all who seek in God their rest
Shall ever find Him near.

4 How God hath built above
A city fair and new,
Where eye and heart shall see and prove
What faith has counted true.

5 My heart for gladness springs;
It cannot more be sad;
For very joy it smiles and sings,—
Sees naught but sunshine glad.

6 The sun that lights mine eyes,
Is Christ, the Lord I love;
I sing for joy of that which lies
Stored up for me above.

Paul Gerhardt, tr.

222 *"Wait thou His time."*

1 Give to the winds thy fears;
Hope on, be not dismayed:
God hears thy sighs and counts thy tears;
God shall lift up thy head.

2 Through waves, and clouds and storms,
He gently clears thy way;
Wait thou His time: the darkest night
Shall end in brightest day.

3 Far, far above thy thought
His counsel shall appear,
When fully He the work hath wrought,
That caused thy needless fear.

4 What though Thou rulest not!
Yet Heaven and earth and hell
Proclaim—God sitteth on the throne,
And ruleth all things well.

Paul Gerhardt, tr.

223 *Doxology.*

1 To the eternal Three,
In will and essence one;
To Father, Son, and Spirit be
Co-equal honor done.

Anon.

A. Williams.

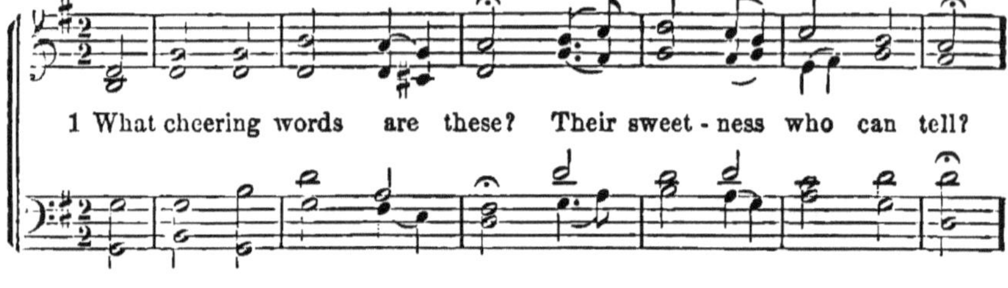

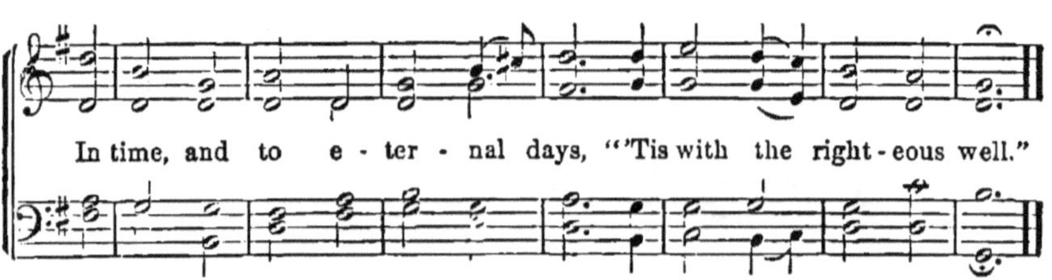

224 *"Say ye to the righteous that it shall be well with him."*

2 In every state secure,
Kept as Jehovah's eye,
'Tis well with them while life endures,
And well, when called to die;

3 'Tis well, when joys arise;
'Tis well, when sorrows flow;
'Tis well, when darkness vails the skies,
And strong temptations grow.

4 'Tis well, when Jesus calls:
"From earth and sin arise,
To join the hosts of ransomed souls,
Made to salvation wise!"

Kent.

225 *"My times are in Thy hand."*

1 "My times are in Thy hand:"
My God, I wish them there;
My life, my friends, my soul, I leave
Entirely to Thy care.

2 "My times are in Thy hand,"
Whatever they may be;
Pleasing or painful, dark or bright,
As best may seem to Thee.

3 "My times are in Thy hand;"
Why should I doubt or fear?
My Father's hand will never cause
His child a needless tear.

4 "My times are in Thy hand,"
Jesus, the crucified!
The hand my cruel sins had pierced,
Is now my guard and guide.

5 "My times are in Thy hand;"
I'll always trust in Thee;
And after death at Thy right hand
I shall forever be.

Anon.

226 *"Goeth forth weeping."*

1 The harvest dawn is near,
The year delays not long;
And he who sows with many a tear,
Shall reap with many a song.

2 Sad to his toil he goes,
His seed with weeping leaves;
But he shall come at twilight's close,
And bring his golden sheaves.

G. Burgess.

MARTYN. 7, D. *S. B. Marsh.*

227 *The sure Refuge.*

2 Other refuge have I none,
  Hangs my helpless soul on Thee:
Leave, ah! leave me not alone,
  Still support and comfort me.
All my trust on Thee is stayed,
  All my help from Thee I bring;
Cover my defenseless head,
  With the shadow of Thy wing.

3 Thou, O Christ, art all I want;
  More than all in Thee I find;
Raise the fallen, cheer the faint,
  Heal the sick, and lead the blind:
Just and holy is Thy name;
  I am all unrighteousness;
False and full of sin I am,
  Thou art full of truth and grace.

4 Plenteous grace with Thee is found,
  Grace to cover all my sin;
Let the healing streams abound,
  Make and keep me pure within.
Thou of life the Fountain art,
  Freely let me take of Thee:
Spring Thou up within my heart,
  Rise to all eternity.

C. Wesley.

228 *"Cast thy burden upon the Lord."*

1 Cast thy burden on the Lord,
Only lean upon His word;
Thou wilt soon have cause to bless
His unchanging faithfulness.

2 He sustains thee by His hand,
He enables thee to stand;
Those whom Jesus once hath loved,
From His grace are never moved.

3 Heaven and earth may pass away,
God's free grace shall not decay:
He hath promised to fulfill
All the pleasure of His will.

4 Jesus! guardian of Thy flock,
Be Thyself our constant rock;
Make us by Thy powerful hand,
Firm as Zion's mountain stand.

Rowland Hill.

YARMOUTH. 7, 6. D. *Lowell Mason.*

229 *Joy and Peace.*

2 In holy contemplation,
We sweetly then pursue
The theme of God's salvation,
And find it ever new:
Set free from present sorrow,
We cheerfully can say,
Let the unknown to-morrow
Bring with it what it may.

3 It can bring with it nothing
But He will bear us through;
Who gives the lilies clothing
Will clothe His people too;
Beneath the spreading heavens,
No creature but is fed;
And He who feeds the ravens
Will give His children bread.

William Cowper.

230 *"Show forth His salvation."*

1 To Thee, my God and Saviour,
My heart exulting sings,
Rejoicing in Thy favor,
Almighty King of kings:
I'll celebrate Thy glory,
With all Thy saints above,
And tell the joyful story,
Of Thy redeeming love.

2 Soon as the morn with roses
Bedecks the dewy east,
And when the sun reposes
Upon the ocean's breast,
My voice in supplication,
Well pleased, Thou shalt hear:
O grant me Thy salvation,
And to my soul draw near.

3 By Thee through life supported,
I pass the dangerous road,
With heavenly hosts escorted
Up to their bright abode;
There cast my crown before Thee;
Now all my conflicts o'er,
And day and night adore Thee:
What can an angel more?

Rev. Thomas Haweis.

RUNDELL. C. H. M. *Lowell Mason.*

231 *"Sorrowing, yet always rejoicing."*

2 Oh, to be brought to Jesus' feet,
Though sorrows fix me there,
Is still a privilege; and sweet
The energy of prayer,
Though sighs and tears its language be,
If Christ be nigh, and smile on me.

3 Then blessed be the hand that gave:
Still blessed when it takes;
Blessed be He who smites to save,
Who heals the heart He breaks:
Perfect and true are all His ways,
Whom Heaven adores and earth obeys.

Conder.

232 *"Fear not, little flock."*

1 In heavenly love abiding,
No change my heart shall fear,
And safe is such confiding,
For nothing changes here:
The storm may roar without me,
My heart may low be laid,
But God is round about me,
And can I be dismayed?

2 Wherever He may guide me,
No want shall turn me back;
My Shepherd is beside me,
And nothing can I lack:
His wisdom ever waketh,
His sight is never dim:
He knows the way he taketh,
And I will walk with him.

3 Green pastures are before me,
Which yet I have not seen;
Bright skies will soon be o'er me,
Where darkest clouds have been:
My hope I cannot measure;
My path to life is free;
My Saviour has my treasure,
And He will walk with me.

Mrs. Waring.

AUTUMN. 8, 7. *Spanish Melody.*

D. S.

All I've sought, and hoped, and known!

233 *Forsaking all for Christ.*

2 Let the world despise and leave me;
They have left my Saviour, too;
Human hearts and looks deceive me;
Thou art not, like man, untrue;
And, while Thou shalt smile upon me,
God of wisdom, love, and might!
Foes may hate, and friends may shun me;
Show Thy face, and all is bright.

3 Go, then, earthly fame and treasure!
Come, disaster, scorn and pain!
In Thy service, pain is pleasure,
With Thy favor, loss is gain:
I have called Thee,—"Abba Father!"
I have stayed my heart on Thee;
Storms may howl, and clouds may gather,
All must work for good to me.

4 Man may trouble and distress me;
'T will but drive me to Thy breast;
Life with trials hard may press me,
Heaven will bring me sweeter rest:
Oh! tis not in grief to harm me,
While Thy love is left to me;
Oh! 't were not in joy to charm me,
Were that joy unmixed with Thee.

H. F. Lyte.

234 *Much Forgiven.*

1 Hail! my ever-blessed Jesus!
Only Thee I wish to sing;
To my soul, Thy name is precious,
Thou, my Prophet, Priest, and King:
Oh! what mercy flows from Heaven!
Oh! what joy and happiness!
Love I much? I've much forgiven;
I'm a miracle of grace.

2 Shout, ye bright angelic choir!
Praise the Lamb enthroned above;
Whilst, astonished, I admire
God's free grace, and boundless love:
That blest moment, I received Him,
Filled my soul with joy and peace:
Love I much? I've much forgiven;
I'm a miracle of grace.

John Wingrove.

FIELD. S. M. *Sab. Hymn & Tune Book.*

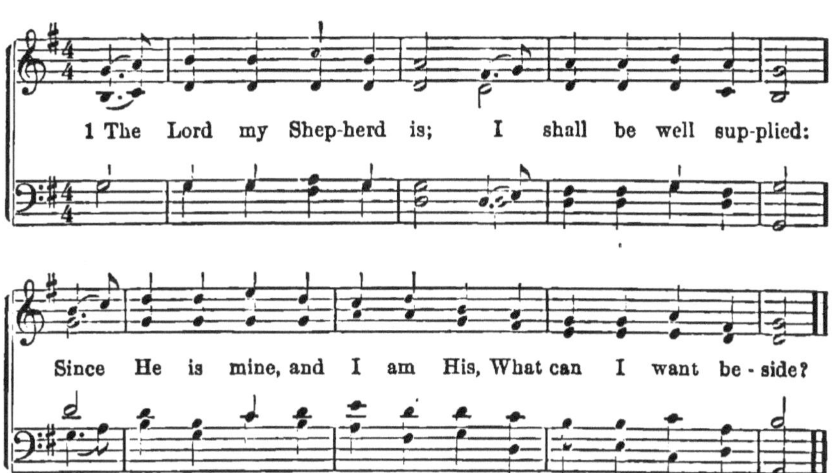

235 *The Lord our Shepherd.*

2 He leads me to the place
Where heavenly pasture grows;
Where living waters gently pass,
And full salvation flows.

3 If e'er I go astray,
He doth my soul reclaim;
And guides me, in His own right way,
For His most holy name.

4 While He affords His aid,
I cannot yield to fear;
Though I should walk through death's dark shade,
My Shepherd's with me there.

5 In spite of all my foes,
Thou dost my table spread;
My cup with blessings overflows,
And joy exalts my head.

6 The bounties of Thy love
Shall crown my following days;
Nor from Thy house will I remove,
Nor cease to speak Thy praise.

I. Watts.

236 *Living by Faith only.*

1 If through unruffled seas
Toward Heaven we calmly sail,
With grateful hearts, O God, to Thee,
We'll own the fostering gale.

2 But should the surges rise,
And rest delay to come,
Blest be the sorrow, kind the storm,
Which drives us nearer home.

3 Soon shall our doubts and fears
All yield to Thy control;
Thy tender mercies shall illume
The midnight of the soul.

4 Teach us, in every state,
To make Thy will our own;
And, when the joys of sense depart,
To live by faith alone.

Anon.

237 *Doxology.*

1 The Father and the Son
And Spirit we adore;
We praise, we bless, we worship Thee,
Both now and evermore!

Anon.

WINFIELD. 7. *Sab. Hymn and Tune Book.*

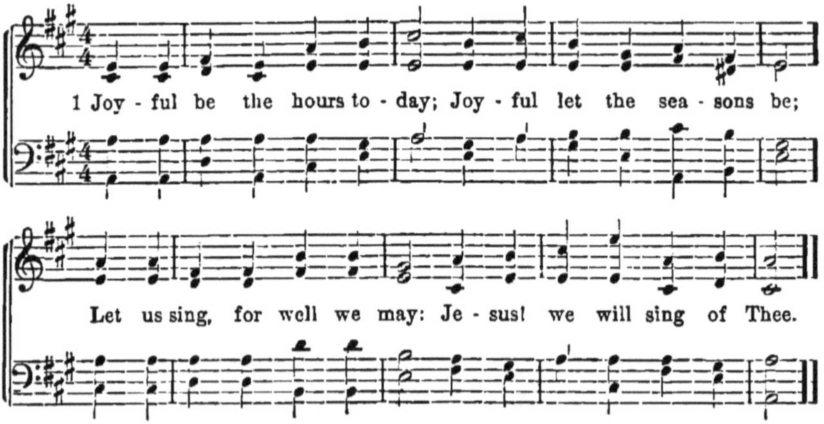

1 Joy - ful be the hours to - day; Joy - ful let the sea - sons be;
Let us sing, for well we may: Je - sus! we will sing of Thee.

238 *Joy in the Lord.*

2 Should Thy people silent be,
Then the very stones would sing:
What a debt we owe to Thee,
Thee our Saviour, Thee our King!

3 Joyful are we now to own,
Rapture thrills us as we trace
All the deeds Thy love hath done,
All the riches of Thy grace.

4 'Tis Thy grace alone can save;
Every blessing comes from Thee—
All we have, and hope to have,
All we are, and hope to be.

5 Thine the name to sinners dear!
Thine the name all names before!
Blessed here and everywhere;
Blessed now and evermore!

T. Kelly.

239 *"For to me to live is Christ."*

1 Christ, of all my hopes the ground,
Christ, the spring of all my joy,
Still in Thee let me be found,
Still for Thee my powers employ.

2 Fountain of o'erflowing grace,
Freely from Thy fullness give;
Till I close my earthly race,
Be it "Christ for me to live."

3 When I touch the blessed shore,
Back the closing waves shall roll;
Death's dark stream shall nevermore
Part from Thee my ravished soul.

4 Thus, oh, thus an entrance give
To the land of cloudless sky!
Having known it "Christ to live,"
Let me know it "gain to die."

Windham.

240 *"The King of kings, and Lord of lords."*

1 Wake the song of jubilee!
Let it echo o'er the sea:
Now is come the promised hour;
Jesus reigns with sovereign power.

2 All ye nations! join and sing,
"Christ, of lords and kings, is King!"
Let it sound from shore to shore,
"Jesus reigns for evermore!"

3 Now the desert lands rejoice,
And the islands join their voice:
Joy! the whole creation sings,
"Jesus is the King of kings!"

L. Bacon.

BROWN. C. M. *W. B. Bradbury.*

241 *Assurance.*

2 Should earth against my soul engage,
And fiery darts be hurled,
Then I can smile at Satan's rage,
And face a frowning world.

3 Let cares like a wild deluge come,
And storms of sorrow fall,
May I but safely reach my home,
My God, my Heaven, my all!

4 There shall I bathe my weary soul
In seas of heavenly rest;
And not a wave of trouble roll
Across my peaceful breast.

I. Watts.

242 *"Altogether Lovely."*

1 My God! the spring of all my joys,
The life of my delights,
The glory of my brightest days,
And comfort of my nights!

2 In darkest shades if He appear,
My dawning is begun:
He is my soul's sweet morning star,
And He my rising sun.

3 The opening heavens around me shine
With beams of sacred bliss,
While Jesus shows His heart is mine,
And whispers, I am His!

4 My soul would leave this heavy clay,
At that transporting word;
Run up with joy the shining way,
T' embrace my dearest Lord!

I. Watts.

243 *"Peace be within thee."*

1 How did my heart rejoice to hear
My friends devoutly say:
"In Zion let us all appear,
And keep the solemn day."

2 I love her gates, I love the road;
The church, adorned with grace,
Stands like a palace, built for God,
To show His milder face.

3 Peace be within this sacred place,
And joy a constant guest!
With holy gifts and heavenly grace
Be her attendants blest!

I. Watts.

HADDAM. **H. M.** *Lowell Mason.*

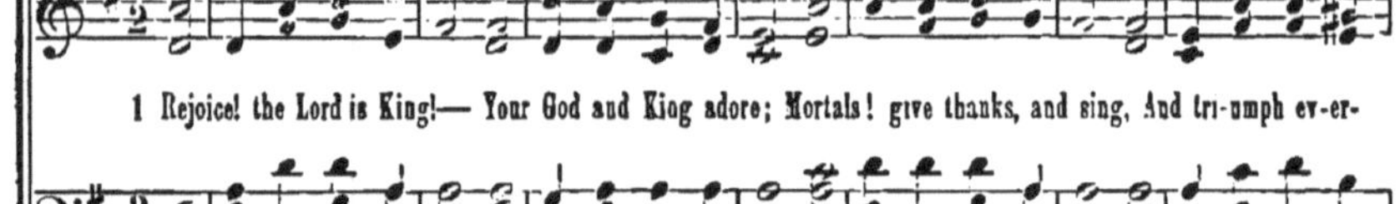

244 *The Reign of Christ.*

2 His kingdom cannot fail;
He rules o'er earth and Heaven;
The keys of death and hell
Are to our Jesus given;
Lift up your hearts,—lift up your voice,
Rejoice! again, I say,—rejoice!

3 He all His foes shall quell,
Shall all our sins destroy;
And every bosom swell
With pure seraphic joy:
Lift up your hearts,—lift up your voice,
Rejoice! again, I say,—rejoice!

C. Wesley.

245 *The Offices of Christ.*

1 Great Prophet of our God!
Our tongues would bless Thy name;
By Thee the joyful news
Of our salvation came:
The joyful news of sins forgiven,
Of hell subdued, and peace with Heaven.

2 Jesus, our great High Priest,
Hath shed His blood and died;
My guilty conscience needs
No sacrifice beside:
His precious blood did once atone;
And now it pleads before the throne.

I. Watts.

246 *The Cross Celebrated.*

1 Ye saints! your music bring,
Attuned to sweetest sound;
Strike every trembling string,
Till earth and Heaven resound:
The triumphs of the cross we sing;
Awake, ye saints! each joyful string.

2 The cross—the cross alone—
Subdued the powers of hell;
Like lightning, from his throne
The prince of darkness fell:
The triumphs of the cross we sing;
Awake, ye saints! each joyful string.

3 The cross has power to save,
From all the foes that rise;
The cross has made the grave
A passage to the skies:
The triumphs of the cross we sing;
Awake, ye saints! each joyful string.

Andrew Reed.

A. Williams.

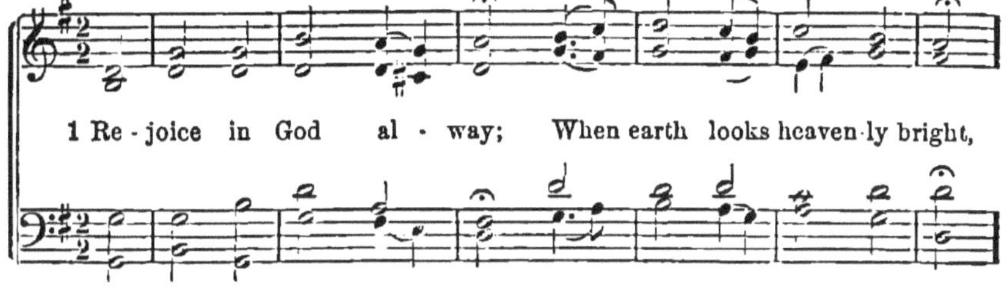

When joy makes glad the live - long day, And peace shuts in the night.

247 *Joy.*

2 Rejoice when care and woe
The fainting soul oppress;
When tears at wakeful midnight flow,
And morn brings heaviness.

3 Rejoice in hope and fear;
Rejoice in life and death;
Rejoice when threatening storms are near,
And comfort languisheth.

4 When should not they rejoice,
Whom Christ His brethren calls,
Who hear and know His guiding voice,
When on their hearts it falls?

5 So, though our path is steep,
And many a tempest lowers,
Shall His own peace our spirits keep,
And Christ's dear love be ours.

Moultrie.

248 *"Jesus is my Friend."*

1 Since Jesus is my friend,
And I to Him belong,
It matters not what foes intend,
However fierce and strong.

2 He whispers in my breast
Sweet words of holy cheer,
How they who seek in God their rest
Shall ever find Him near;—

3 How God hath built above
A city fair and new,
Where eye and heart shall see and prove
What faith has counted true.

4 My heart for gladness springs;
It cannot more be sad;
For very joy it smiles and sings,—
Sees naught but sunshine glad.

5 The sun that lights mine eyes
Is Christ, the Lord I love;
I sing for joy of that which lies
Stored up for me above.

C. Winkworth, tr.

SHIRLAND. **S. M.** *S. Stanley.*

249 *Blessing of Christian Unity.*

2 Blest is the pious house
Where zeal and friendship meet:
Their songs of praise, their mingled vows,
Make their communion sweet.

3 From those celestial springs
Such streams of pleasure flow,
As no increase of riches brings,
Nor honors can bestow.

4 Thus on the heavenly hills
The saints are blest above;
Where joy, like morning dew, distills,
And all the air is love!

I. Watts.

250 *"The Spirit of God dwelleth in you."*

1 Blest are the pure in heart,
For they shall see their God:
The secret of the Lord is theirs;
Their soul is Christ's abode.

2 The Lord, who left the Heavens,
Our life and peace to bring;
To dwell in lowliness with men,
Their Pattern and their King;—

3 He to the lowly soul
Doth still Himself impart,
And for His dwelling, and His throne,
Chooseth the pure in heart.

4 Lord, we Thy presence seek:
May ours this blessing be:
Oh, give the pure and lowly heart,
A temple meet for Thee!

Anon.

251 *"Then would I fly away and be at rest."*

1 Oh cease, my wandering soul,
On restless wing to roam;
All this wide world, to either pole,
Hath not for thee a home.

2 Behold the ark of God!
Behold the open door!
Oh haste to gain that dear abode,
And rove, my soul, no more.

3 There safe thou shalt abide,
There sweet shall be thy rest;
And every longing satisfied,
With full salvation blest.

Muhlenberg.

EVAN. C. M. *Wm. H. Havergal.*

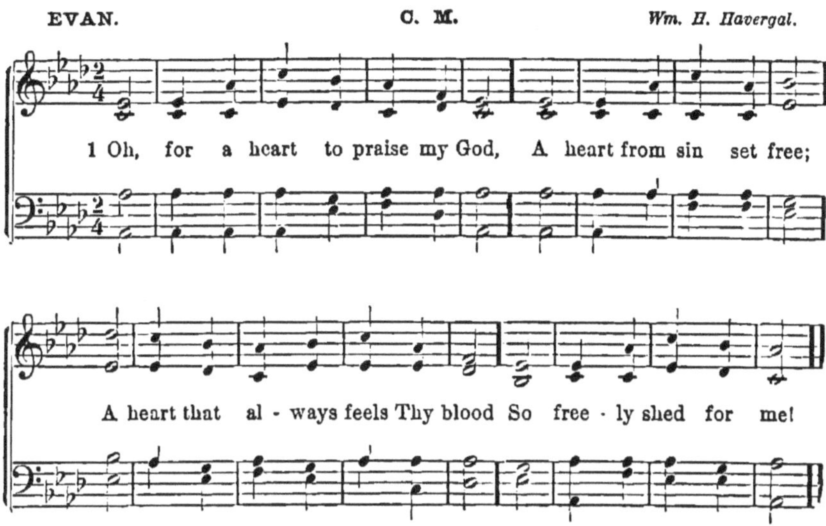

252 *"A clean heart."*

2 A heart resigned, submissive, meek,
My dear Redeemer's throne;
Where only Christ is heard to speak,
Where Jesus reigns alone!

3 Oh, for a lowly, contrite heart,
Believing, true, and clean!
Which neither life nor death can part
From Him that dwells within.

4 A heart in every thought renewed,
And filled with love divine;
Perfect, and right, and pure, and good;
An image, Lord, of Thine.

5 Thy nature, gracious Lord, impart;
Come quickly from above;
Write Thy new name upon my heart,—
Thy new, best name of Love.

C. Wesley.

253 *Walking with God.*

1 Oh! for a closer walk with God,
A calm and heavenly frame,
A light, to shine upon the road,
That leads me to the Lamb.

2 Where is the blessedness I knew
When first I saw the Lord?
Where is the soul-refreshing view
Of Jesus, and His word?

3 What peaceful hours I once enjoyed!
How sweet their memory still!
But they have left an aching void,
The world can never fill.

4 Return, O holy Dove! return,
Sweet Messenger of rest;
I hate the sins that made Thee mourn,
And drove Thee from my breast.

5 The dearest idol I have known,
Whate'er that idol be,
Help me to tear it from Thy throne,
And worship only Thee.

6 So shall my walk be close with God,
Calm and serene my frame;
So purer light shall mark the road
That leads me to the Lamb.

William Cowper.

MILLBURN. 7, 6. *R. S. Thain.*

254 *I Need Thee.*

2 I need Thee, blessed Jesus!
For I am very poor;
A stranger and a pilgrim,
I have no earthly store;
I need the love of Jesus
To cheer me on my way,
To guide my doubting footsteps,
To be my strength and stay.

3 I need Thee, blessed Jesus!
I need a friend like Thee;
A friend to soothe and pity,
A friend to care for me;
I need the heart of Jesus
To feel each anxious care
To tell my every trial,
And all my sorrows share.

4 I need Thee, blessed Jesus!
And hope to see Thee soon,
Encircled with the rainbow,
And seated on Thy throne:
There with Thy blood-bought children,
My joy shall ever be
To sing Thy praise, Lord Jesus,
To gaze, my Lord, on Thee.

Frederick Whitfield.

255 *"He satisfieth the longing soul."*

1 O Jesus! friend unfailing!
How dear art Thou to me!
Are cares or fears assailing?
I find my strength in Thee:
Why should my feet grow weary
Of this my pilgrim way?
Rough though the path and dreary,
It ends in perfect day!

2 Nought, nought I court as pleasure,
Compared, O Christ, with Thee!
Thy sorrow without measure,
Earned peace and joy for me!
I love to own, Lord Jesus!
Thy claims o'er me divine,
Bought with Thy blood most precious,
Whose can I be but Thine!

3 What fills my heart with gladness?
'Tis Thy abounding grace!
Where can I look, in sadness,
But, Jesus, on Thy face?
My all is Thy providing,—
Thy love can ne'er grow cold;
In Thee, my Refuge, hiding,—
No good wilt Thou withhold.

Anon.

MORE LOVE TO THEE, O CHRIST. *W. H. Doane, by per.*

1 More love to Thee, O Christ, More love to Thee; Hear Thou the prayer I make On bend-ed knee; This is my earn-est plea, More love, O Christ, to Thee, More love to Thee! More love to Thee!

256 *"Continue ye in My love."*

2 Once earthly joy I craved,
Sought peace and rest;
Now Thee alone I seek,
Give what is best:
This all my prayer shall be,
More love, O Christ, to Thee, etc.

3 Let sorrow do its work,
Send grief and pain;
Sweet are Thy messengers,
Sweet their refrain,
When they can sing with me,—
More love, O Christ, to Thee, etc.

4 Then shall my latest breath,
Whisper Thy praise,
This be the parting cry
My heart shall raise;
This still its prayer shall be:
More love, O Christ, to Thee, etc.

Mrs. Elizabeth Prentiss.

SEVERN. 6. 5.

257 *"I have longed for Thy Salvation, O Lord."*

2 Calmer yet and calmer,
Trial bear and pain,
Surer yet and surer
Peace at last to gain;
Suff'ring still and doing,
To His will resigned,
And to God subduing
Heart and will and mind.

3 Higher yet and higher,
Out of clouds and night,
Nearer yet and nearer
Rising to the light—
Light serene and holy,
Where my soul may rest,
Purified and lowly,
Sanctified and blest;

4 Quicker yet and quicker
Ever onward press,
Firmer yet and firmer
Step as I progress:
Oft these earnest longings
Swell within my breast,
Yet their inner meaning
Ne'er can be expressed.

Anon.

PETERBOROUGH. C. M. *Rev. Ralph Harrison.*

258 *The Refining Fire of the Holy Spirit.*

2 Oh, that in me the sacred fire
Might now begin to glow;
Burn up the dross of base desire,
And make the mountains flow.

3 Oh, that it now from Heaven might fall,
And all my sins consume:
Come, Holy Ghost, for Thee I call;
Spirit of burning, come.

4 Refining fire, go through my heart;
Illuminate my soul;
Scatter Thy life through every part,
And sanctify the whole.

5 My steadfast soul, from falling free,
Shall then no longer move:
While Christ is all the world to me,
And all my heart is love.

C. Wesley.

259 *Breathing after Holiness.*

1 Oh, that the Lord would guide my ways,
To keep His statutes still:
Oh, that my God would grant me grace
To know and do His will!

2 Order my footsteps by Thy word,
And make my heart sincere:
Let sin have no dominion, Lord,
But keep my conscience clear.

3 Make me to walk in Thy commands,
'Tis a delightful road:
Nor let my head, or heart, or hands,
Offend against my God.

I. Watts.

260 *Living with Christ.*

1 Oh, could I find, from day to day,
A nearness to my God!
Then should my hours glide sweet away,
While leaning on His word.

2 Lord, I desire with Thee to live
Anew from day to day;
In joys the world can never give,
Nor ever take away.

3 Blest Jesus! come and rule my heart,
And make me wholly Thine,
That I may never more depart,
Nor grieve Thy love divine.

4 Thus, till my last, expiring breath,
Thy goodness I'll adore;
And when my frame dissolves in death,
My soul shall love Thee more.

B. Cleveland.

NILLEN. 6.

261 *No Rest, but in God.*

2 Of so divine a Guest
Unworthy though I be,
Yet hath my heart no rest
Until it come to Thee!

3 Until it come to Thee,
In vain I look around;
In all that I can see
No rest is to be found!

4 No rest is to be found,
But in Thy bleeding love:
Oh, let my wish be crowned,
And send it from above!

Anon.

262 *"Choose Thou for me."*

1 Thy way, not mine, O Lord,
However dark it be!
Lead me by Thine own hand;
Choose out the path for me.

2 I dare not choose my lot:
I would not, if I might;
Choose Thou for me, my God,
So shall I walk aright.

3 The kingdom that I seek
Is Thine: so let the way
That leads to it be Thine,
Else I must surely stray.

4 Take Thou my cup, and it
With joy or sorrow fill,
As best to Thee may seem;
Choose Thou my good and ill.

5 Choose Thou for me my friends,
My sickness or my health;
Choose Thou my cares for me,
My poverty or wealth.

6 Not mine, not mine the choice,
In things or great or small;
Be Thou my Guide, my Strength,
My Wisdom, and my All.

Anon.

AVON. C. M. *Hugh Wilson.*

263 *Blessedness of the Communion of Saints.*

2 The church triumphant in Thy love,—
Their mighty joys we know:
They sing the Lamb in hymns above,
And we, in hymns below.

3 Thee, in Thy glorious realm, they praise,
And bow before Thy throne:
We, in the kingdom of Thy grace;—
The kingdoms are but one.

4 The holy to the holiest leads;
From thence our spirits rise:
And he that in Thy statutes treads
Shall meet Thee in the skies.

C. Wesley.

264 *"Of one heart and of one soul."*

1 Blest be the dear, uniting love,
That will not let us part:
Our bodies may far off remove;
We still are one in heart.

2 Joined in one spirit to our Head,
Where He appoints we go;
We still in Jesus' footsteps tread,
And show His praise below.

3 Oh, may we ever walk in Him,
And nothing know beside!
Nothing desire, nothing esteem,
But Jesus crucified!

4 Partakers of the Saviour's grace,
The same in mind and heart,
Not joy, nor grief, nor time, nor place,
Nor life, nor death, can part.

C. Wesley.

265 *"Weep with them that weep."*

1 Lord, may our sympathizing breasts
The generous pleasure know,
Kindly to share in others' joys,
And weep for others' woe!

2 Where'er the helpless sons of grief
In low distress are laid,
Soft be our hearts, their pains to feel,
And swift our hands to aid.

3 Thus may the sacred law of love
Through all our actions shine,
And force a scoffing world to own
The Christian name divine.

Anon.

HEBER. C. M. *G. Kingsley.*

266 *"One as We are one."*

2 The love the Father bears to Thee,
His own eternal Son,
Fill all Thy saints, till all shall be
In pure affection one.

3 As Thou for us didst stoop so low,
Warmed by love's holy flame,
So let our deeds of kindness flow
To all that bear Thy name.

4 One blessed fellowship of love,
Thy living church should stand,
Till, faultless, she at last above
Shall shine at Thy right hand.

5 Oh, glorious day, when she, the Bride,
With her dear Lord appears!
Then, robed in beauty at His side,
She shall forget her tears!

Ray Palmer.

267 *1 John 4:21.*

1 How sweet, how heavenly is the sight,
When those who love the Lord
In one another's peace delight,
And so fulfill His word!

2 When each can feel his brother's sigh,
And with him bear a part!
When sorrow flows from every eye,
And joy from heart to heart!

3 When, free from envy, scorn, and pride,
Our wishes all above,
Each can his brother's failings hide,
And show a brother's love!

4 Let love, in one delightful stream,
Through every bosom flow;
And union sweet, and dear esteem
In every action glow.

5 Love is the golden chain that binds
The happy souls above;
And he's an heir of Heaven who finds
His bosom glow with love.

J. Swain.

DENNIS. S. M. *Lowell Mason.*

268 *Brotherly Love.*

2 Before our Father's throne
We pour our ardent prayers:
Our fears, our hopes, our aims are one,
Our comforts and our cares.

3 We share our mutual woes;
Our mutual burdens bear;
And often for each other flows
The sympathizing tear.

4 When we asunder part,
It gives us inward pain;
But we shall still be joined in heart,
And hope to meet again.

Rev. John Fawcett.

269 *Christian Union.*

1 Let party names no more
The Christian world o'erspread;
Gentile and Jew, and bond and free,
Are one in Christ their head.

2 Among the saints on earth,
Let mutual love be found;
Heirs of the same inheritance,
With mutual blessings crowned.

3 Thus will the church below
Resemble that above;
Where streams of pleasure ever flow,
And every heart is love.

B. Beddome.

270 *Thanks for all Saints.*

1 For all Thy saints, O God,
Who strove in Christ to live,
Who followed Him, obeyed, adored,
Our grateful hymn receive.

2 For all Thy saints, O God,
Accept our thankful cry,
Who counted Christ their great reward,
And yearned for Him to die.

3 They all, in life and death,
With Him, their Lord, in view,
Learned from Thy Holy Spirit's breath
To suffer and to do.

4 For this, Thy name we bless,
And humbly pray that we
May follow them in holiness,
And live and die in Thee.

Richard Mant.

ERNAN. **L. M.** *Lowell Mason.*

271 *"How blest the sacred tie."*

2 To each the soul of each how dear!
What jealous care, what holy fear!
How doth the generous flame within,
Refine from earth and cleanse from sin!

3 Their streaming tears together flow
For human guilt and human woe;
Their ardent prayers united rise,
Like mingling flames in sacrifice.

4 Together oft they seek the place
Where God reveals His awful face;
How high, how strong their raptures swell
There's none but kindred minds can tell.

5 Nor shall the glowing flame expire
Mid nature's drooping, sickening fire:
Soon shall they meet in realms above,
A Heaven of joy, because of love.

Mrs. Barbauld.

272 *"Kindred in Christ."*

1 Kindred in Christ, for His dear sake,
A hearty welcome here receive;
May we together now partake
The joys which only He can give.

2 May He, by whose kind care we meet,
Send His good Spirit from above,
Make our communications sweet,
And cause our hearts to burn with love.

3 Forgotten be each worldly theme,
When Christians see each other thus;
We only wish to speak of Him
Who lived, and died, and reigns for us

4 We'll talk of all He did and said,
And suffered for us here below;
The path He marked for us to tread,
And what He's doing for us now.

5 Thus, as the moments pass away,
We'll love, and wonder, and adore;
And hasten on the glorious day
When we shall meet to part no more.

Newton.

"WORK, FOR THE NIGHT IS COMING." *Lowell Mason.*

273 *"Work, for the night is coming."*

2 Work, for the night is coming,
Work through the sunny noon;
Fill brightest hours with labor,—
Rest comes sure and soon:
Give every flying minute
Something to keep in store;
Work, for the night is coming,
When man works no more.

3 Work, for the night is coming,
Under the sunset skies;
While their bright tints are glowing,
Work, for the daylight flies:
Work till the last beam fadeth,
Fadeth to shine no more;
Work while the night is dark'ning,
When man's work is o'er.

4 Work, for the night is coming,
Work while the fields are white;
Work, for thy sands are running,
Work while hopes are bright:
Gather thy sheaves at morning:
Rest not thy hand at noon;
Labor and strive till evening;
Rest when daylight's gone.

Lowell Mason.

STOCKWELL. 8, 7. *D. E. Jones.*

274 *Psalm 126: 6.*

2 Soft descend the dews of Heaven,
Bright the rays celestial shine;
Precious fruits will thus be given,
Through an influence all divine.

3 Sow thy seed, be never weary,
Let no fears thy soul annoy;
Be the prospect ne'er so dreary,
Thou shalt reap the fruits of joy.

4 Lo, the scene of verdure brightening!
See the rising grain appear;
Look again! the fields are whitening,
For the harvest time is near.

T. Hastings.

275 *Eccl. 11:1.*

1 Cast thy bread upon the waters,
Thinking not 'tis thrown away;
God himself saith, thou shalt gather
It again some future day.

2 Cast thy bread upon the waters;
Wildly though the billows roll,
They but aid thee as thou toilest
Truth to spread from pole to pole.

3 As the seed by billows floated,
To some distant island lone,
So to human souls benighted,
That thou flingest may be borne.

4 Cast thy bread upon the waters;
Why wilt thou still doubting stand?
Bounteous shall God send the harvest,
If thou sow'st with liberal hand.

J. H. Hanaford.

276 *Progress.*

1 Like the eagle, upward, onward,
Let my soul in faith be borne:
Calmly gazing, skyward, sunward,
Let my eye unshrinking turn!

2 Where the cross, God's love revealing,
Sets the fettered spirit free,
Where it sheds its wondrous healing,
There, my soul, thy rest shall be!

3 Oh, may I no longer, dreaming,
Idly waste my golden day,
But, each precious hour redeeming,
Upward, onward, press my way!

H. Bonar.

ROCKINGHAM. **L. M.** *Lowell Mason.*

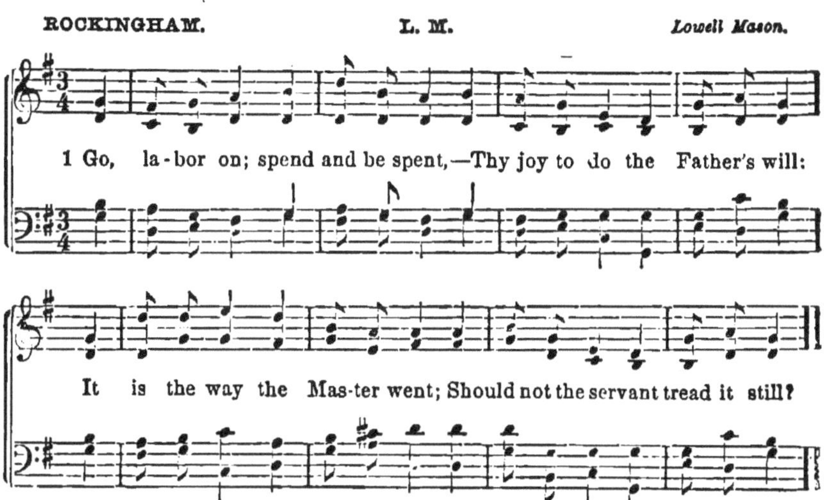

277 *"Go, labor on."*

2 Go, labor on; 'tis not for naught;
Thine earthly loss is heavenly gain;
Men heed Thee, love Thee, praise Thee not;
The Master praises,—what are men?

3 Go, labor on; enough, while here,
If He shall praise thee, if He deign
Thy willing heart to mark and cheer:
No toil for Him shall be in vain.

4 Toil on, and in thy toil rejoice;
For toil comes rest, for exile home;
Soon shalt thou hear the Bridegroom's voice,
The midnight peal: "Behold, I come!"

H. Bonar.

278 *"Faint not."*

1 Go, labor on; your hands are weak,
Your knees are faint, your soul cast down;
Yet falter not; the prize you seek
Is near,—a kingdom and a crown!

2 Go, labor on, while it is day;
The world's dark night is hastening on;
Speed, speed thy work,—cast sloth away!
It is not thus that souls are won.

3 Men die in darkness at your side,
Without a hope to cheer the tomb:
Take up the torch and wave it wide—
The torch that lights time's thickest gloom.

4 Toil on,—faint not,—keep watch and pray!
Be wise the erring soul to win;
Go forth into the world's highway;
Compel the wanderer to come in.

H. Bonar.

279 *Faith and Works.*

1 One cup of healing oil and wine,
One offering laid on mercy's shrine,
Is thrice more grateful, Lord, to Thee,
Than lifted eye or bended knee.

2 In true and inward faith we trace
The source of every outward grace;
Within the pious heart it plays,
A living fount of joy and praise.

3 Kind deeds of peace and love betray
Where'er the stream has found its way;
But, where these spring not rich and fair,
The stream has never wandered there.

W. H. Drummond.

RESCUE THE PERISHING. *W. H. Doane.*

280 *"Go out into the highways and hedges, and compel them to come in."*

2 Though they are slighting Him,
Still He is waiting,
Waiting the penitent child to receive.
Plead with them earnestly,
Plead with them gently:
He will forgive if they only believe.

3 Down in the human heart,
Crushed by the tempter,
Feelings lie buried that grace can restore:
Touched by a loving heart,
Wakened by kindness,
Chords that were broken will vibrate once more.

4 Rescue the perishing,
Duty demands it;
Strength for thy labor the Lord will provide;
Back to the narrow way
Patiently win them;
Tell the poor wanderer a Saviour has died.

Fanny J. Crosby.

SESSIONS. L. M. *L. O. Emerson.*

281 *Encouragement.*

2 Yet ours the grateful service whence
Comes, day by day, the recompense;
The hope, the trust, the purpose stayed,
The fountain, and the noonday shade.

3 And were this life the utmost span,
The only end and aim of man,
Better the toil of fields like these
Than waking dream and slothful ease.

4 But life, though falling like our grain,
Like that revives and springs again;
And, early called, how blest are they
Who wait, in Heaven, their harvest day!

J. G. Whittier.

282 *Our Cross.*

1 "Take up thy cross," the Saviour said,
"If thou wouldst My disciple be;
Deny thyself, the world forsake,
And humbly follow after Me."

2 Take up thy cross; let not its weight
Fill thy weak spirit with alarm;
His strength shall bear thy spirit up,
And brace thy heart and nerve thine arm.

3 Take up thy cross, nor heed the shame;
Nor let thy foolish pride rebel;
Thy Lord for thee the cross endured,
To save thy soul from death and hell.

4 Take up thy cross, and follow Christ;
Nor think till death to lay it down;
For only he who bears the cross
May hope to wear the glorious crown.

C. W. Everest.

283 *Jesus, the Model of Benevolence.*

1 When Jesus dwelt in mortal clay,
What were His works from day to day,
But miracles of power and grace,
That spread salvation through our race?

2 Teach us, O Lord! to keep in view
Thy pattern, and Thy steps pursue;
Let alms bestowed, let kindness done,
Be witnessed by each rolling sun.

3 That man may last, but never lives,
Who much receives, but nothing gives,
Whom none can love, whom none can thank,—
Creation's blot, creation's blank:

4 But he who marks, from day to day,
In generous acts his radiant way,
Treads the same path the Saviour trod,
The path to glory and to God.

Thomas Gibbons.

GOLDEN HILL. **S. M.** *Annanias Davisson.*

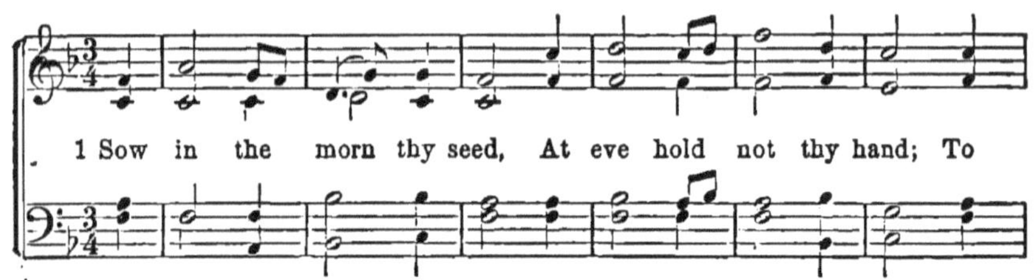

284 *Sowing beside all Waters.*

2 Beside all waters sow,
The highway furrows stock,
Drop it where thorns and thistles grow,
Scatter it on the rock.

3 The good, the fruitful ground
Expect not here nor there;
O'er hill and dale alike 'tis found;
Go forth, then, everywhere.

4 And duly shall appear,
In verdure, beauty, strength,
The tender blade, the stalk, the ear,
And the full corn at length.

5 Thou canst not toil in vain;
Cold, heat, the moist and dry,
Shall foster and mature the grain
For garners in the sky.

6 Then, when the glorious end,
The day of God shall come,
The angel-reapers shall descend,
And Heaven sing "Harvest-home!"

J. Montgomery.

285 *Expedition.*

1 Work while it is to-day!
This was our Saviour's rule;
With docile minds let us obey,
As learners in His school.

2 Lord Christ, we humbly ask
Of Thee the power and will,
With fear and meekness, every task
Of duty to fulfill.

3 At home, by word and deed,
Adorn redeeming grace;
And sow abroad the precious seed
Of truth in every place:—

4 That thus the wilderness
May blossom like the rose,
And trees spring up of righteousness,
Where'er life's river flows.

5 For Thee our all to spend,
Still may we watch and pray,
And, persevering to the end,
Work while it is to day.

J. Montgomery.

GREENVILLE. 8, 7, D. *Rosseau.*

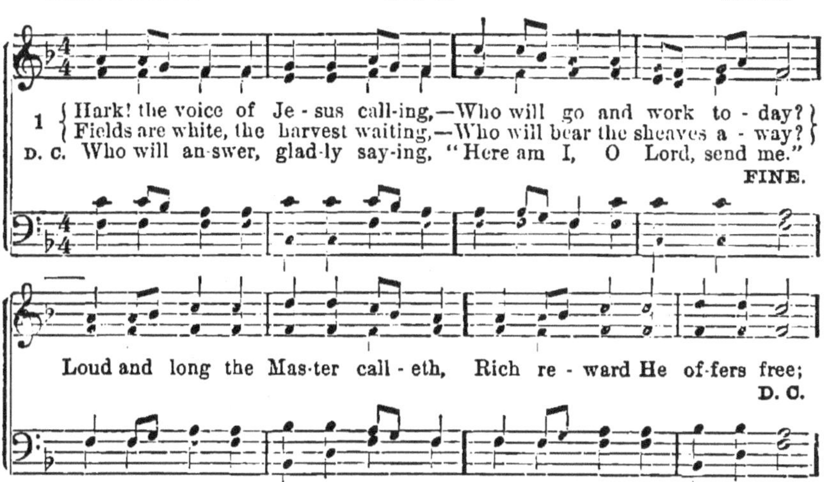

286 *"The laborers are few."*

2 If you cannot cross the ocean
And the heathen lands explore,
You can find the heathen nearer,
You can help them at your door;
If you cannot speak like angels,
If you cannot preach like Paul,
You can tell the love of Jesus,
You can say He died for all.

3 While the souls of men are dying,
And the Master calls for you,
Let none hear you idly saying,
"There is nothing I can do!"
Gladly take the task He gives you,
Let His work your pleasure be;
Answer quickly when He calleth,
"Here am I, O Lord, send me."

D. March.

287 *"What thy hand findeth to do."*

1 If you cannot on the ocean
Sail among the swiftest fleet,
Rocking on the highest billows,
Laughing at the storms you meet.
You can stand among the sailors,
Anchored yet within the bay,
You can lend a hand to help them
As they launch their boat away.

2 If you are too weak to journey
Up the mountain steep and high,
You can stand within the valley
While the multitude go by;
You can chant in happy measure,
As they slowly pass along;
Though they may forget the singer,
They will not forget the song.

3 If you have not gold and silver
Ever ready to command;
If you cannot toward the needy
Reach an ever open hand,
You can visit the afflicted,
O'er the erring you can weep;
You can be a true disciple
Sitting at the Saviour's feet.

4 If you cannot in the harvest
Garner up the richest sheaf,—
Many a grain both ripe and golden
Will the careless reapers leave,—
Go and glean among the briars,
Growing rank against the wall,
For it may be that the shadow
Hides the heaviest wheat of all.

E. H. Gates.

LATTER DAY. 8, 7. D. *Unknown.*

288

Reform.

1 We are living, we are dwelling,
In a grand and awful time,
In an age on ages telling—
To be living is sublime!
Hark! the waking up of nations,
Gog and Magog to the fray!
Hark! what soundeth? is creation
Groaning for its latter day!

2 Worlds are charging, heaven beholding,
Thou hast but an hour to fight;
Now the blazoned cross unfolding,
On—right onward, for the right!
On! let all the soul within you
For the truth's sake go abroad!
Strike! let every nerve and sinew
Tell on ages—tell for God!

WEBB. 7, 6. D. *George James Webb.*

289 *"Stand up, stand up for Jesus."*

2 Stand up, stand up for Jesus,
The trumpet call obey;
Forth to the mighty conflict,
In this His glorious day:
"Ye that are men, now serve Him"
Against unnumbered foes;
Let courage rise with danger,
And strength to strength oppose.

3 Stand up, stand up for Jesus,
Stand in His strength alone;
The arm of flesh will fail you,
Ye dare not trust your own:
Put on the gospel armor,
Each piece put on with prayer;
Where duty calls, or danger,
Be never wanting there.

4 Stand up, stand up for Jesus,
The strife will not be long;
This day the noise of battle,
The next the victor's song:
To him that overcometh,
A crown of life shall be;
He with the King of Glory
Shall reign eternally.

Rev. George Duffield, Jr.

290 *"Go forward, Christian soldier."*

1 Go forward, Christian soldier,
Beneath His banner true:
The Lord Himself, thy Leader,
Shall all thy foes subdue.
Trust only Christ, thy Captain,
Cease not to watch and pray;
Heed not the treach'rous voices,
That lure thy soul astray.

2 Go forward, Christian soldier,
Nor dream of peaceful rest,
Till Satan's host is vanquished,
And Heaven is all possessed;
Till Christ Himself shall call thee
To lay thine armor by,
And wear in endless glory,
The crown of victory.

3 Go forward, Christian soldier,
Fear not the gathering night;
The Lord has been thy shelter,
The Lord will be thy light;
When morn His face revealeth,
Thy dangers all are past;
Oh, pray that faith and virtue
May keep thee to the last.

Rev. Lawrence Tuttiett.

SPANISH HYMN. **7. D.** *Spanish Melody.*

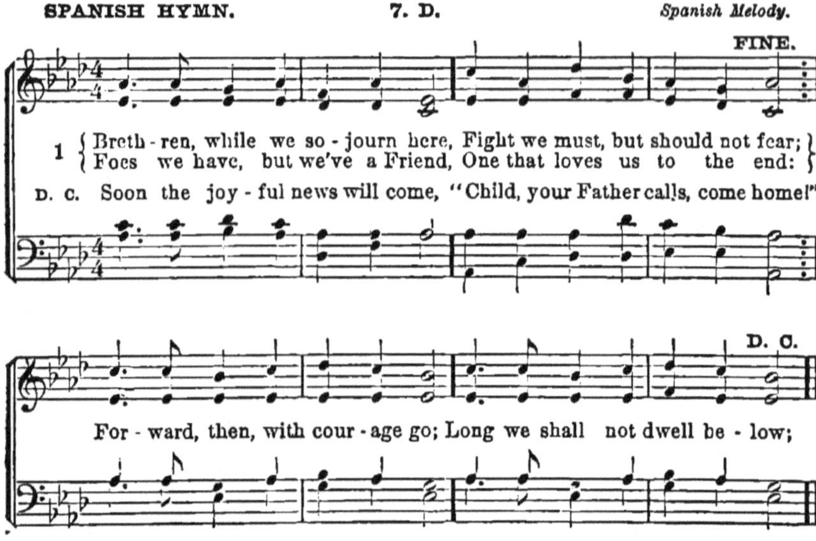

291 *The Conflict soon Over.*

2 In the way a thousand snares
Lie, to take us unawares;
Satan, with malicious art,
Watches each unguarded part:
But, from Satan's malice free,
Saints shall soon victorious be;
Soon the joyful news will come,
"Child, your Father calls, come home!"

3 But of all the foes we meet,
None so oft mislead our feet,
None betray us into sin,
Like the foes that dwell within;
Yet let nothing spoil our peace,
Christ shall also conquer these;
Soon the joyful news will come,
"Child, your Father calls, come home!"

Rev. Joseph Swain.

292 *"Thou art my Rock."*

1 Lord, Thou art my Rock of strength,
And my home is in Thine arms;
Thou wilt send me help at length,
And I feel no wild alarms.
Sin nor death can pierce the shield
Thy defense has o'er me thrown;
Up to Thee myself I yield,
And my sorrows are Thine own.

2 When my trials tarry long,
Unto Thee I look and wait,
Knowing none, though keen and strong,
Can my trust in Thee abate.
And this faith I long have nursed
Comes alone, O God, from Thee;
Thou my heart didst open first,
Thou didst set this hope in me.

1 Let Thy mercy's wings be spread
O'er me, keep me close to Thee;
In the peace Thy love doth shed,
Let me dwell eternally.
Be my All; in all I do,
Let me only seek Thy will.
Where the heart to Thee is true,
All is peaceful, calm and still.

Rev. A. H. Franke.

CHRISTMAS. C. M. *George Frederick Handel.*

293 *"Quit you like Men."*

2 Must I be carried to the skies
On flowery beds of ease,
While others fought to win the prize,
And sailed through bloody seas?

3 Are there no foes for me to face?
Must I not stem the flood?
Is this vile world a friend to grace,
To help me on to God?

4 Sure I must fight, if I would reign;
Increase my courage, Lord;
I'll bear the toil, endure the pain,
Supported by Thy word.

5 Thy saints, in all this glorious war,
Shall conquer though they die;
They view the triumph from afar,
And seize it with their eye.

6 When that illustrious day shall rise,
And all Thine armies shine
In robes of victory through the skies,
The glory shall be Thine.

I. Watts.

294 *Pressing on.*

1 Awake, my soul, stretch every nerve,
And press with vigor on;
A heavenly race demands thy zeal,
And an immortal crown.

2 A cloud of witnesses around
Hold thee in full survey:
Forget the steps already trod,
And onward urge thy way.

3 'Tis God's all-animating voice
That calls thee from on high;
'Tis His own hand presents the prize
To thine aspiring eye:—

4 That prize with peerless glories bright,
Which shall new lustre boast,
When victors' wreaths and monarchs' gems
Shall blend in common dust.

5 Blest Saviour, introduced by Thee,
Have I my race begun;
And, crowned with victory, at Thy feet
I'll lay my honors down.

Rev. Philip Doddridge.

LABAN. **S. M.** *Lowell Mason.*

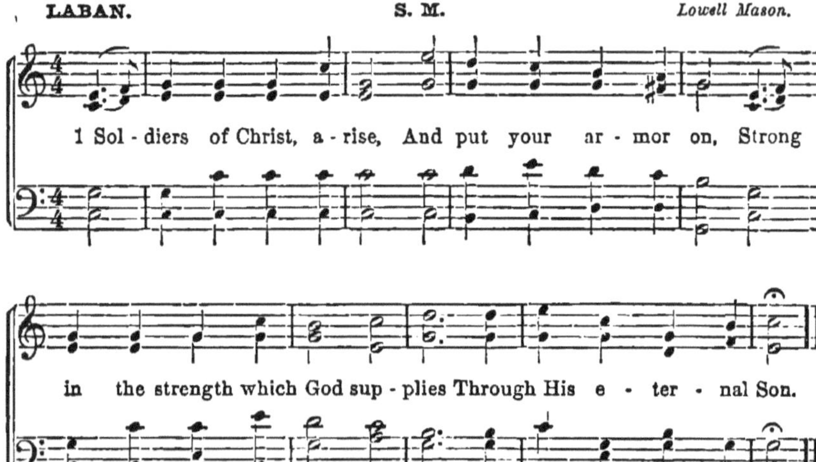

295 *"The whole armor."*

2 Strong in the Lord of hosts,
And in His mighty power,
Who in the strength of Jesus trusts,
Is more than conqueror.

3 Stand, then, in His great might,
With all His strength endued,
And take, to arm you for the fight,
The panoply of God:

4 That, having all things done,
And all your conflicts past,
Ye may o'ercome thro' Christ alone,
And stand entire at last.

C. Wesley.

296 *"Be on thy guard."*

1 My soul, be on thy guard;
Ten thousand foes arise,
And hosts of sin are pressing hard
To draw thee from the skies.

2 O watch, and fight, and pray,
The battle ne'er give o'er;
Renew it boldly every day,
And help divine implore.

3 Ne'er think the victory won,
Nor once at ease sit down;
Thine arduous work will not be done
Till thou receive thy crown.

4 Fight on, my soul, till death
Shall bring thee to thy God;
He'll take thee at thy parting breath,
To His divine abode.

George Heath.

297 *"Weigh not thy life."*

1 My soul, weigh not thy life
Against thy heavenly crown;
Nor suffer Satan's deadliest strife
To beat thy courage down.

2 With prayer and crying strong,
Hold on the fearful fight,
And let the breaking day prolong
The wrestling of the night.

3 The battle soon will yield,
If thou thy part fulfill;
For strong as is the hostile shield,
Thy sword is stronger still.

4 Thine armor is divine,
Thy feet with victory shod;
And on thy head shall quickly shine
The diadem of God.

Anon.

298 *"Fight the good fight."*

2 Like a mighty army
Moves the church of God;
Brothers, we are treading
Where the saints have trod;
We are not divided;
All one body we,
One in hope and doctrine,
One in charity.

3 Crowns and thrones may perish,
Kingdoms rise and wane,
But the church of Jesus
Constant will remain;
Gates of hell can never
'Gainst that church prevail;
We have Christ's own promise,
And that cannot fail.

4 Onward, then, ye people,
Join our happy throng;
Blend with ours your voices
In the triumph-song;
Glory, laud, and honor,
Unto Christ the King;
This through countless ages,
Men and angels sing.

S. Baring Gould.

SOLITUDE. **7.** *L. T. Downs.*

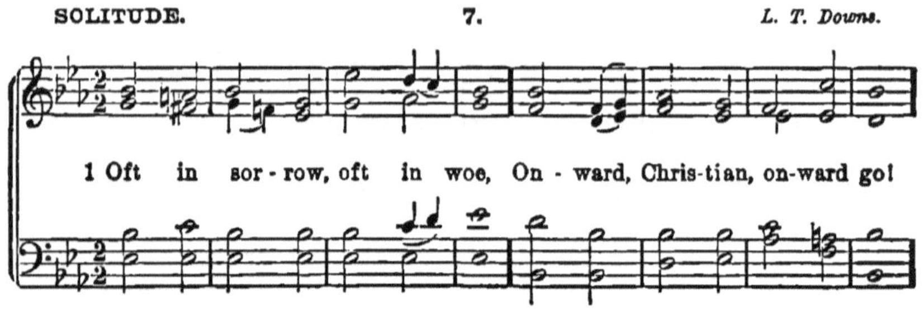

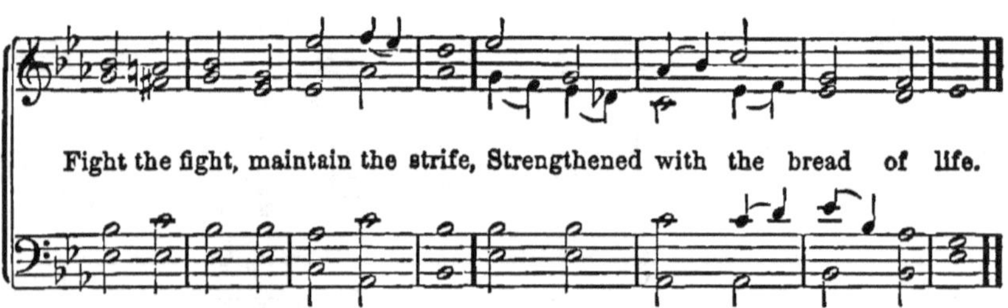

299 *Onward Go.*

2 Onward, Christian, onward go!
Join the war and face the foe:
Will you flee in danger's hour?
Know you not your Captain's power?

3 Let your drooping heart be glad;
March, in heavenly armor clad;
Fight! nor think the battle long;
Soon shall vict'ry tune your song.

4 Let not sorrow dim your eye;
Soon shall every tear be dry:
Let not fears your course impede;
Great your strength, if great your need.

5 Onward, then, to battle move!
More than conq'ror you shall prove;
Though opposed by many a foe,
Christian soldier, onward go!

Anon.

300 *"Let us not sleep, as do others."*

1 Sleep not, soldier of the cross!
Foes are lurking all around;
Look not here to find repose:
This is but thy battle-ground.

2 Up! and take thy shield and sword;
Up! it is the call of Heaven:
Shrink not faithless from thy Lord;
Nobly strive as He hath striven.

3 Break through all the force of ill;
Tread the might of passion down,—
Struggling onward, onward still,
To the conq'ring Saviour's crown!

4 Through the midst of toil and pain,
Let this thought ne'er leave thy breast,
Every triumph thou dost gain
Makes more sweet thy coming rest.

W. Gaskell.

301 *Doxology.*

Sing we to our God above,
Praise eternal as His love;
Praise Him, all ye heavenly host,
Father, Son, and Holy Ghost.

Anon.

WEBB. 7, 6. D. *George James Webb.*

1 The morning light is breaking, The darkness disappears; The sons of earth are wak - ing
D. S. Of na - tions in com - mo-tion,

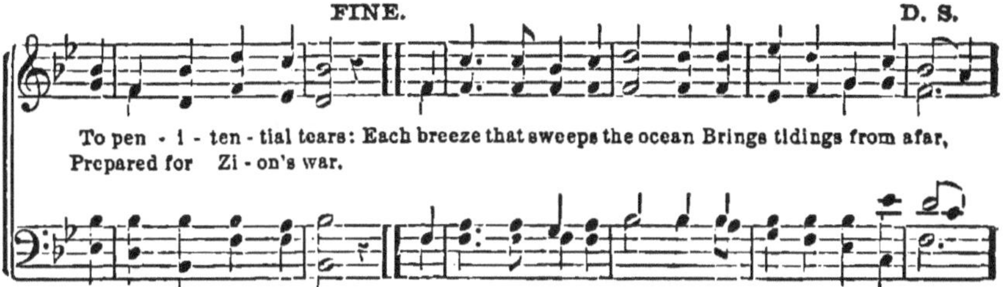

302 *"The morning light is breaking."*

2 See heathen nations bending
Before the God we love,
And thousand hearts ascending,
In gratitude above;
While sinners, now confessing,
The gospel call obey,
And seek the Saviour's blessing,
A nation in a day.

3 Blest river of salvation,
Pursue thine onward way;
Flow thou to every nation,
Nor in thy riches stay:
Stay not, till all the lowly
Triumphant reach their home;
Stay not, till all the holy
Proclaim, "The Lord is come."

Rev. S. F. Smith.

303 *"Hail to the Lord's Anointed!"*

1 Hail to the Lord's Anointed,
Great David's greater Son;
Hail, in the time appointed,
His reign on earth begun!
He comes to break oppression,
To set the captive free,
To take away transgression,
And rule in equity.

2 He comes with succor speedy
To those who suffer wrong;
To help the poor and needy,
And bid the weak be strong;
To give them songs for sighing,
Their darkness turn to light,
Whose souls, condemned and dying,
Were precious in His sight.

3 For Him shall prayer unceasing
And daily vows ascend:
His kingdom still increasing,
A kingdom without end:
The tide of time shall never
His covenant remove;
His name shall stand forever,
That name to us is Love.

James Montgomery.

ZION. 8, 7, 4. *Thos. Hastings.*

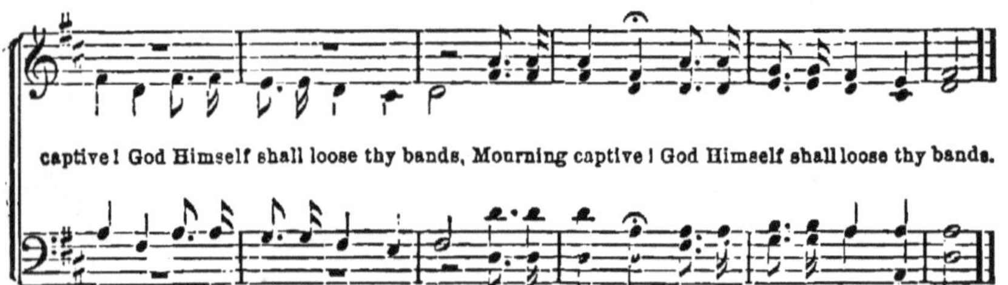

304 *The Gospel Herald.*

1 On the mountain's top appearing,
Lo! the sacred herald stands,
Welcome news to Zion bearing—
Zion long in hostile lands:
Mourning captive!
God Himself shall loose thy bands.

2 Has thy night been long and mournful?
Have thy friends unfaithful proved?
Have thy foes been proud and scornful?
By thy sighs and tears unmoved?
Cease thy mourning;
Zion still is well beloved.

3 God, thy God, will now restore thee;
He Himself appears thy Friend;
All thy foes shall flee before thee;
Here their boasts and triumphs end:
Great deliverance
Zion's King will surely send.

T. Kelly.

305 *Sun of Righteousness.*

1 O'er the gloomy hills of darkness,
Cheered by no celestial ray,
Sun of righteousness! arising,
Bring the bright, the glorious day;
Send the gospel
To the earth's remotest bound.

2 Kingdoms wide that sit in darkness,—
Grant them, Lord, the glorious light:
And from eastern coast to western,
May the morning chase the night;
And redemption,
Freely purchased, win the day.

3 Fly abroad, thou mighty gospel!
Win and conquer, never cease;
May thy lasting, wide dominions
Multiply and still increase;
Sway thy sceptre,
Saviour, all the world around.

W. Williams.

OVIO. 8, 7. *Sab. Hymn & Tune Book.*

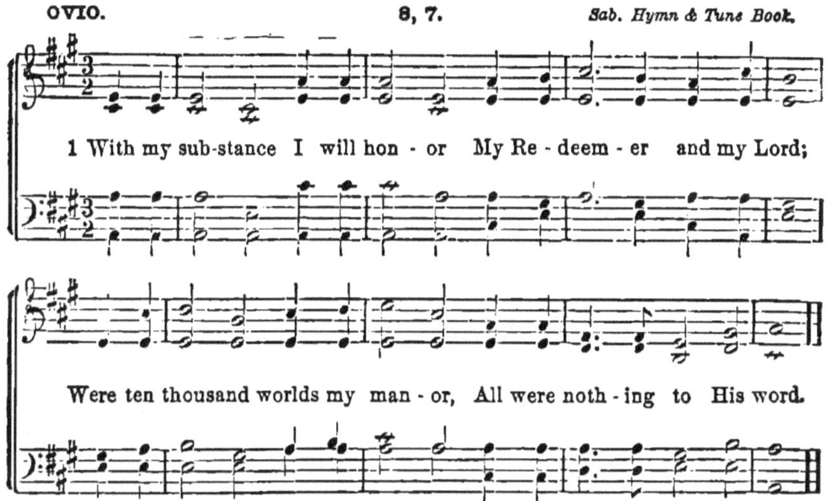

306 *"Bring ye all the tithes into the storehouse."*

2 While the heralds of salvation
His abounding grace proclaim,
Let His friends, of every station,
Gladly join to spread His fame.

3 Be His kingdom now promoted,
Let the earth her Monarch know;
Be my all to Him devoted;
To my Lord my all I owe.

4 Praise the Saviour, all ye nations!
Praise Him, all ye hosts above!
Shout, with joyful acclamations,
His divine, victorious love!

Francis.

307 *"Zion, city of our God."*

1 Glorious things of thee are spoken,
Zion, city of our God;
He whose word can ne'er be broken
Chose thee for His own abode.

2 Lord, Thy church is still Thy dwelling,
Still is precious in Thy sight;
Judah's temple far excelling,
Beaming with the gospel's light.

3 On the Rock of Ages founded,
What can shake her sure repose?
With salvation's wall surrounded,
She can smile at all her foes.

4 Glorious things of thee are spoken,
Zion, city of our God;
He whose word can ne'er be broken
Chose thee for His own abode.

Newton.

308 *"And the light shineth in darkness."*

1 Light of those whose dreary dwelling
Borders on the shades of death!
Rise on us, Thyself revealing,
Rise and chase the clouds beneath.

2 Thou, of heaven and earth Creator!
In our deepest darkness rise;
Scatter all the night of nature;
Pour the day upon our eyes.

3 By Thine all-sufficient merit,
Every burdened soul release;
Every weary, wandering spirit,
Guide into Thy perfect peace.

Anon.

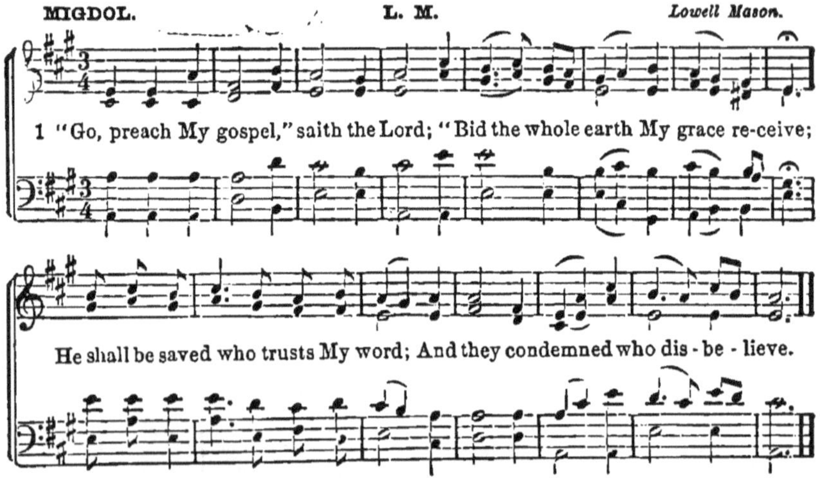

309 *"Go, preach My Gospel."*

2 "I'll make your great commission known,
And ye shall prove My gospel true
By all the works that I have done,
By all the wonders ye shall do.

3 "Teach all the nations My commands;
I'm with you till the world shall end;
All power is trusted in My hands;
I can destroy, and I defend."

4 He spake, and light shone round His head;
On a bright cloud to heaven he rode;
They to the farthest nations spread
The grace of their ascended God.

I. Watts.

310 *The Song of Triumph.*

1 Soon may the last glad song arise
Through all the millions of the skies—
That song of triumph which records
That all the earth is now the Lord's!

2 Let thrones and powers and kingdoms be
Obedient, mighty God, to Thee!
And, over land and stream and main,
Wave Thou the scepter of Thy reign!

3 Oh, let that glorious anthem swell,
Let host to host the triumph tell,
That not one rebel heart remains,
But over all the Saviour reigns!

Mrs. Voke.

311 *Missionary Convocation.*

1 Assembled at Thy great command;
Before Thy face, dread King, we stand;
The voice that marshaled every star,
Has called Thy people from afar.

2 We meet, through distant lands to spread
The truth for which the martyrs bled;
Along the line, to either pole,
The thunder of Thy praise to roll.

3 Our prayers assist, accept our praise,
Our hopes revive, our courage raise;
Our counsels aid, to each impart
The single eye, the faithful heart.

4 Forth with Thy chosen heralds come,
Recall the wandering spirits home;
From Zion's mount send forth the sound,
To spread the spacious earth around.

W. B. Collyer.

NORMAN. 6, 4. *Sab. Hymn and Tune Book.*

312 *Called to Missionary Work.*

2 Far over sea and land,
'Tis our Lord's own command,
Bear ye His name;
Bear it to every shore,
Regions unknown explore,
Enter at every door;
Silence is shame.

3 Speed on the wings of love,
Jesus, who reigns above,
Bid us to fly;
They who His message bear
Should neither doubt nor fear,
He will their Friend appear,
He will be nigh.

Rev. Thomas Kelly.

313 *"Let there be light."*

1 Thou, whose almighty word
Chaos and darkness heard,
And took their flight,
Hear us, we humbly pray,
And where the Gospel's day
Sheds not its glorious ray,
"Let there be light!"

2 Thou, who didst come to bring
On Thy redeeming wing
Healing and sight,
Health to the sick in mind,
Sight to the inly blind,
O, now to all mankind
"Let there be light."

3 Spirit of truth and love,
Life-giving, holy Dove,
Speed forth Thy flight:
Move o'er the waters' face,
Bearing the lamp of grace,
And in earth's darkest place
"Let there be light."

4 Blessed and Holy Three,
Glorious Trinity,
Wisdom, Love, Might:
Boundless as ocean's tide,
Rolling in fullest pride,
Through the world, far and wide,
"Let there be light!"

Rev. John Marriott.

HERALD ANGELS. 7. D. *Felix M. Bartholdy.*

314 *"Go, ye messengers of God."*

2 Go to many a tropic isle,
In the bosom of the deep,
Where the skies forever smile,
And th' oppressed forever weep.
O'er the negro's night of care
Pour the living light of Heaven;
Chase away the fiend despair,
Bid him hope to be forgiven.

3 Where the golden gates of day
Open on the palmy East,
Wide the bleeding cross display,
Spread the gospel's richest feast.
Bear the tidings round the ball,
Visit every soil and sea;
Preach the cross of Christ to all,
Christ, whose love is full and free.

Rev. Joshua Marsden.

315 *The Victory Anticipated.*

1 Hasten, Lord, the glorious time,
When beneath Messiah's sway,
Every nation, every clime,
Shall the gospel call obey,
Mightiest kings His power shall own,
Heathen tribes His name adore;
Satan and his host o'erthrown,
Bound in chains, shall hurt no more.

2 Then shall wars and tumults cease,
Then be banished grief and pain;
Righteousness, and joy, and peace,
Undisturbed shall ever reign.
Time shall sun and moon obscure,
Seas be dried, and rocks be riven,
But His reign shall still endure,
Endless as the days of Heaven.

Miss Harriet Auber.

OLIVET. 6, 4. *Lowell Mason.*

316 *"Christ for the World."*

2 Christ for the world we sing;
The world to Christ we bring,
With fervent prayer:
The wayward and the lost,
By restless passion tossed,
Redeemed, at countless cost,
From dark despair.

3 Christ for the world we sing;
The world to Christ we bring,
With one accord;
With us the work to share,
With us reproach to dare,
With us the cross to bear,
For Christ our Lord.

4 Christ for the world we sing;
The world to Christ we bring,
With joyful song;
The new-born souls, whose days,
Reclaimed from error's ways,
Inspired with hope and praise,
To Christ belong.

Rev. Samuel Wolcott.

317 *"Speed on Thy Word."*

1 Lord of all power and might;
Father of love and light;
Speed on Thy word:
Oh let the Gospel sound
All the wide world around,
Wherever man is found:
God speed His word.

2 Hail, blessed Jubilee:
Thine, Lord, the glory be;
Hallelujah!
Thine was the mighty plan,
From Thee the work began;
Away with praise of man,
Glory to God!

3 Onward shall be our course,
Despite of fraud or force;
God is before:
His word ere long shall run
Free as the noon-day sun;
His purpose must be done:
God bless His word.

Rev. Hugh Stowell.

MISSIONARY HYMN. 7, 6. D. *Lowell Mason.*

318 *"From Greenland's icy mountains."*

2 What though the spicy breezes
Blow soft o'er Ceylon's isle,
Though every prospect pleases,
And only man is vile:
In vain with lavish kindness
The gifts of God are strown,
The heathen in his blindness
Bows down to wood and stone.

3 Can we, whose souls are lighted
With wisdom from on high,
Can we to men benighted
The lamp of life deny?
Salvation, oh, salvation!
The joyful sound proclaim,
'Till each remotest nation
Has learnt Messiah's name.

4 Waft, waft, ye winds, His story,
And you, ye waters, roll,
Till, like a sea of glory,
It spreads from pole to pole;
Till o'er our ransomed nature,
The Lamb for sinners slain,
Redeemer, King, Creator,
In bliss returns to reign.

Bp. Reginald Heber.

319 *The Final Reign of Christ.*

1 When shall the voice of singing
Flow joyfully along,
When hill and valley, ringing
With one triumphant song,
Proclaim the contest ended,
And Him who once was slain,
Again to earth descended,
In righteousness to reign?

2 Then from the craggy mountains
The sacred shout shall fly;
And shady vales and fountains
Shall echo the reply:
High tower and lowly dwelling
Shall send the chorus round,
All hallelujah swelling
In one eternal sound.

J. Edmeston.

320 *The Gospel Banner.*

1 Now be the gospel banner
In every land unfurled,
And be the shout, "Hosanna!"
Re echoed through the world:
Till every isle and nation,
Till every tribe and tongue,
Receive the great salvation,
And join the happy throng. *Anon.*

DUKE STREET. L. M. *John Hatton.*

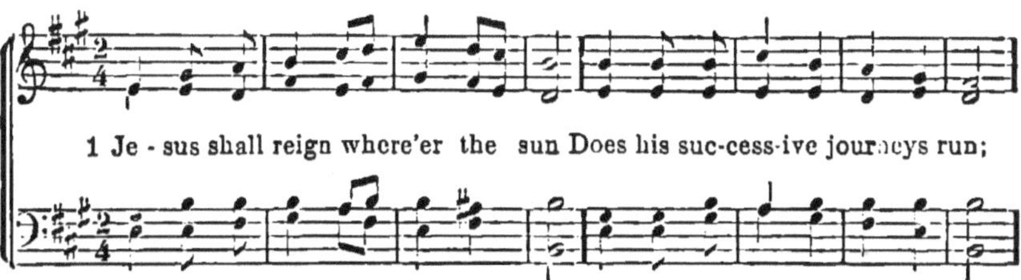

321 *Christ's Dominion.*

2 To Him shall endless prayer be made,
And praises throng to crown His head;
His name, like sweet perfume, shall rise
With every morning sacrifice.

3 People and realms of every tongue
Dwell on His love with sweetest song;
And infant voices shall proclaim
Their early blessings on His name.

4 Blessings abound where'er He reigns;
The prisoner leaps to loose his chains;
The weary find eternal rest,
And all the sons of want are blest.

5 Let every creature rise and bring
Peculiar honors to our King;
Angels descend with songs again,
And earth repeat the loud Amen.

I. Watts.

322 *The Holy City Purified and Guarded.*

1 Triumphant Zion, lift thy head
From dust, and darkness, and the dead:
Tho' humbled long, awake at length,
And gird thee with thy Saviour's strength.

2 Put all thy beauteous garments on,
And let thy various charms be known:
The world thy glories shall confess,
Decked in the robes of righteousness.

3 No more shall foes unclean invade,
And fill thy hallow'd walls with dread:
No more shall hell's insulting host
Their victory and thy sorrows boast.

4 God from on high thy groans will hear;
His hand thy ruins shall repair;
Nor will thy watchful Monarch cease
To guard thee in eternal peace.

Philip Doddridge.

DOWNS. C. M. *Lowell Mason.*

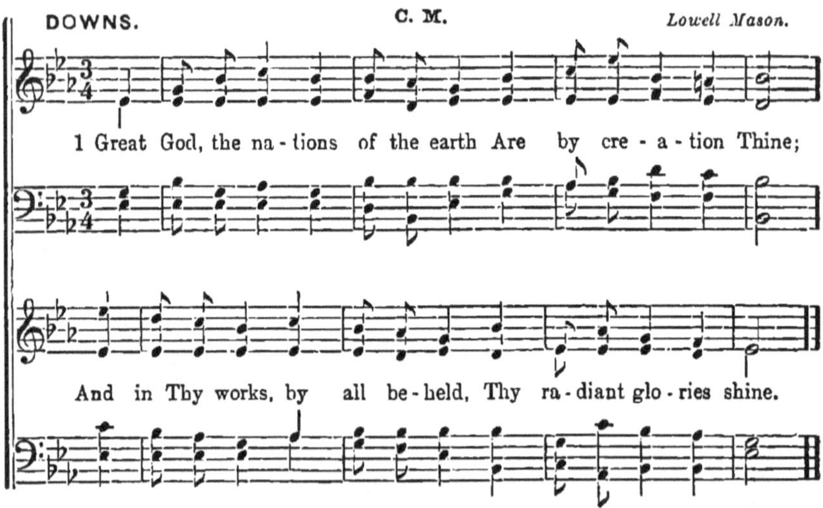

323 *The Gospel for all Nations.*

2 But, Lord, Thy greater love has sent
Thy gospel to mankind,
Unveiling what rich stores of grace
Are treasured in Thy mind.

3 Lord, when shall these glad tidings spread
The spacious earth around,
Till every tribe and every soul,
Shall hear the joyful sound?

4 Smile, Lord, on each divine attempt
To spread the gospel's rays,
And build on sin's demolished throne
The temples of Thy praise.

Rev. Thomas Gibbons.

324 *Prayer Heard, and Zion Restored.*

1 Let Zion and her sons rejoice;
Behold the promised hour:
Her God hath heard her mourning voice,
And comes t' exalt His power.

2 Her dust and ruins that remain
Are precious in our eyes;
Those ruins shall be built again,
And all that dust shall rise.

3 The Lord will raise Jerusalem,
And stand in glory there;
Nations shall bow before His name,
And kings attend with fear.

I. Watts.

325 *Prayer for Home Missions.*

1 On Zion and on Lebanon,
On Carmel's blooming height,
On Sharon's fertile plains, once shone
The glory pure and bright.

2 From thence its mild and cheering ray
Streamed forth from land to land;
And empires now behold its day;
And still its beams expand.

3 But ah, our deserts deep and wild
See not this heavenly light;
No sacred beams, no radiance mild,
Dispel their dreary night.

4 Thou, who didst lighten Zion's hill,
On Carmel who didst shine,
Our deserts let Thy glory fill,
Thy excellence divine.

Bp. H. U. Onderdonk.

BOYLSTON. **S. M.** *Lowell Mason.*

326 *"I love Thy kingdom, Lord."*

2 I love Thy church, O God!
Her walls before Thee stand,
Dear as the apple of Thine eye,
And graven on Thy hand.

3 For her my tears shall fall,
For her my prayers ascend;
To her my cares and toils be given,
Till toils and cares shall end.

4 Beyond my highest joy
I prize her heavenly ways,
Her sweet communion, solemn vows,
Her hymns of love and praise.

5 Jesus, Thou Friend divine,
Our Saviour and our King,
Thy hand from every snare and foe
Shall great deliverance bring.

6 Sure as Thy truth shall last,
To Zion shall be given
The brightest glories earth can yield,
And brighter bliss of Heaven.

Dwight.

327 *"Thou shalt arise, and have mercy upon Zion."*

1 O Lord our God! arise;
The cause of truth maintain;
And wide o'er all the peopled world
Extend her blessed reign.

2 Thou Prince of life! arise,
Nor let Thy glory cease;
Far spread the conquests of Thy grace,
And bless the earth with peace.

3 Thou Holy Ghost! arise,
Extend Thy healing wing,
And o'er a dark and ruined world
Let light and order spring.

4 O all ye nations! rise,—
To God, the Saviour, sing;
From shore to shore, from earth to heaven,
Let echoing anthems ring!

Anon.

MORNING STAR. 7. D. *Lowell Mason.*

328 *"What of the night?"*

2 Watchman, tell us of the night;
  Higher yet that star ascends:
Traveler, blessedness and light,
  Peace and truth, its course portends.
Watchman, will its beams alone
  Gild the spot that gave them birth?
Traveler, ages are its own,
  See, it bursts o'er all the earth.

8 Watchman, tell us of the night,
  For the morning seems to dawn;
Traveler, darkness takes its flight,
  Doubt and terror are withdrawn.
Watchman, let thy wanderings cease;
  Hie thee to thy quiet home:
Traveler, lo, the Prince of Peace,
  Lo, the Son of God is come!

Sir John Bowring.

329 *"All, and in all."*

1 Hark! the song of Jubilee,
  Loud as mighty thunders roar,
Or the fullness of the sea,
  When it breaks upon the shore!
Hallelujah! for the Lord
  God Omnipotent shall reign:
Hallelujah! let the word
  Echo round the earth and main

2 Hallelujah! hark! the sound,
  From the centre to the skies,
Wakes above, beneath, around,
  All creation's harmonies.
See Jehovah's banner furled,
  Sheathed His sword, He speaks—
    't is done;
And the kingdoms of this world
  Are the kingdoms of His Son.

Montgomery.

BADEA. **S. M.** *German Melody.*

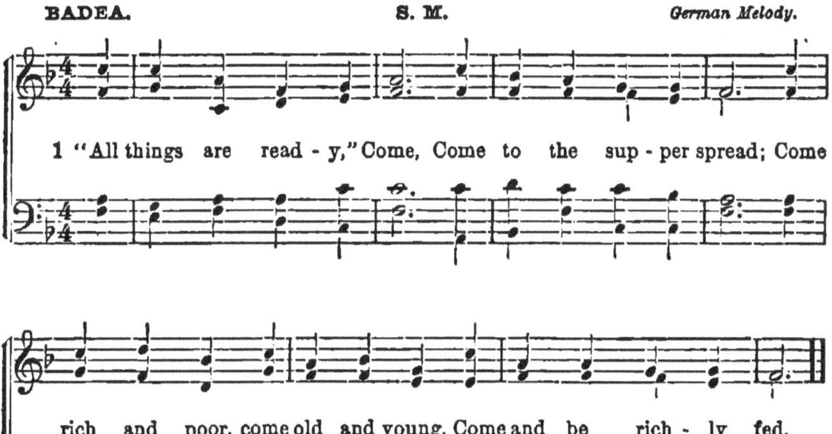

330 *"All things are ready."*

2 "All things are ready," Come,
The invitation's given,
Through Him who now in glory sits,
At God's right hand in Heaven.

3 "All things are ready," Come,
The door is open wide;
Oh, feast upon the love of God,
For Christ His Son has died.

4 "All things are ready," Come,
All hindrance is removed;
And God in Christ His precious love
To fallen man has proved.

5 "All things are ready," Come,
To-morrow may not be;
O sinner, come, the Saviour waits
This hour to welcome thee.

Anon.

331 *"Ye must be born again."*

1 How solemn are the words,
And yet to faith how plain,
Which Jesus uttered while on earth—
"Ye must be born again!"

2 "Ye must be born again!"
For so hath God decreed;
No reformation will suffice—
'Tis *life* poor sinners need.

3 "Ye must be born again!"
And life in Christ must have;
In vain the soul elsewhere may go—
'Tis He alone can save.

4 "Ye must be born again!"
Or never enter Heaven;
'Tis only blood-wash'd ones are there—
The ransomed and forgiven.

5 "Ye must be born again!"
Then look to Christ and live;
He is "the life," and waits in Heaven
Eternal life to give.

Anon.

HEBER. C. M. *G. Kingsley.*

332 *Boundless Grace.*

2 It tells the weary soul of rest
The poor of heavenly wealth,
Of joy to heal the mourning breast;
It brings the sin-sick health.

3 It speaks of boundless grace, by which
The vilest are forgiven;
To sinners it proclaims a rich
Inheritance in Heaven.

Anon.

333 *The Gospel Feast.*

1 Come, sinner, to the gospel feast:
Oh, come without delay;
For there is room on Jesus' breast
For all who will obey.

2 There's room in God's eternal love
To save thy precious soul;—
Room in the Spirit's grace above,
To heal and make thee whole.

3 There's room within the church redeem'd
With blood of Christ divine—
Room 'mid the white-robed throng convened,
For that dear soul of thine.

4 There's room in Heav'n among the choir,
And harps and crowns of gold;
And glorious palms of vict'ry there,
And joys that ne'er were told.

5 There's room around the Father's board
For thee, and thousands more;
Oh, come and welcome to the Lord—
Yes, come this very hour.

Anon.

334 *"I will give you rest."*

1 Come unto Me, all ye who mourn,
With guilt and fear oppressed;
Resign to Me the willing heart,
And I will give you rest.

2 Take up My yoke, and learn of Me
A meek and lowly mind;
And thus your weary, troubled souls
Repose and peace shall find.

3 For light and gentle is My yoke:
The burden I impose
Shall ease the heart which groaned before
Beneath a load of woes.

Anon.

GERMANY. L. M. *From Beethoven.*

335 *"Brought nigh by the blood of Christ."*

2 The Saviour died, and by His blood
Brought rebel sinners home to God;
He died to set the captives free,
And why, my soul—why not for thee?

3 The blood of Christ! how sweet it sounds,
To cleanse and heal the sinner's wounds!
The streams thereof are rich and free,
And why, my soul—why not for thee?

4 Eternal life by Christ is given,
And ruined rebels raised to Heaven;
Then sing of grace so rich and free,
And shout, my soul—'tis all for thee!

Anon.

336 *"God calling yet."*

1 God calling yet! shall I not hear?
Earth's pleasures shall I still hold dear?
Shall life's swift passing years all fly,
And still my soul in slumber lie?

2 God calling yet! shall I not rise?
Can I His loving voice despise,
And basely His kind care repay?
He calls me still; can I delay?

3 God calling yet! I cannot stay;
My heart I yield without delay;
Vain world, farewell! from thee I part;
The voice of God hath reached my heart.

J. Borthwick.

337 *"Why not to-night?"*

1 Oh, do not let the word depart,
And close thine eyes against the light;
Poor sinner, harden not thy heart:
Thou wouldst be saved; why not to-night?

2 To-morrow's sun may never rise
To bless thy long-deluded sight;
This is the time; oh, then be wise!
Thou wouldst be saved; why not to-night?

3 Our God in pity lingers still;
And wilt thou thus His love requite?
Renounce at length thy stubborn will;
Thou wouldst be saved; why not to-night?

4 Our blessed Lord refuses none
Who would to Him their souls unite;
Then be the work of grace begun:
Thou wouldst be saved; why not to-night?

H. Bonar.

ST. MARTIN'S. C. M. *Wm. Tansur.*

338 *A Revival Sought.*

2 Shine, dearest Lord, from realms of day,
Disperse the gloom of night;
Chase all our clouds and doubts away,
And turn the shades to light.

3 Revive, O God, desponding saints,
Who languish, droop and sigh;
Refresh the soul that tires and faints,
Fill mourning hearts with joy.

4 Make known Thy power, victorious King!
Subdue each stubborn will;
Then sovereign grace we'll join to sing
On Zion's sacred hill.

Anon.

339 "*Light in Thy light.*"

1 Eternal Sun of righteousness,
Display Thy beams divine,
And cause the glory of Thy face
Upon my heart to shine.

2 Light, in Thy light, oh, may I see,
Thy grace and mercy prove,
Revived, and cheered, and blest by Thee
The God of pardoning love.

3 Lift up Thy countenance serene,
And let Thy happy child
Behold, without a cloud between,
The Father reconciled.

C. Wesley.

340 "*Come, Lord!*"

1 Come, Thou Desire of all Thy saints!
Our humble strains attend,
While with our praises and complaints,
Low at Thy feet we bend.

2 How should our songs, like those above,
With warm devotion rise!
How should our souls, on wings of love,
Mount upward to the skies!

3 Come, Lord! Thy love alone can raise
In us the heavenly flame;
Then shall our lips resound Thy praise,
Our hearts adore Thy name.

4 Dear Saviour, let Thy glory shine,
And fill Thy dwellings here,
Till life, and love, and joy divine
A heaven on earth appear.

A. Steele.

 8, 7. D. *English Melody.*

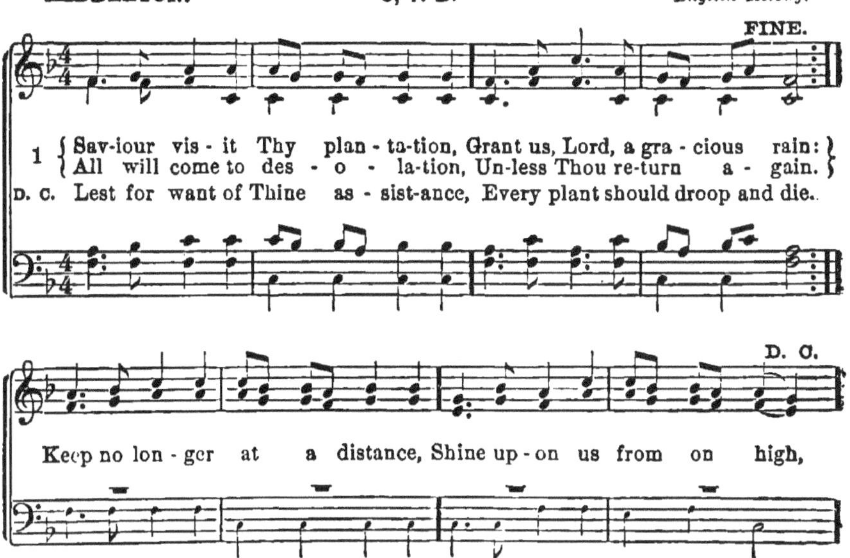

341 *Prayer for Revival.*

1 Saviour, visit thy plantation,
Grant us, Lord, a gracious rain;
All will come to desolation,
Unless Thou return again.
Keep no longer at a distance,
Shine upon us from on high,
Lest, for want of Thine assistance,
Every plant should droop and die.

2 Once, O Lord, Thy garden flourished;
Every part looked gay and green;
Then Thy word our spirits nourished:
Happy seasons we have seen.
But a drought has since succeeded,
And a sad decline we see:
Lord, Thy help is greatly needed,
Help can only come from Thee.

3 Let our mutual love be fervent;
Make us prevalent in prayer;
Let each one esteemed Thy servant
Shun the world's bewitching snare.
Break the tempter's fatal power,
Turn the stony heart to flesh,
And begin from this good hour
To revive Thy work afresh.

Newton.

342 *"Wash me, and I shall be whiter than snow."*

1 Jesus! who on Calv'ry's mountain
Poured Thy precious blood for me,
Wash me in its flowing fountain,
That my soul may spotless be.
I have sinned, but, oh, restore me;
For, unless Thou smile on me,
Dark is all the world before me,
Darker yet eternity!

2 In Thy word I hear Thee saying,
"Come, and I will give you rest;"
Glad the gracious call obeying,
See, I hasten to Thy breast.
Grant, oh, grant Thy spirit's teaching,
That I may not go astray,
Till, the gate of Heaven reaching,
Earth and sin are passed away!

Anon.

MORNINGTON. S. M. *G. W. Mornington.*

343 *Prayer for Revival.*

2 Oh! let Thy chosen few
Awake to earnest prayer;
Their covenant again renew,
And walk in filial fear.

3 Thy Spirit then will speak
Through lips of humble clay,
Till hearts of adamant shall break,
Till rebels shall obey.

4 Now lend Thy gracious ear:
Now listen to our cry;
Oh! come and bring salvation near;
Our souls on Thee rely.

Mrs. Phœbe H. Brown.

344 *A Revival Sought.*

1 Revive Thy work, O Lord!
Thy mighty arm make bare;
Speak with the voice that wakes the dead,
And make Thy people hear.

2 Revive Thy work, O Lord!
Disturb this sleep of death:
Quicken the smouldering embers now,
By Thine almighty breath.

3 Revive Thy work, O Lord!
Exalt Thy precious name;
And, by the Holy Ghost, our love
For Thee and Thine inflame.

4 Revive Thy work, O Lord!
And give refreshing showers;
The glory shall be all Thine own,
The blessing, Lord! be ours.

Albert Midlane.

345 *Longing for a Revival.*

1 Oh! for the happy hour
When God will hear our cry;
And send with a reviving power,
His Spirit from on high!

2 We meet, we sing, we pray,
We listen to the word,
In vain; we see no cheering ray,
No cheering voice is heard.

3 While many seek Thy house,
How few around Thy board,
Meet to recount their solemn vows,
And bless Thee as their Lord!

4 Come, then, with power divine,
Spirit of life and love!
Then shall our people all be Thine,
Our church, like that above.

G. W. Bethune.

HORTON. 7 *Xavier Schnyder Von Wartensee.*

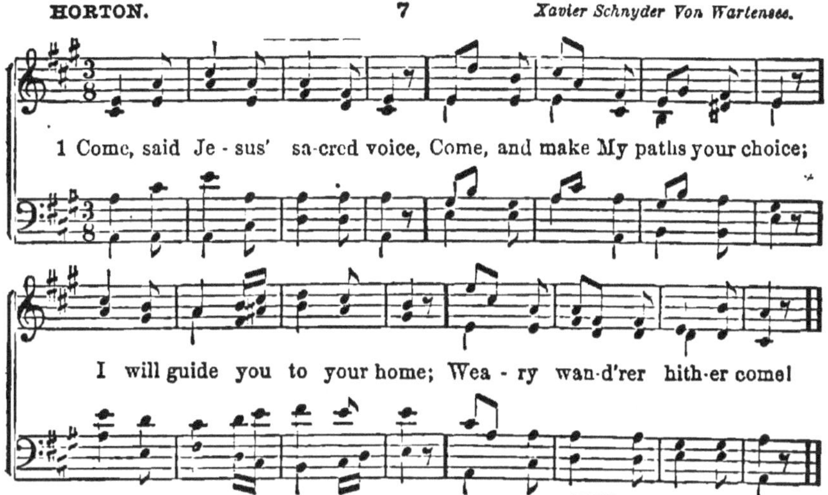

346 *The Voice of Jesus.*

2 Thou who, homeless and forlorn,
Long hast borne the proud world's scorn,
Long hast roamed the barren waste,
Weary wanderer, hither haste;

3 Ye who, tossed on beds of pain,
Seek for ease; but seek in vain;
Ye, by fiercer anguish torn,
In remorse for guilt who mourn:—

4 Hither come! for here is found
Balm that flows for every wound;
Peace that ever shall endure,
Rest eternal, sacred, sure.

Mrs. Barbauld.

347 *"Now is the day of salvation."*

1 Haste, O sinner! now be wise;
Stay not for the morrow's sun:
Wisdom if you still despise,
Harder is it to be won.

2 Haste, and mercy now implore:
Stay not for the morrow's sun,
Lest thy season should be o'er
Ere the morrow is begun.

3 Haste, O sinner! now return:
Stay not for the morrow's sun,
Lest thy lamp should cease to burn
Ere salvation's work is done.

4 Lord! do Thou the sinner turn—
Turn him from his fearful state;
Let him not Thy counsel spurn,
Nor lament his choice too late!

T. Scott.

348 *The Test.*

1 Hark, my soul! it is the Lord;
'Tis thy Saviour; hear His word;
Jesus speaks, and speaks to thee:
"Say, poor sinner, lovest thou Me?

2 "Mine is an unchanging love,
Higher than the heights above,
Deeper than the depths beneath,
Free and faithful, strong as death.

3 "Thou shalt see My glory soon,
When the work of grace is done;
Partner of My throne shalt be;
Say, poor sinner, lovest thou Me?"

Cowper.

AVA. 6, 4. *Thomas Hastings.*

Grieve not that love
Which from above,
Child of sin and sorrow,
Would bring thee nigh.

349 *"Child of sin and sorrow."*

2 Child of sin and sorrow,
Why wilt thou die?
Come while thou canst borrow
Help from on high:

3 Child of sin and sorrow,
Thy moments glide,
Like the flitting arrow,
Or the rushing tide;
Ere time is o'er,
Heaven's grace implore;
Child of sin and sorrow,
In Christ confide.

Thomas Hastings.

STEPHANOS. 8, 5, 8, 3. *William Henry Monk.*

350 *"If we suffer we shall also reign."*

2 Hath He marks to lead me to Him,
If He be my Guide?
"In His feet and hands are wound-prints,
And His side."

3 Is there diadem, as Monarch,
That His brow adorns?
"Yea, a crown in very surety,
But of thorns!"

4 If I still hold closely to Him,
What hath He at last?
"Sorrow vanquished, labor ended,
Jordan past!"

5 If I ask Him to receive me,
Will He say me nay?
"Not till earth, and not till heaven
Pass away!"

Stephen of St. Sabas.

OLNEY. S. M. *Lowell Mason.*

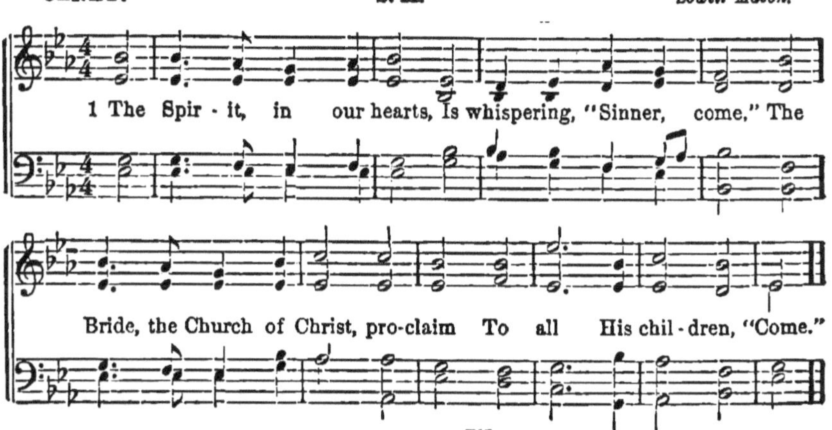

351 *"The Spirit and the Bride say, Come."*

2 Let him that heareth, say
To all about him, "Come;"
Let him that thirsts for righteousness,
To Christ, the Fountain, come.

3 Yes, whosoever will,
Oh, let him freely come,
And freely drink the stream of life:
'Tis Jesus bids him come.

4 Lo, Jesus, who invites,
Declares, "I quickly come;"
Lord, even so; I wait Thine hour;
Jesus, my Saviour, come.

Bp. Onderdonk.

352 *"The land of peace."*

1 Come to the land of peace;
From shadows come away;
Where all the sounds of weeping cease,
And storms no more have sway.

2 Fear hath no dwelling here;
But pure repose and love
Breathe through the bright, celestial air
The spirit of the dove.

3 Come to the bright and blest,
Gathered from every land;
For here thy soul shall find its rest
Amid the shining band.

J. Montgomery.

353 *The Accepted Time.*

1 Now is the accepted time,
Now is the day of grace;
O sinners! come, without delay,
And seek the Saviour's face.

2 Now is the accepted time,
The Saviour calls to-day;
To-morrow it may be too late;—
Then why should you delay?

3 Now is the accepted time,
The gospel bids you come;
And every promise in His word
Declares there yet is room.

4 Lord, draw reluctant souls,
And feast them with Thy love;
Then will the angels spread their wings,
And bear the news above.

J. Dobell.

BELMONT. 8, 7, 4. *Jeremiah Ingalls.*

354 *"Come, and welcome."*

2 Let not conscience make you linger,
Nor of fitness fondly dream;
All the fitness He requireth
Is to feel your need of Him:
This He gives you;
'Tis the Spirit's rising beam.

3 Come, ye weary, heavy-laden,
Bruised and mangled by the fall;
If you tarry till you're better,
You will never come at all:
Not the righteous,
Sinners, Jesus came to call.

4 Lo, the Incarnate God, ascended,
Pleads the merit of His blood:
Venture on Him, venture wholly,
Let no other trust intrude;
None but Jesus
Can do helpless sinners good.

Rev. Joseph Hart.

355 *"Hear, and live."*

1 Sinners, will you scorn the message
Sent in mercy from above?
Every sentence, oh, how tender!
Every line is full of love:
Listen to it;
Every line is full of love.

2 Hear the heralds of the gospel
News from Zion's King proclaim:
"Pardon to each rebel sinner,
Free forgiveness in His name:"
How important!
"Free forgiveness in His name."

3 O ye angels, hovering round us,
Waiting spirits, speed your way;
Haste ye to the court of Heaven,
Tidings bear without delay,
Rebel sinners
Glad the message will obey.

Rev. Jonathan Allen.

COME, YE DISCONSOLATE. 11, 10. *Samuel Webbe.*

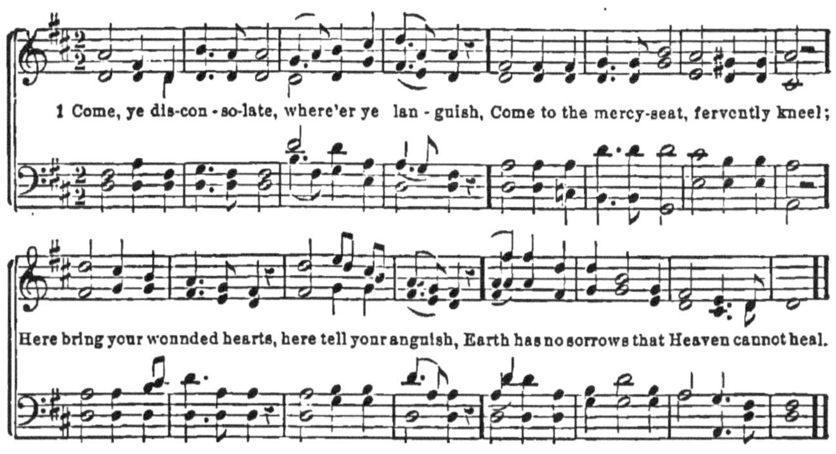

356

"Come, ye disconsolate."

2 Joy of the desolate, Light of the straying,
Hope of the penitent, fadeless and pure,
Here speaks the Comforter, tenderly saying,
Earth has no sorrows that Heaven cannot cure.

3 Here see the Bread of Life, see waters flowing
Forth from the throne of God, pure from above;
Come to the feast prepared, come, ever knowing
Earth has no sorrows but Heaven can remove.

Thomas Moore.

TO-DAY. 6, 4. *Lowell Mason.*

357 *"To-day."*

2 To-day the Saviour calls:
Oh, hear Him now;
Within these sacred walls
To Jesus bow.

3 To-day the Saviour calls:
For refuge fly;
The storm of justice falls,
And death is nigh.

4 The Spirit calls to-day:
Yield to His power;
Oh, grieve Him not away,
'Tis mercy's hour.

Rev. S. F. Smith.

EXPOSTULATION. 11. *J. Hopkins.*

358 *"Why will ye die?*

2 In riches, in pleasures, what can you obtain,
To soothe your affliction, or banish your pain?
To bear up your spirit when summoned to die,
Or waft you to mansions of glory on high?

3 And now Christ is ready your souls to receive,
Oh, how can you question, if you will believe?
If sin is your burden, why will you not come?
'Tis you He bids welcome; He bids you come home.

J. Hopkins.

359 *"I made haste."*

1 Delay not, delay not, O sinner, draw near,
The waters of life are now flowing for thee;
No price is demanded, the Saviour is here;
Redemption is purchased, salvation is free.

2 Delay not, delay not, O sinner, to come,
For Mercy still lingers and calls thee to-day:
Her voice is not heard in the vale of the tomb;
Her message unheeded will soon pass away.

3 Delay not, delay not, the Spirit of grace,
Long grieved and resisted, may take His sad flight,
And leave thee in darkness to finish thy race,
To sink in the gloom of eternity's night.

4 Delay not, delay not, the hour is at hand,
The earth shall dissolve and the heavens shall fade,
The dead, small and great, in the judg-ment shall stand;
What power then, O sinner, will lend thee its aid!

T. Hastings.

ALPHEUS. C. M. *Max. Eberwein, arr.*

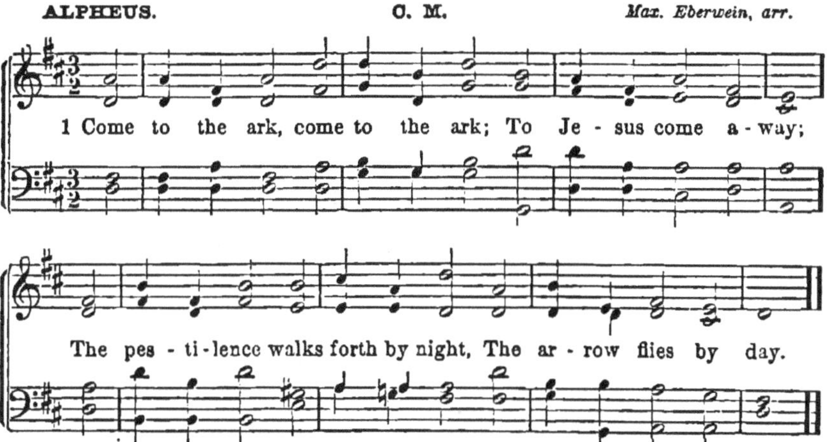

360 "*Come to the ark.*"

2 Come to the ark: the waters rise,
The seas their billows rear;
While darkness gathers o'er the skies,
Behold a refuge near!

3 Come to the ark, all, all that weep
Beneath the sense of sin:
Without, deep calleth unto deep,
But all is peace within.

4 Come to the ark, ere yet the flood
Your lingering steps oppose;
Come, for the door, which open stood,
Is now about to close.

Anon.

361 "*Return, O wanderer.*"

1 Return, O wanderer, now return,
And seek thy Father's face!
Those new desires which in thee burn,
Were kindled by His grace.

2 Return, O wanderer, now return!
He hears thy humble sigh;
He sees thy softened spirit mourn,
When no one else is nigh.

3 Return, O wanderer, now return!
Thy Saviour bids thee live:
Go to His bleeding feet, and learn
How freely He'll forgive.

4 Return, O wanderer, now return,
And wipe the falling tear!
Thy Father calls—no longer mourn.
His love invites thee near.

W. B. Collyer.

362 *The Prodigal Son.*

1 Return, O wanderer, to thy home,
Thy Father calls for thee:
No longer now an exile roam
In guilt and misery.

2 Return, O wanderer, to thy home,
Thy Saviour calls for thee:
"The Spirit and the Bride say, Come;"
Oh, now for refuge flee!

3 Return, O wanderer, to thy home,
'Tis madness to delay:
There are no pardons in the tomb;
And brief is mercy's day!

T. Hastings.

ZEPHYR. L. M. *W. B. Bradbury.*

363 *Christ's Invitation.*

2 They shall find rest, that learn of Me;
I'm of a meek and lowly mind;
But passion rages like the sea,
And pride is restless as the wind.

3 Blest is the man whose shoulders take
My yoke, and bear it with delight;
My yoke is easy to his neck,
My grace shall make the burden light.

4 Jesus, we come at Thy command;
With faith, and hope, and humble zeal;
Resign our spirits to Thy hand,
To mould and guide us at Thy will.

I. Watts.

364 *Rest for the Weary.*

1 Come, weary souls! with sin distressed,
The Saviour offers heavenly rest;
The kind, the gracious call obey,
And cast your gloomy fears away.

2 Here mercy's boundless ocean flows,
To cleanse your guilt, and heal your woes;
Pardon, and life, and endless peace;—
How rich the gift, how free the grace!

3 Lord! we accept, with thankful heart,
The hope Thy gracious words impart;
We come, with trembling; yet rejoice,
And bless the kind inviting voice.

4 Dear Saviour, let Thy powerful love
Confirm our faith, our fears remove;
And sweetly influence every breast,
And guide us to eternal rest.

Anne Steele.

365 *"Behold, I stand at the door and knock."*

1 Behold! a stranger's at the door!
He gently knocks, has knocked before;
Has waited long—is waiting still;
You treat no other friend so ill.

2 But will He prove a friend indeed?
He will—the very friend you need;
The Man of Nazareth—'tis He,
With garments dyed at Calvary.

3 Oh! lovely attitude!—He stands
With melting heart, and laden hands:
Oh! matchless kindness!—and He shows
This matchless kindness to His foes.

4 Admit Him, ere His anger burn;
His feet departed ne'er return;
Admit Him,—or the hour's at hand,
When, at His door, denied you'll stand.

Joseph Grigg.

SHINING SHORE. 8, 7. *Geo. F. Root.*

366 *Jordan's Strand.*

2 We'll gird our loins, my brethren dear!
Our heavenly home discerning;
Our absent Lord has left us word,—
"Let every lamp be burning:"

3 Should coming days be cold and dark,
We need not cease our singing;
That perfect rest nought can molest,
Where golden harps are ringing:

4 Let sorrow's rudest tempest blow,
Each cord on earth to sever;
Our King says,—"Come!"—and there's our home,
Forever, oh! forever!

D. Nelson.

367 *Wayfarers.*

1 Wayfarers in the wilderness,
By morn, and noon, and even,
Day after day, we journey on,
With weary feet toward Heaven:

CHORUS.

O land above! O land of love!
The glory shineth o'er thee;
O Christ, our King! in mercy bring
Us thither, we implore Thee!

2 By day the cloud before us goes,
By night the cloud of fire,
To guide us o'er the trackless waste,
To Canaan ever nigher:

3 Each morning find we, as he said,
The dew of daily manna;
And ever, when a foe appears,
Confronts him Christ, our banner:

4 The sea was riven for our feet,
And so shall be the river;
And, by the King's highway brought home,
We'll praise His name forever:

A. R. Thompson.

368 "*There remaineth therefore a rest.*"

2 Spend and be spent would we,
While lasteth time's brief day;
No turning back in coward fear,
No lingering by the way.

3 Onward we press in haste,
Upward our journey still;
Ours is the path the Master trod
Through good report and ill.

4 The way may rougher grow,
The weariness increase,
We gird our loins and hasten on,—
The end, the end is peace.

H. Bonar.

BETHANY. 6, 4. *Lowell Mason.*

369 *"Nearer, my God, to Thee."*

2 Though like a wanderer,
Daylight all gone,
Darkness be over me,
My rest a stone,
Yet in my dreams I'd be
Nearer, my God, to Thee,
Nearer to Thee.

3 There let the way appear
Steps up to Heaven;
All that thou sendest me
In mercy given;
Angels to beckon me
Nearer, my God, to Thee,
Nearer to Thee.

4 Then with my waking thoughts,
Bright with Thy praise,
Out of my stony griefs,
Bethel I'll raise;
So by my woes to be
Nearer, my God, to Thee,
Nearer to Thee.

5 Or if on joyful wing,
Cleaving the sky,
Sun, moon, and stars forgot,
Upward I fly,
Still all my song shall be,
Nearer, my God, to Thee,
Nearer to Thee.

Sarah Fowler Adams.

ARCADIA. **C. M.** *Thomas Hastings.*

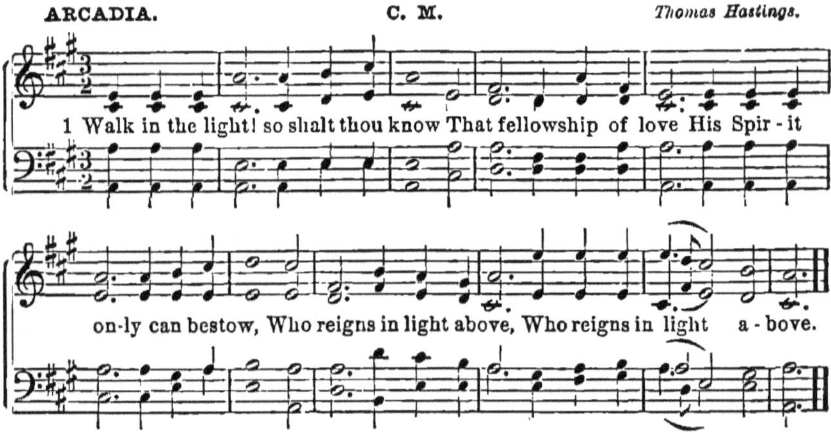

370 *"Walk in the light."*

2 Walk in the light! and thou shalt own
Thy darkness passed away,
Because that light on thee hath shone
In which is perfect day.

3 Walk in the light! and ev'n the tomb
No fearful shade shall wear:
Glory shall chase away its gloom,
For Christ hath conquered there.

4 Walk in the light! and thine shall be
A path, though thorny, bright;
For God, by grace, shall dwell in thee,
And God Himself is light!

Barton.

371 *"The Way, the Truth, and the Life."*

1 Thou art the Way: to Thee alone
From sin and death we flee;
And he who would the Father seek,
Must seek Him, Lord, by Thee.

2 Thou art the Truth: Thy word alone
True wisdom can impart;
Thou only canst instruct the mind,
And purify the heart.

3 Thou art the Life: the rending tomb
Proclaims Thy conquering arm;
And those who put their trust in Thee
Nor death nor hell shall harm.

4 Thou art the Way, the Truth, the Life:
Grant us to know that Way;
That Truth to keep, that Life to win,
Which leads to endless day,

Bp. Doane.

372 *The Happy Home.*

1 Happy the home, when God is there,
And love fills every breast;
Where one their wish, and one their prayer,
And one their heavenly rest.

2 Happy the home where Jesus' name
Is sweet to every ear;
Where children early lisp His fame,
And parents hold Him dear.

3 Happy the home where prayer is heard,
And praise is wont to rise;
Where parents love the sacred word,
And live but for the skies.

4 Lord! let us in our homes agree,
This blessed peace to gain;
Unite our hearts in love to Thee,
And love to all will reign.

Mrs. W——.

BONAR. **S. M. D.** *Lowell Mason.*

373 *The Church in the Wilderness.*

2 It is the oft-told tale
  Of sin and weariness,
Of grace and love yet flowing down
  To pardon and to bless.
No wider is the gate,
  No broader is the way,
No smoother is the ancient path,
  That leads to life and day.

3 No sweeter is the cup,
  Nor less our lot of ill:
'Twas tribulation ages since,
  'Tis tribulation still.
No slacker grows the fight,
  No feebler is the foe,
Nor less the need of armor tried,
  Of shield, and spear, and bow.

4 Thus onward still we press,
  Through evil and through good,—
Through pain, and poverty, and want,
  Through peril and through blood.
Still faithful to our God,
  And to our Captain true,
We follow where He leads the way,
  The kingdom in our view.

H. Bonar.

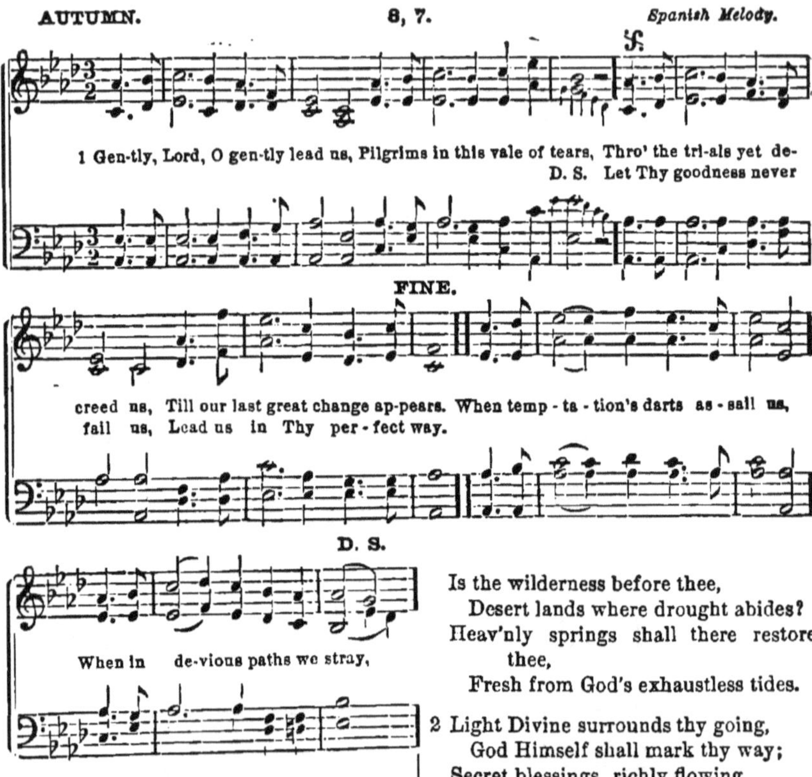

374 *"Lead us."*

2 In the hour of pain and anguish,
In the hour when death draws near,
Suffer not our hearts to languish,
Suffer not our souls to fear;
And, when mortal life is ended,
Bid us in Thine arms to rest,
Till, by angel bands attended,
We awake among the blest.

Thomas Hastings.

375 *Through the Wilderness.*

1 Rise, my soul, thy God directs thee;
Stranger hands no more impede;
Pass thou on, His hand protects thee—
Strength that has the captive freed.
Is the wilderness before thee,
Desert lands where drought abides?
Heav'nly springs shall there restore thee,
Fresh from God's exhaustless tides.

2 Light Divine surrounds thy going,
God Himself shall mark thy way;
Secret blessings, richly flowing,
Lead to everlasting day.
Though thy way be long and dreary,
Eagle-strength He'll still renew;
Garments fresh, and feet unweary,
Tell how God hath brought thee through.

3 When to Canaan's long loved dwelling
Love Divine thy foot shall bring,
There, with shouts of triumph swelling
Zion's songs in rest to sing,
There, no stranger God shall meet thee—
Stranger thou in courts above!
He who to His rest shall greet thee,
Greets thee with a well-known love.

Anon.

AMSTERDAM. 7, 6. D. *James Nares.*

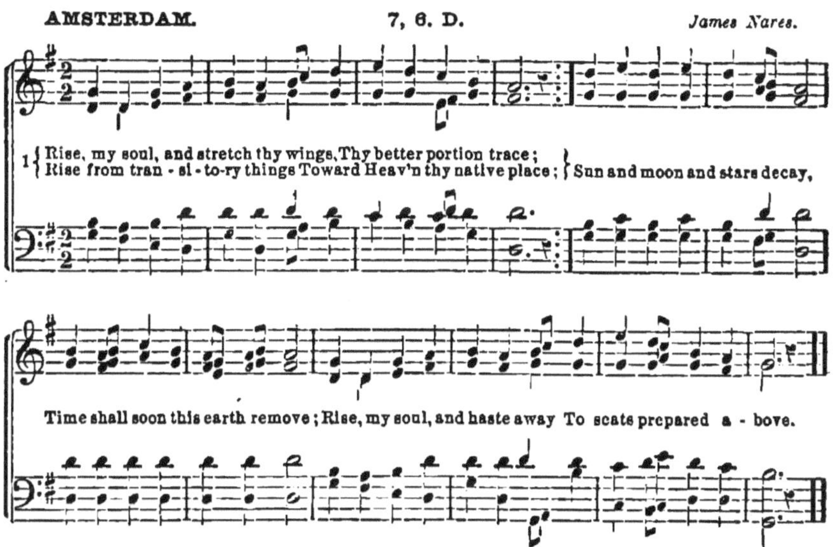

376 *The Pilgrim's Song.*

2 Rivers to the ocean run,
Nor stay in all their course;
Fire, ascending, seeks the sun;
Both speed them to their source:
So, a soul that's born of God,
Pants to view His glorious face,
Upward tends to His abode,
To rest in His embrace.

3 Fly me, riches, fly me, cares,
Whilst I that coast explore;
Flattering world, with all thy snares,
Solicit me no more!
Pilgrims fix not here their home:
Strangers tarry but a night;
When the last dear morn is come,
They'll rise to joyful light.

4 Cease, ye pilgrims, cease to mourn,
Press onward to the prize;
Soon our Saviour will return,
Triumphant in the skies:
Yet a season, and you know
Happy entrance will be given,
All our sorrows left below,
And earth exchanged for Heaven.

Rev. Robert Seagrave.

377 *"Time is winging us away."*

1 Time is winging us away
To our eternal home;
Life is but a winter's day,
A journey to the tomb;
Youth and vigor soon will flee,
Blooming beauty lose its charms;
All that's mortal soon shall be
Enclosed in death's cold arms.

2 Time is winging us away
To our eternal home;
Life is but a winter's day,
A journey to the tomb;
But the Christian shall enjoy
Health and beauty soon, above,
Far beyond the world's annoy,
Secure in Jesus' love.

John Burton.

NUREMBURG. 7. *Johann Rudolph Ahle.*

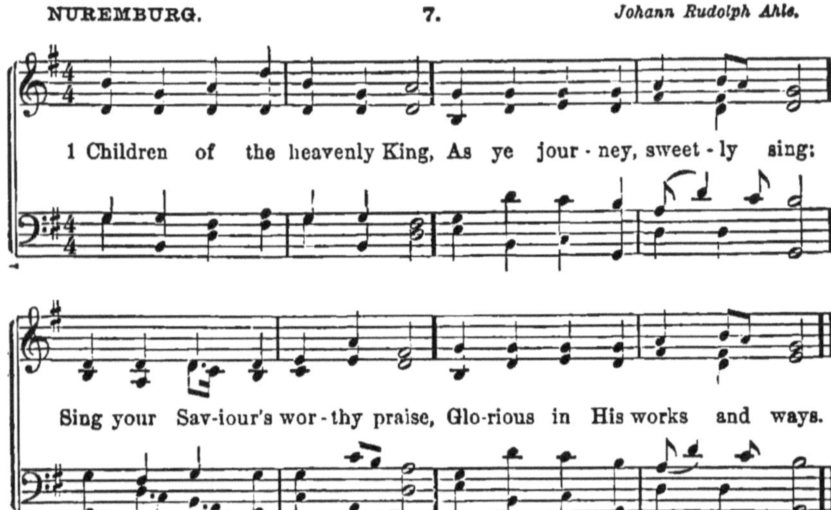

378 *Rejoicing on our Way.*

2 We are traveling home to God,
In the way the fathers trod:
They are happy now, and we
Soon their happiness shall see.

3 Shout, ye little flock, and blest,
You on Jesus' throne shall rest;
There your seat is now prepared,
There your kingdom and reward.

4 Fear not, brethren, joyful stand
On the borders of your land;
Jesus Christ, your Father's Son,
Bids you undismayed go on.

5 Lord, obediently we go,
Gladly leaving all below;
Only Thou our Leader be,
And we still will follow Thee.

Rev. John Cennick.

379 *Redeeming Love.*

1 Now begin the heavenly theme,
Sing aloud in Jesus' name;
Ye who Jesus' kindness prove,
Triumph in redeeming love.

2 Ye who see the Father's grace
Beaming in the Saviour's face,
As to Canaan on ye move,
Praise and bless redeeming love.

3 Mourning souls, dry up your tears;
Banish all your guilty fears;
See your guilt and curse remove,
Cancelled by redeeming love.

4 Welcome, all by sin oppressed,
Welcome to His sacred rest;
Nothing brought Him from above,
Nothing but redeeming love.

5 Hither, then, your music bring,
Strike aloud each joyful string;
Mortals, join the host above,
Join to praise redeeming love.

Rev. Martin Madan.

HE LEADETH ME. **L. M.** *W. B. Bradbury.*

380 *"He leadeth me."*

2 Sometimes 'mid scenes of deepest gloom,
Sometimes where Eden's bowers bloom,
By waters still, o'er troubled sea,
Still 'tis His hand that leadeth me.

3 Lord, I would clasp Thy hand in mine,
Nor ever murmur nor repine;
Content, whatever lot I see,
Since 'tis my God that leadeth me.

4 And when my task on earth is done,
When, by Thy grace, the victory's won,
E'en death's cold wave I will not flee,
Since God through Jordan leadeth me.

Rev. Joseph H. Gilmore.

SICILY. 8, 7, 4. *Sicilian Melody.*

381 *Guidance.*

2 Open Thou the crystal fountain
Whence the healing streams do flow;
Let the fiery, cloudy pillar
Lead me all my journey through;
Strong Deliverer,
Be Thou still my Strength and Shield.

3 When I tread the verge of Jordan,
Bid my anxious fears subside;
Death of death! and hell's Destruction!
Land me safe on Canaan's side;
Songs of praises
I will ever give to Thee.

W. Williams.

382 *"Lead us!"*

1 Lead us, Heavenly Father, lead us
O'er the world's tempestuous sea;
Guard us, guide us, keep us, feed us,
For we have no help but Thee;
Yet possessing Every blessing,
If our God our Father be.

2 Saviour, breathe forgiveness o'er us;
All our weakness Thou dost know;
Thou didst tread this earth before us;
Thou didst feel its keenest woe;
Lone and dreary, Faint and weary,
Through the desert thou didst go.

3 Spirit of our God, descending,
Fill our hearts with heavenly joy;
Love with every passion blending,
Pleasure that can never cloy;
Thus provided, Pardoned, guided,
Nothing can our peace destroy.

J. Edmeston.

383 *"Keep us, Lord."*

1 Keep us, Lord, oh, keep us ever!
Vain our hope, if left by Thee;
We are Thine; oh, leave us never,
Till Thy glorious face we see!
Then to praise Thee
Through a bright eternity.

2 Precious is Thy word of promise,
Precious to Thy people here;
Never take Thy presence from us,
Jesus, Saviour, still be near:
Living, dying,
May Thy name our spirits cheer.

Anon.

SHEPARD. 8, 7, 4. *W. B. Bradbury.*

384 *Prayer for Guidance.*

2 We are Thine, do Thou befriend us,
Be the guardian of our way;
Keep Thy flock, from sin defend us,
Seek us when we go astray;
Blessed Jesus,
Hear the children when they pray.

3 Thou hast promised to receive us,
Poor and sinful though we be;
Thou hast mercy to relieve us,
Grace to cleanse and power to free;
Blessed Jesus,
Let us early turn to Thee.

4 Early let us seek Thy favor,
Early let us do Thy will;
Holy Lord, our only Saviour,
With Thy grace our bosoms fill;
Blessed Jesus,
Thou hast loved us, love us still.

Miss Dorothy Ann Thrupp.

385 *The Pilgrim's Prayer.*

1 Shepherd of Thine Israel! lead us,
Pilgrims o'er this barren sand;
Thou who hast from bondage freed us,
Guard us by Thine outstretched hand:
Guide Thy chosen
Safely to the promised land.

2 Feed us with the heavenly manna;
Fainting, may we feel thy might;
Go before us as our banner,
Cloud by day and fire by night:
Great Redeemer,
Shine around us;—thou art light.

3 When we come to death's dark river,
Bid the swelling stream divide;
Thou who canst our life deliver,
Bear us through the sundered tide:
Praises, praises
Will we sing on Canaan's side!

From the Welsh.

LEBANON. S. M. *J. Zundel.*

386 *Our Shepherd.*

2 The Shepherd sought His sheep,
The Father sought His child;
They followed me o'er vale and hill,
O'er deserts waste and wild:
They found me nigh to death,
Famished, and faint, and lone;
They bound me with the bands of love,
They saved the wandering one.

3 They spoke in tender love,
They raised my drooping head;
They gently closed my bleeding wounds.
My fainting soul they fed:
They washed my filth away,
They made me clean and fair;
They brought me to my home in peace,
The long-sought wanderer.

4 Jesus my Shepherd is,
'T was He that loved my soul,
'T was He that washed me in His blood,
'T was He that made me whole:
'T was He that sought the lost,
That found the wandering sheep,
'T was He that brought me to the fold—
'T is He that still doth keep.

5 No more a wandering sheep,
I love to be controlled,
I love my tender Shepherd's voice,
I love the peaceful fold:
No more a wayward child,
I seek no more to roam,
I love my Heavenly Father's voice—
I love, I love His home.

H. Bonar.

387 *"Not my will, but Thine."*

2 My Jesus, as Thou wilt!
Though seen through many a tear,
Let not my star of hope
Grow dim or disappear;
Since Thou on earth hast wept,
And sorrowed oft alone,
If I must weep with Thee,
My Lord, Thy will be done!

3 My Jesus, as Thou wilt!
All shall be well for me;
Each changing future scene
I gladly trust with Thee:
Straight to my home above
I travel calmly on,
And sing in life or death,
My Lord, Thy will be done!

J. Borthwick.

388 *"He knoweth the way."*

1 Thy way, not mine, O Lord,
However dark it be!
Lead me by Thine own hand;
Choose out my path for me.
I dare not choose my lot:
I would not if I might;
Choose Thou for me, my God,
So shall I walk aright.

2 The kingdom that I seek
Is Thine: so let the way
That leads to it be Thine,
Else I must surely stray.
Take Thou my cup, and it
With joy or sorrow fill,
As best to Thee may seem;
Choose Thou my good or ill.

H. Bonar.

BARBY. C. M. *Wm. Tansur.*

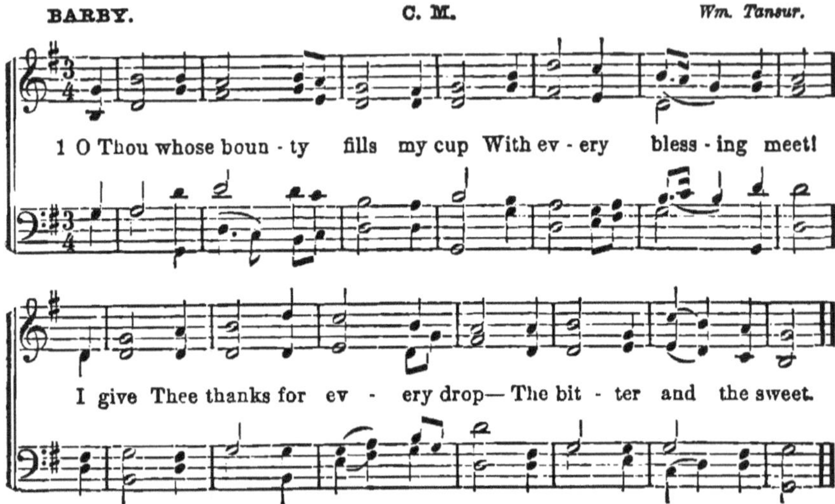

389 *Thanks for All.*

2 I praise Thee for the desert road,
And for the river-side;
For all Thy goodness hath bestowed,
And all Thy grace denied.

3 I thank Thee for both smile and frown,
And for the gain and loss;
I praise Thee for the future crown,
And for the present cross.

4 I thank Thee for the wing of love,
Which stirred my worldly nest;
And for the stormy clouds which drove
The flutterer to Thy breast.

5 I bless Thee for the glad increase,
And for the waning joy;
And for this strange, this settled peace,
Which nothing can destroy.

J. Crewdson.

390 *"I firmly trust."*

1 One prayer I have—all prayers in one—
When I am wholly Thine;
Thy will, my God, Thy will be done,
And let that will be mine.

2 All-wise, almighty, and all-good,
In Thee I firmly trust;
Thy ways, unknown or understood,
Are merciful and just.

3 May I remember that to Thee
Whate'er I have I owe;
And back, in gratitude, from me
May all Thy bounties flow.

4 And though Thy wisdom takes away,
Shall I arraign Thy will?
No, let me bless Thy name, and say,
"The Lord is gracious still."

5 A pilgrim through the earth I roam,
Of nothing long possessed;
And all must fail when I go home,
For this is not my rest.

J. Montgomery.

391 *"Sweet to lie passive."*

1 When languor and disease invade
This trembling house of clay,
'Tis sweet to look beyond my pain,
And long to fly away;—

2 Sweet to look inward and attend
The whispers of His love;
Sweet to look upward to the place
Where Jesus pleads above;—

3 Sweet on His faithfulness to rest,
Whose love can never end;
Sweet on His covenant of grace
For all things to depend;—

4 Sweet, in the confidence of faith,
To trust His firm decrees;
Sweet to lie passive in His hands,
And know no will but His.

A. M. Toplady.

392 *"I know the Lord can save."*

1 Affliction is a stormy deep,
Where wave resounds to wave;
Though o'er my head the billows roll,
I know the Lord can save.
The hand that now withholds my joys
Can soon restore my peace;
And He who bade the tempest rise
Can bid that tempest cease.

2 In darkest scenes, when sorrows rose
And pressed on every side,
The Lord has still sustained my steps,
And still has been my guide.
Here will I rest, and build my hope,
Nor murmur at His rod!
He's more than all the world to me—
My Health, my Life, my God!

Anon.

HENLEY. 11, 10. *Lowell Mason.*

393 *"Come unto me."*

2 Ye who have mourned when the spring-flowers were taken,
When the ripe fruit fell richly to the ground,
When the loved slept, in brighter homes to waken,
Where their pale brows with spirit-wreaths are crowned.

3 Large are the mansions in thy Father's dwelling,
Glad are the homes that sorrows never dim;
Sweet are the harps in holy music swelling,
Soft are the tones which raise the heavenly hymn;

4 There, like an Eden blossoming in gladness,
Bloom the fair flowers the earth too rudely pressed;
Come unto Me, all ye who droop in sadness,
Come unto Me, and I will give you rest!

Anon.

WALES. 8, 4. *Sab. Hymn & Tune Book.*

394 *"It is well."*

2 Though we pass through tribulation,
All will be well:
Ours is such a full salvation;
All, all is well:
Happy, still in God confiding,
Fruitful, if in Christ abiding,
Holy, through the Spirit's guiding,
All must be well.

3 We expect a bright to-morrow;
All will be well:
Faith can sing through days of sorrow,
All, all is well:
On our Father's love relying,
Jesus every need supplying,
Or in living, or in dying,
All must be well.

Anon.

395 *"Weep not for me."*

1 When the spark of life is waning,
Weep not for me;
When the languid eye is straining,
Weep not for me;
When the feeble pulse is ceasing,
Start not at its swift decreasing;
'Tis the fettered soul's releasing;
Weep not for me.

2 When the pangs of death assail me,
Weep not for me;
Christ is mine—He cannot fail me;
Weep not for me;
Yes, though sin and doubt endeavor
From His love my soul to sever,
Jesus is my strength forever:
Weep not for me.

Dale.

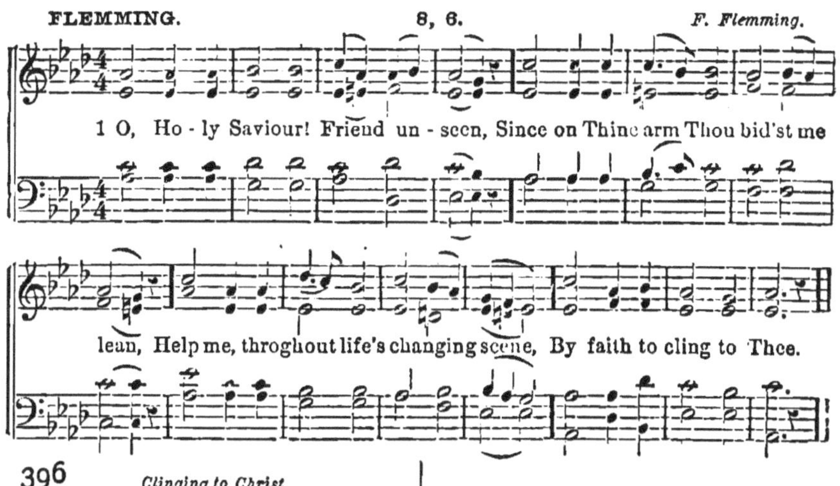

396 *Clinging to Christ.*

2 What though the world deceitful prove,
And earthly friends and hopes remove;
With patient, uncomplaining love,
Still would I cling to Thee.

4 Though faith and hope are often tried,
I ask not, need not, aught beside;
So safe, so calm, so satisfied,
The soul that clings to Thee!

C. Elliott.

397 *A Will Resigned.*

1 I ask not now for gold to gild,
With mocking shine, an aching frame;
The yearning of the mind is stilled—
I ask not now for fame.

2 But, bowed in lowliness of mind,
I make my humble wishes known;
I only ask a will resigned,
O Father, to Thine own.

4 And now my spirit sighs for home,
And longs for light whereby to see;
And, like a weary child, would come,
O Father, unto Thee.

J. G. Whittier.

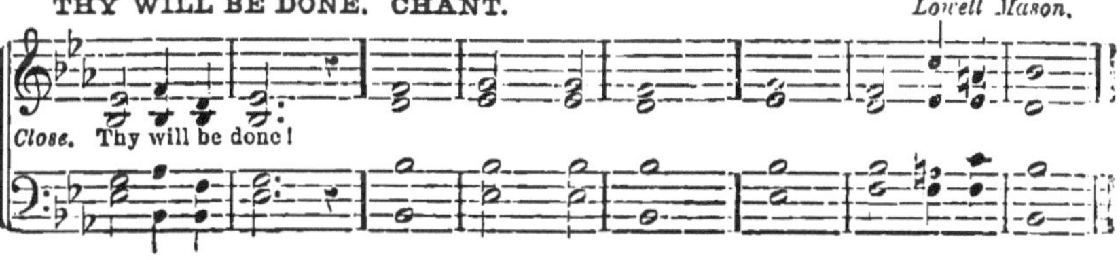

398 *Mark 14: 36.*

1 "Thy will be | done!" ‖ In devious way
The hurrying stream of | life may | run; ‖
Yet still our grateful hearts shall say, |
"Thy will be | done."

2 "Thy will be | done!" ‖ If o'er us shine
A gladdening and a | prosperous | sun, ‖
This prayer will make it more divine— |
"Thy will be | done!"

3 Thy will be | done! ‖ Tho' shrouded o'er
Our | path with | gloom, | one comfort—one
Is ours:—to breathe, while we adore, |
"Thy will be | done."

J. Bowring.

FREDERICK. 11. *Geo. Kingsley.*

399 *"I would not live alway."*

2 I would not live alway, thus fettered by sin—
Temptation without, and corruption within:
Ev'n the rapture of pardon is mingled with fears,
And the cup of thanksgiving with penitent tears.

3 I would not live alway; no, welcome the tomb;
Since Jesus hath lain there, I dread not its gloom;
There sweet be my rest till He bid me arise
To hail Him in triumph descending the skies.

4 Who, who would live alway, away from his God,
Away from yon Heaven, that blissful abode,
Where the rivers of pleasure flow o'er the bright plains,
And the noontide of glory eternally reigns?

5 Where the saints of all ages in harmony meet,
Their Saviour and brethren transported to greet;
While the anthems of rapture unceasingly roll,
And the smile of the Lord is the feast of the soul.

W. A. Muhlenberg.

DUNDEE. C. M. *Scotch Psalter.*

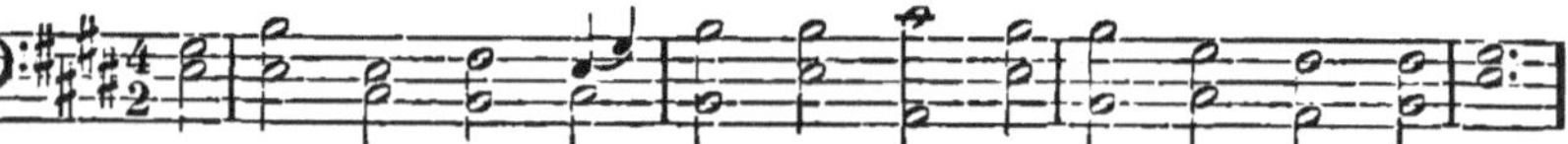

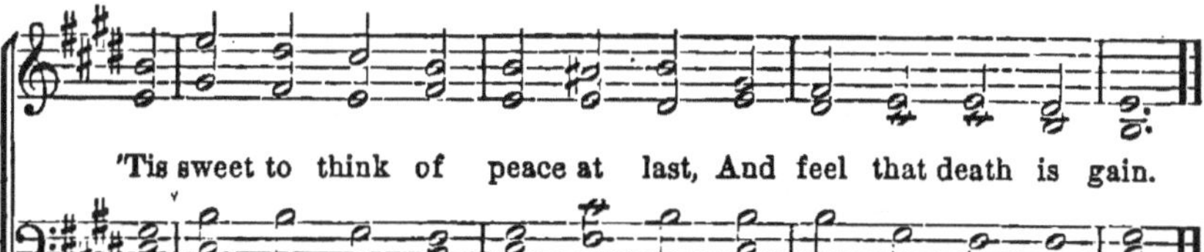

400 *Death is Gain.*

2 'Tis not that murmuring thoughts arise,
And dread a Father's will;
'Tis not that meek submission flies,
And would not suffer still:

3 It is that heaven-born faith surveys
The path that leads to light,
And longs her eagle plumes to raise,
And lose herself in sight.

4 Oh, let me wing my hallowed flight
From earth-born woe and care,
And soar above these clouds of night,
My Saviour's bliss to share!

Noel.

401 *"That I may know how frail I am."*

1 Teach me the measure of my days,
Thou Maker of my frame;
I would survey life's narrow space,
And learn how frail I am.

2 A span is all that we can boast,
An inch or two of time!
Man is but vanity and dust,
In all his flower and prime.

I. Watts.

402 *Resurrection Sure.*

1 When downward to the darksome tomb
I thoughtful turn my eyes,
Frail nature trembles at the gloom,
And anxious fears arise.

2 Why shrinks my soul?—in death's embrace
Once Jesus captive slept:
And angels, hovering o'er the place,
His lowly pillow kept.

3 Thus shall they guard my sleeping dust,
And, as the Saviour rose,
The grave again shall yield her trust,
And end my deep repose.

4 My Lord, before to glory gone,
Shall bid me come away;
And calm and bright shall break the dawn
Of Heaven's eternal day.

5 Then let my faith each fear dispel,
And gild with light the grave;
To Him my loftiest praises swell,
Who died, from death to save.

Ray Palmer.

NAOMI. **C. M.** *Lowell Mason.*

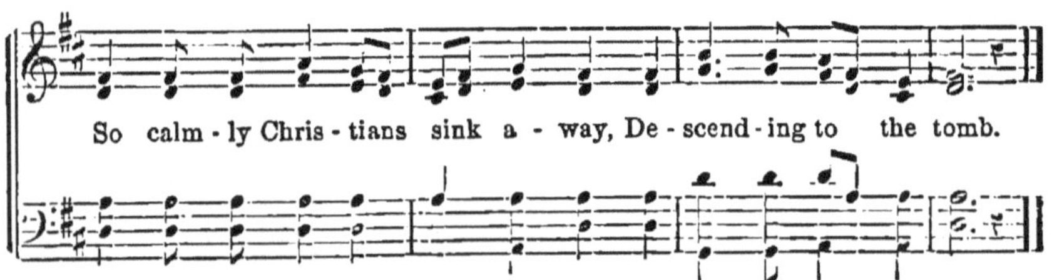

403 *"He fell asleep."*

2 The winds breathe low, the withering leaf
Scarce whispers from the tree:
So gently flows the parting breath,
When good men cease to be.

3 How beautiful on all the hills
The crimson light is shed!
'Tis like the peace the Christian gives
To mourners round his bed.

4 How mildly on the wandering cloud
The sunset beam is cast!
'Tis like the memory left behind,
When loved ones breathe their last.

W. B. C. Peabody.

404 *"Sorrow not, even as others which have no hope."*

1 Dear as thou wert, and justly dear,
We will not weep for thee:
One thought shall check the starting tear:
It is, that thou art free.

2 And thus shall faith's consoling power
The tears of love restrain:
Oh, who that saw thy parting hour,
Could wish thee back again?

3 Angels shall guard thy sleeping dust,
And, as thy Saviour rose,
The grave again shall yield her trust,
And end thy deep repose.

405 *2. Cor. 4:11.*

1 Thro' sorrow's night and danger's path,
Amid the deepening gloom,
We, followers of our suffering Lord,
Are marching to the tomb.

2 There, when the turmoil is no more,
And all our powers decay,
Our cold remains in solitude
May sleep the years away.

3 Our labors done, securely laid
In this our last retreat,
Unheeded o'er our silent dust,
The storms of earth shall beat.

4 Yet not thus buried or extinct,
The vital spark shall lie;
For o'er life's wreck that spark shall rise
To seek its kindred sky.

Anon.

406 *1 Thess. 4: 13.*

1 'Tis sweet to think of those at rest,
  Who slept in Christ the Lord;
Whose spirits now with Him are bless'd
  According to His word.

2 They once were pilgrims here with us,
  In Jesus now they sleep:
And we for them, while resting thus,
  As hopeless cannot weep.

3 How bright the resurrection morn
  On all the saints will break!
The Lord Himself will then return,
  His ransom'd church to take.

4 Or raised or changed His saints will meet,
  All grief and care removed:
What joy 'twill be to us to greet
  Each saint whom here we loved.

5 Our Lord Himself we then shall see,
  Whose blood for us was shed;
With Him forever we shall be,
  Made like our glorious Head.

6 We cannot linger o'er the tomb:
  The resurrection day
To faith shines bright beyond its gloom,
  Christ's glory to display.

ENOS. 7, 6. *Uzziah C. Burnap.*

407 *"Non, ce n'est pas mourir."*

2 No, no, it is not dying
  To hear this gracious word,
"Receive a Father's blessing,
For evermore possessing
  The favor of thy Lord."

3 No, no, it is not dying
  The Shepherd's voice to know;
His sheep He ever leadeth,
His peaceful flock He feedeth,
  Where living pastures grow.

4 No, no, it is not dying
  To wear a lordly crown;
Among God's people dwelling,
The glorious triumph swelling
  Of Him whose sway we own.

5 Oh, no, this is not dying,
  Thou Saviour of mankind;
There, streams of love are flowing,
No hindrance ever knowing;
  Here, drops alone we find.

Cæsar Malan.

REST. L. M. *W. B. Bradbury.*

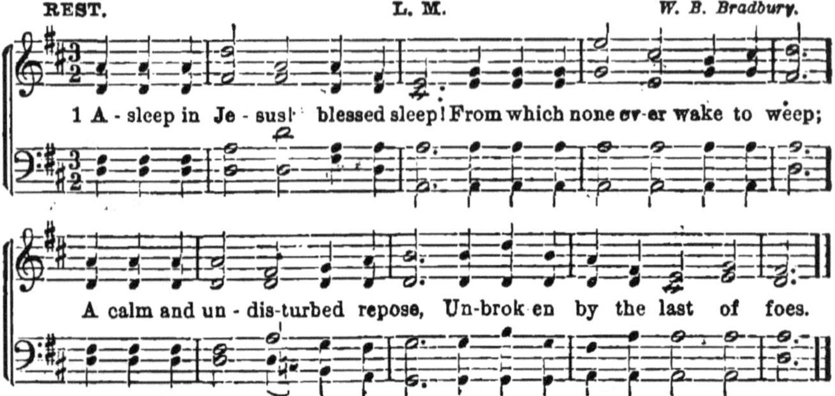

408 *"Asleep in Jesus."*

2 Asleep in Jesus! oh, how sweet
To be for such a slumber meet!
With holy confidence to sing
That death hath lost its venomed sting!

3 Asleep in Jesus! peaceful rest!
Whose waking is supremely blest;
No fear, no woe, shall dim that hour
Which manifests the Saviour's power.

4 Asleep in Jesus! oh, for me
May such a blissful refuge be!
Securely shall my ashes lie,
And wait the summons from on high.

Margaret Mackay.

409 *Psalm* 17.

1 What sinners value, I resign;
Lord! 'tis enough that Thou art mine;
I shall behold Thy blissful face,
And stand complete in righteousness.

2 This life's a dream—an empty show;
But the bright world to which I go,
Hath joys substantial and sincere;
When shall I wake, and find me there?

3 Oh, glorious hour! oh, blest abode!
I shall be near, and like my God;
And flesh and sin no more control
The sacred pleasure of the soul.

4 My flesh shall slumber in the ground,
Till the last trumpet's joyful sound;
Then burst the chains, with sweet surprise,
And in my Saviour's image rise!

I. Watts.

410 *"Why should we weep for those who die?"*

1 Why should we weep for those who die,
Those blessed ones who weep no more?
Jesus hath called them to the sky,
And gladly have they gone before.

2 A few short days they lingered here,
Th' appointed span of trial knew;
Dropped—early dropped the parting tear,
And early now have parted, too.

3 Up, up, in swift ascent, they rise,
Star after star of living light!
Why should we mourn that midnight skies
Become with added glories bright?

4 Far in the distant heavens they shine,
But still with borrowed lustre glow:
Saviour, the beams are only thine,
Of saints above, or saints below.

5 For them no bitter tear we shed—
Their night of pain and grief is o'er,—
But weep our lonely path to tread,
And see the forms we love, no more.

Mrs. Gilbert.

MALVERN. L. M. *Lowell Mason.*

411 *"His beloved sleep."*

2 The pains, the groans, the dying strife
Fright our approaching souls away;
We still shrink back again to life,
Fond of our prison and our clay.

3 Oh, if my Lord would come and meet,
My soul should stretch her wings in haste,
Fly fearless through death's iron gate,
Nor feel the terrors as she passed.

4 Jesus can make a dying bed
Feel soft as downy pillows are,
While on His breast I lean my head,
And breathe my life out sweetly there!

I. Watts.

412 *Death of the Righteous.*

1 How blest the righteous when he dies,—
When sinks a weary soul to rest!
How mildly beam the closing eyes!
How gently heaves the expiring breast!

2 So fades a summer-cloud away;
So sinks the gale when storms are o'er;
So gently shuts the eye of day;
So dies a wave along the shore.

3 A holy quiet reigns around,—
A calm which life nor death destroys;
And naught disturbs that peace profound,
Which his unfettered soul enjoys.

4 Life's labor done, as sinks the clay,
Light from its load the spirit flies;
While heaven and earth combine to say,—
"How blest the righteous when he dies!"

A. L. Barbauld.

413 *Death of an Infant.*

1 So fades the lovely, blooming flower,—
Frail, smiling solace of an hour!
So soon our transient comforts fly,
And pleasure only blooms to die.

2 Is there no kind, no lenient art,
To heal the anguish of the heart?
Spirit of grace! be ever nigh,
Thy comforts are not made to die.

3 Thy powerful aid supports the soul,
And nature owns thy kind control;
While we peruse the sacred page,
Our fiercest griefs resign their rage.

4 Then gentle patience smiles on pain,
And dying hope revives again;
Hope wipes the tear from sorrow's eye,
And faith points upward to the sky.

A. Steele.

AUBURN. C. M. *Thos. Hastings.*

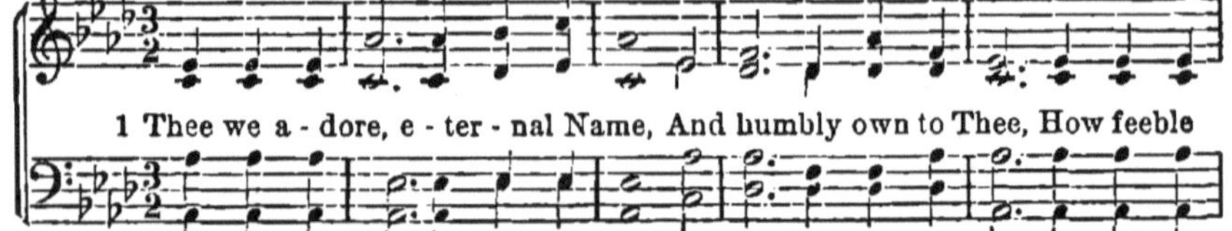

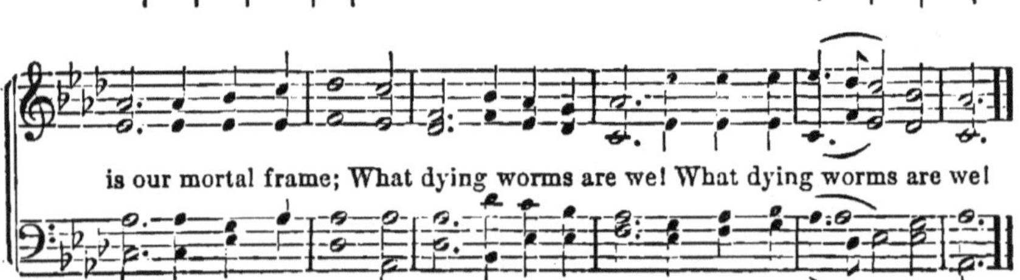

414 *"We all do fade as a leaf."*

2 The year rolls round and steals away
The breath that first it gave;
Whate'er we do, where'er we be,
We're traveling to the grave.

3 Infinite joy or endless woe
Attends on every breath;
And yet how unconcerned we go
Upon the brink of death!

4 Waken, O Lord, our drowsy sense,
To walk this dangerous road;
And if our souls are hurried hence,
May they be found with God.

Anon.

415 *"A name better than of sons and daughters."*

1 Ye mourning saints, whose streaming tears
Flow o'er your children dead,
Say not, in transports of despair,
That all your hopes are fled.

2 While, cleaving to that darling dust,
In deep distress ye lie,
Rise, and with joy and reverence view
A heavenly Par nt nigh!

3 "Transient and vain is every hope
A rising race can give;
In endless honor and delight
My children all shall live."

4 We welcome, Lord, those rising tears
Through which Thy face we see;
And bless those wounds which through our hearts
Prepare a way for Thee.

Anon.

416 *"For what is your life? It is even a vapor."*

1 Beneath our feet and o'er our head
Is equal warning given:
Beneath us lie the countless dead,
Above us is the heaven.

2 Their names are graven on the stone,
Their bones are in the clay;
And ere another day is gone,
Ourselves may be as they.

3 Death rides on every passing breeze,
And lurks in every flower;
Each season has its own disease,
Its peril every hour.

TAMWORTH. 8, 7, 4. *Charles Lockhart.*

417 *"Surely I come quickly."*

2 Long, too long, in sin and sadness,
Far away from Thee I pine;
When, oh, when, shall I the gladness
Of Thy Spirit feel in mine?
O my Saviour,
When shall I be wholly Thine?

3 Nearer is my soul's salvation,
Spent the night, the day at hand;
Keep me in my lowly station,
Watching for Thee, till I stand,
O my Saviour,
In Thy bright and promised land.

4 With my lamp well-trimmed and burning,
Swift to hear, and slow to roam,
Watching for Thy glad returning
To restore me to my home;
Come, my Saviour,
O my Saviour, quickly come.

Rev. John S. B. Monsell.

418 *The Lord's Return.*

1 Lo, He comes, with clouds descending,
Once for favored sinners slain;
Thousand thousand saints attending
Swell the triumph of His train:
Hallelujah!
God appears on earth to reign.

2 Every eye shall now behold Him,
Robed in dreadful majesty;
Those who set at nought and sold Him,
Pierced and nailed Him to the tree,
Deeply wailing,
Shall the true Messiah see.

3 Now redemption, long expected,
See in solemn pomp appear:
All His saints, by men rejected,
Now shall meet Him in the air:
Hallelujah!
See the day of God appear.

4 Yea, amen; let all adore Thee,
High on Thine eternal throne:
Saviour, take the power and glory;
Claim the kingdom for Thine own;
Oh, come quickly,
Hallelujah! come, Lord, come.

C. Wesley.

ELL. S. M. *Sab. Hymn and Tune Book.*

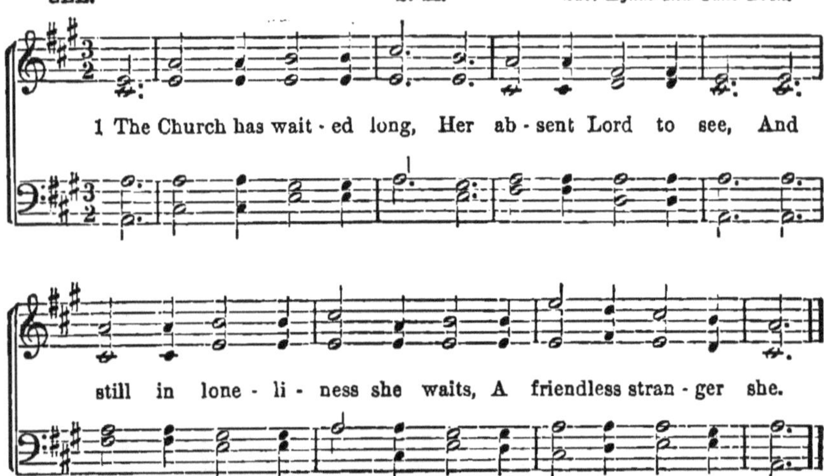

419 *"How long, O Lord, holy and true?"*

2 How long, O Lord our God,
Holy and true and good,
Wilt Thou not judge Thy suffering church,
Her sighs and tears and blood?

3 Saint after saint on earth
Has lived, and loved, and died;
And as they left us one by one,
We laid them side by side.

4 We laid them down to sleep,
But not in hope forlorn;
We laid them but to ripen there,
Till the last glorious morn.

5 We long to hear Thy voice,
To see Thee face to face,
To share Thy crown and glory then,
As now we share Thy grace.

6 Come, Lord! and wipe away
The curse, the sin, the stain,
And make this blighted world of ours
Thine own fair world again.

H. Bonar.

420 *"Even so, come, Lord Jesus."*

1 Come, Lord! and tarry not;
Bring the long-looked-for day;
Oh! why these years of waiting here,
These ages of delay?

2 Come! for creation groans,
Impatient of Thy stay,
Worn out with these long years of ill,
These ages of delay.

3 Come, and make all things new,
Build up this ruined earth;
Restore our faded Paradise—
Creation's second birth!

4 Come, and begin Thy reign
Of everlasting peace;
Come, take the kingdom to Thyself,
Great King of righteousness!

H. Bonar.

HARWELL. 8, 7. D. *Lowell Mason.*

421 *Worshiped of Angels.*

2 King of glory, reign forever!
Thine an everlasting crown;
Nothing from Thy love shall sever
Those whom Thou hast made Thine own;
Happy objects of Thy grace,
Destined to behold Thy face.

3 Saviour, hasten Thine appearing;
Bring, oh, bring the glorious day,
When the awful summons hearing,
Heaven and earth shall pass away:
Then, with golden harps, we'll sing,
"Glory, glory to our King!"

Rev. Thomas Kelly.

422 *"Who stand before God's Throne."*

1 Who are these like stars appearing,
These, before God's throne who stand?
Each a golden crown is wearing,
Who are all this glorious band?
Alleluia! hark, they sing,
Praising loud their heavenly King.

2 These are they who have contended
For their Saviour's honor long,
Wrestling on till life was ended,
Following not the sinful throng:
These, who well the fight sustained,
Triumph thro' the Lamb have gained.

3 These, like priests have watched and waited,
Offering up to Christ their will,
Soul and body consecrated,
Day and night they serve Him still:
Now, in God's most holy place,
Blest they stand before His face.

4 Lo, the Lamb Himself now feeds them
On Mount Zion's pastures fair;
From His central throne He leads them
By the living fountain there:
Lamb and Shepherd, Good Supreme,
Free He gives the cooling stream.

Rev. H. T. Schenk.

MENDEBRAS. 7, 6. D. *Lowell Mason, arr.*

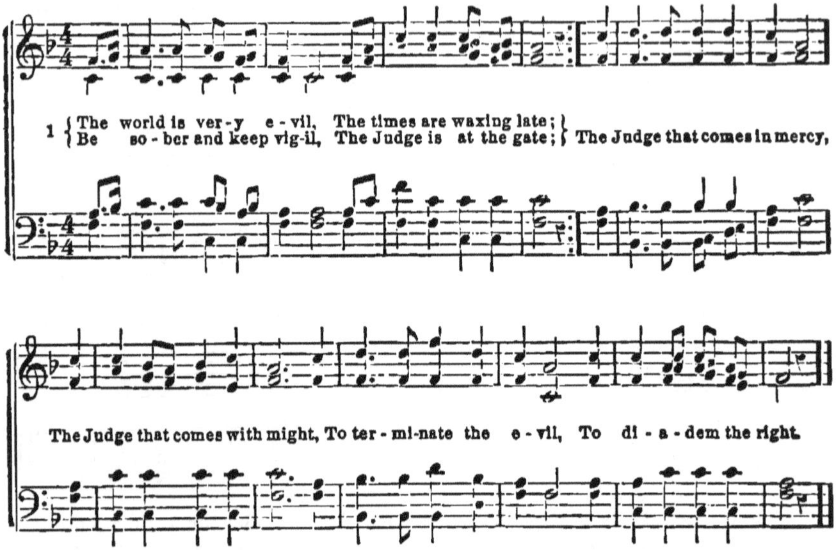

1 { The world is ver-y e-vil, The times are waxing late; / Be so-ber and keep vig-il, The Judge is at the gate; } The Judge that comes in mercy, The Judge that comes with might, To ter-mi-nate the e-vil, To di-a-dem the right.

423 *"Hora novissima."*

2 Arise, arise, good Christian,
Let right to wrong succeed;
Let penitential sorrow
To heavenly gladness lead;
To light that hath no evening,
That knows no moon nor sun,
The light so new and golden,
The light that is but one.

3 Oh, home of fadeless splendor,
Of flowers that fear no thorn,
Where they shall dwell as children
Who here as exiles mourn.
'Midst power that knows no limit,
Where wisdom has no bound,
The beatific vision
Shall glad the saints around.

Bernard of Cluny.

424 *"Ermuntert euch, ihr Frommen."*

1 Rejoice, rejoice, believers,
And let your lights appear;
The evening is advancing,
And darker night is near.
The Bridegroom is arising,
And soon He will draw nigh;
Up, pray, and watch, and wrestle,
At midnight comes the cry.

2 See that your lamps are burning,
Replenish them with oil;
Look now for your salvation,
The end of sin and toil.
The watchers on the mountain
Proclaim the Bridegroom near,
Go meet Him as He cometh,
With hallelujahs clear.

3 Our hope and expectation,
O Jesus, now appear;
Arise, Thou Sun so longed for,
O'er this benighted sphere.
With hearts and hands uplifted,
We plead, O Lord, to see
The day of earth's redemption,
And ever be with Thee.

Laurentius Laurenti.

BRADFORD. C. M. *Handel.*

425 *Acts 3:20, 21.*

2 Come, blessed Lord! bid every shore
And answering island sing
The praises of Thy royal name,
And own Thee as their king.

3 Lord, Lord, Thy fair creation groans—
The air, the earth, the sea,
In unison with all our hearts,
And calls aloud for Thee.

4 Come, then, with all Thy quickening power,
With one awakening smile,
And bid the serpent's trail no more
Thy beauteous realms defile.

5 Thine was the cross, with all its fruits
Of grace and peace divine;
Be Thine the crown of glory now,
The palm of vict'ry Thine.

Anon.

426 *"When Christ, who is our life, shall appear."*

1 Long hath the night of sorrow reigned,
The dawn shall bring us light:
Christ shall appear; and we shall rise
With gladness in His sight.

2 Then shall we see our absent Lord—
Shall know Him and rejoice:
His coming like the morn shall be,
Like morning songs His voice.

3 As dew upon the tender herb,
Diffusing fragrance round;
As showers that usher in the spring
And cheer the thirsty ground;

4 So shall His presence bless our souls,
And shed a joyful light:
That hallowed morn shall chase away
The sorrows of the night.

Anon.

427 *"Until He come."*

1 Until He come! like music tones
Are these most precious words,
'Mid all the noise and din of earth,
To those who are the Lord's.

2 They mark the time when life's dark sea,
Whose storms so fiercely roar,
Shall toss upon its troubled waves,
The Christian's bark no more.

3 O glorious hour! what rapturous strains
Shall ring with grand accord,
When from the ransomed throng shall burst—
"Forever with the Lord!"

Anon.

LISBON. S. M. *D. Read.*

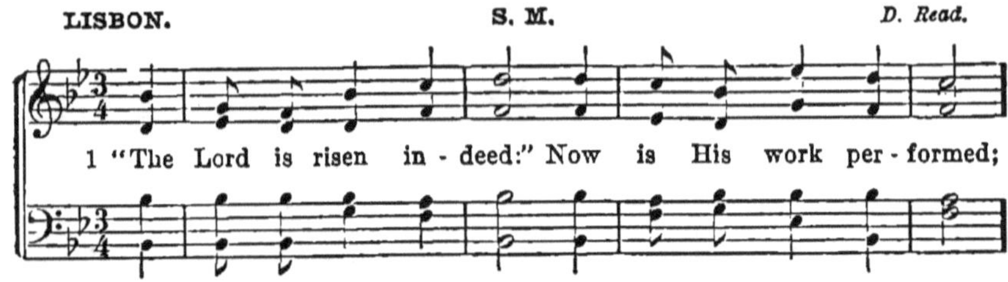

428 *"The Lord is risen indeed."*

2 "The Lord is risen indeed:"
The grave has lost his prey;
With Him is risen the ransomed seed
To reign in endless day.

3 "The Lord is risen indeed:"
He lives, to die no more;
He lives, the sinner's cause to plead,
Whose curse and shame He bore.

4 "The Lord is risen indeed:"
Attending angels, hear;
Up to the courts of Heaven, with speed,
The joyful tidings bear.

5 Then take your golden lyres,
And strike each cheerful chord;
Join all the bright, celestial choirs,
To sing our risen Lord!

Kelly.

429 *Resurrection.*

1 Oh, for the death of those
Who slumber in the Lord!
Oh, be like theirs my last repose,
Like theirs my last reward!

2 Their bodies in the ground,
In silent hope may lie,
Till the last trumpet's joyful sound
Shall call them to the sky.

3 Their ransomed spirits soar
On wings of faith and love,
To meet the Saviour they adore,
And reign with Him above.

4 With us their names shall live
Through long succeeding years,
Embalmed with all our hearts can give,
Our praises and our tears.

S. F. Smith.

430 *Doxology.*

To God, the Father, Son,
And Spirit, glory be,
As was, and is, and shall remain
Through all eternity!

TEN THOUSAND TIMES. *Ira D. Sankey.*

431 *"The number of them was ten thousand times ten thousand."*

2 What rush of hallelujahs
Fills all the earth and sky!
What ringing of a thousand harps
Bespeaks the triumphs nigh!
Oh, day for which creation
And all its tribes were made!
Oh joy, for all its former woes
A thousand-fold repaid!

3 Oh, then what raptured greetings
On Canaan's happy shore!
What knitting severed friendships up,
Where partings are no more!
Then eyes with joy shall sparkle,
That brimmed with tears of late;
Orphans no longer fatherless,
Nor widows desolate.

Henry Alford, D. D.

LISCHER. H. M. *Friedrich Schneider.*

432 *The Resurrection of Christ.*

2 Lo! the angelic bands
In full assembly meet,
To wait His high commands,
And worship at His feet:
Joyful they come, and wing their way,
From realms of day, to such a tomb.

3 Then back to Heaven they fly,
And the glad tidings bear;
Hark! as they soar on high,
What music fills the air!
Their anthems say,—"Jesus, who bled,
Hath left the dead;—He rose to-day."

4 All hail! triumphant Lord!
Who sav'st us with Thy blood:
Wide be Thy name adored,
Thou rising, reigning God!
With Thee we rise, with Thee we reign,
And empires gain, beyond the skies.

Philip Doddridge.

433 *The Condescension and Love of Christ.*

1 Come every pious heart,
That loves the Saviour's name!
Your noblest powers exert,
To celebrate His fame;
Tell all above, and all below,
The debt of love to Him you owe.

2 He left His starry crown,
And laid His robes aside;
On wings of love came down,
And wept, and bled, and died;
What He endured, oh! who can tell,
To save our souls from death and hell?

3 From the dark grave He rose,
The mansion of the dead;
And thence His mighty foes,
In glorious triumph led;
Up through the sky the Conqueror rode,
And reigns on high, the Saviour God.

4 Jesus! we ne'er can pay
The debt we owe Thy love,
Yet tell us how we may
Our gratitude approve:
Our hearts, our all, to Thee we give;
The gift, though small, Thou wilt receive.

Samuel Stennett.

HENDON. 7. *Rev. Cæsar Malan.*

434 *"Christ, the first-fruits."*

2 Love's redeeming work is done,
Fought the fight, the battle won:
Lo! our sun's eclipse is o'er;
Lo! he sets in blood no more.

3 Vain the stone, the watch, the seal—
Christ hath burst the gates of hell:
Death in vain forbids His rise,
Christ hath opened paradise.

4 Lives again our glorious King!
Where, O Death, is now thy sting?
Once He died, our souls to save
Where's thy vict'ry, boasting Grave?

5 Soar we now where Christ hath led,
Following our exalted Head:
Made like Him, like Him we rise,
Ours the cross, the grave, the skies!

Cudworth.

435 *Morning at the Tomb.*

1 Morning breaks upon the tomb;
Jesus scatters all its gloom:
Day of triumph through the skies!
See the glorious Saviour rise!

2 Christian! dry your flowing tears;
Chase those unbelieving fears:
Look on His deserted grave;
Doubt no more His power to save.

3 Ye, who are of death afraid,
Triumph in the scattered shade;
Drive your anxious cares away:
See the place where Jesus lay!

4 Lo! the rising sun appears,
Shedding radiance o'er the spheres;
Lo! returning beams of light
Chase the terrors of the night.

Collyer.

436 *"He hath risen, as He said."*

1 Christ, the Lord, is risen again,
Christ hath broken every chain:
Hark, the angels shout for joy,
Singing evermore on high.

2 He who bore all pain and loss
Comfortless upon the cross,
Lives in glory now on high,
Pleads for us, and hears our cry.

3 He who slumbered in the grave,
Is exalted now to save;
Now through Christendom it rings,
That the Lamb is King of kings.

M. Weisse.

ROTHWELL. **L. M.** *Wm. Tansur.*

437

Psalm 24.

2 There His triumphal chariot waits,
And angels chant the solemn lay:
"Lift up your heads, ye heavenly gates!
Ye everlasting doors! give way."

3 Loose all your bars of massy light,
And wide unfold the ethereal scene:
He claims these mansions as His right;
Receive the King of glory in.

4 Who is this King of glory—who?
The Lord who all our foes o'ercame;
Who sin, and death, and hell o'erthrew;
And Jesus is the conqueror's name.

5 Lo! his triumphal chariot waits,
And angels chant the solemn lay:—
"Lift up your heads, ye heavenly gates!
Ye everlasting doors! give way."

6 Who is this King of glory—who?
The Lord of boundless power possessed;
The King of saints and angels, too,
God over all, forever blessed.

C. Wesley.

438

"He lives."

1 "I know that my Redeemer lives:"
What comfort this sweet sentence gives,
He lives, He lives, who once was dead,
He lives, my ever-living Head.

2 He lives to bless me with His love,
He lives to plead for me above,
He lives my hungry soul to feed,
He lives to help in time of need.

3 He lives to silence all my fears,
He lives to stoop and wipe my tears,
He lives to calm my troubled heart,
He lives all blessings to impart.

4 He lives, my kind, my faithful Friend,
He lives and loves me to the end,
He lives, and while He lives I'll sing,
He lives, my Prophet, Priest, and King.

5 He lives, all glory to His name;
He lives, my Jesus, still the same:
Oh, the sweet joy this sentence gives,
"I know that my Redeemer lives."

Rev. Samuel Medley.

HOME OVER THERE.

T. C. O'Kane, by per.

JOYFUL SOUND. C. M. D. *E. L. White.*

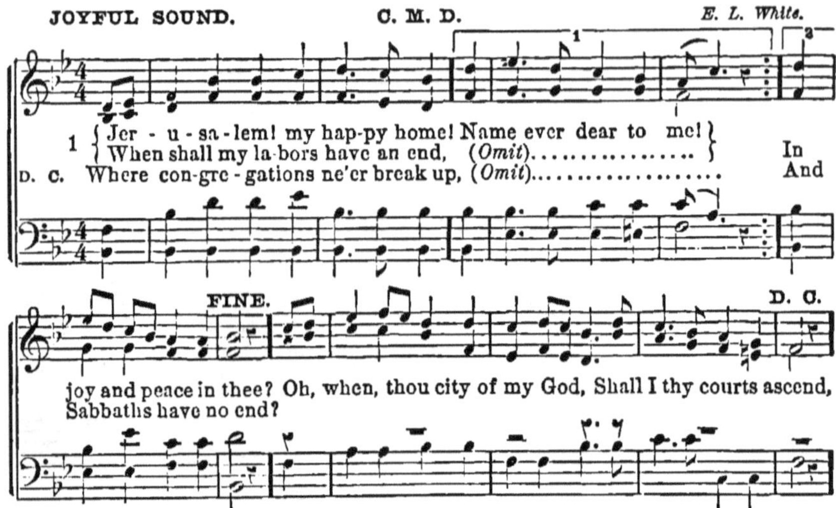

440 *The New Jerusalem.*

2 There happier bow'rs than Eden's bloom
Nor sin nor sorrow know: [scenes,
Blest seats! thro' rude and stormy
I onward press to you.
Why should I shrink at pain and woe,
Or feel, at death, dismay?
I've Canaan's goodly land in view,
And realms of endless day.

3 Apostles, martyrs, prophets there,
Around my Saviour stand;
And soon my friends in Christ below,
Will join the glorious band.
Jerusalem! my happy home!
My soul still pants for thee;
Then shall my labors have an end,
When I thy joys shall see.

Anon.

441 *"O Mother dear, Jerusalem."*

1 O mother dear, Jerusalem,
When shall I come to thee?
When shall my sorrows have an end?
Thy joys when shall I see?
O happy harbor of God's saints,
O sweet and pleasant soil;
In thee no sorrow can be found,
Nor grief, nor care, nor toil.

2 No dimming cloud o'ershadows thee,
Nor gloom, nor darksome night;
But every soul shines as the sun,
For God Himself gives light.
Thy walls are made of precious stone,
Thy bulwarks diamond-square,
Thy gates are all of orient pearl:
O God, if I were there!

3 Right through thy streets with pleasing sound
The flood of life doth flow,
And on the banks, on either side,
The trees of life do grow.
Those trees each month yield ripened fruit;
For evermore they spring,
And all the nations of the earth
To Thee their honors bring.

4 There the blest souls that hardly 'scaped
The snare of death and hell,
Triumph in joy eternally,
Whereof no tongue can tell.
O mother dear, Jerusalem,
When shall I come to thee?
When shall my sorrows have an end?
Thy joys when shall I see?

Rev. Francis Baker.

ONE SWEETLY SOLEMN THOUGHT. *Philip Phillips.*

442 *"Now they desire a better country than this, an heavenly."*

2 Nearer my Father's house,
Where many mansions be;
Nearer the great white throne to-day,
Nearer the crystal sea.

3 Nearer the bound of life,
Where burdens are laid down;
Nearer to leave the cross to-day,
And nearer to the crown.

4 Be near me when my feet
Are slipping o'er the brink;
For I am nearer home to-day,
Perhaps, than now I think.

Miss Phœbe Carey.

"LET ME GO." 8, 7. D. *Rev. L. Hartsough.*

443 *Let Me Go.*

2 Let me go where none are weary,
Where is raised no wail of woe,
Let me go, and bathe my spirit
In the raptures angels know:
Let me go, for bliss eternal
Lures my soul away, away,
And the victor's song triumphant,
Thrills my heart, I cannot stay.

3 Let me go, why should I tarry?
What has earth to bind me here?
What, but cares, and toils, and sorrows,
What, but death, and pain and fear?
Let me go, for hopes most cherished,
Blasted, round me often lie;
Oh! I've gathered brightest flowers,
But to see them fade and die.

4 Let me go where tears and sighing
Are forever more unknown,
Where the joyous songs of glory
Call me to a happier home.
Let me go, I'd cease this dying,
I would gain life's fairer plains;
Let me join the myriad harpers,
Let me chant their rapturous strains.

5 Let me go, oh, speed my journey,
Saints and seraphs lure away;
Oh, I almost feel the raptures,
That belong to endless day.
Oft methinks I hear the singing
That is only heard above:
Let me go, oh, speed my going,
Let me go where all is love.

Rev. L. Hartsough.

BEULAH. 7. D. *E. Ives.*

444 "*Who are these?*"

1 Who are these in bright array,
  This innumerable throng
Round the altar, night and day
  Hymning one triumphant song?—
"Worthy is the Lamb, once slain,
  Blessing, honor, glory, power,
Wisdom, riches, to obtain,
  New dominion every hour."

2 These through fiery trials trod;
  These from great afflictions came:
Now, before the throne of God,
  Sealed with His almighty name.
Clad in raiment pure and white,
  Victor palms in every hand,
Through their dear Redeemer's might,
  More than conquerors they stand.

3 Hunger, thirst, disease unknown,
  On immortal fruits they feed;
Them the Lamb, amid the throne,
  Shall to living fountains lead:
Joy and gladness banish sighs—
  Perfect love dispels all fears—
And forever from their eyes
  God shall wipe away the tears.

Anon.

445 "*God shall wipe away all tears from their eyes.*"

1 High in yonder realms of light,
  Dwell the raptured saints above;
Far beyond our feeble sight,
  Happy in Immanuel's love:
Pilgrims in this vale of tears,
  Once they knew like us below,
Gloomy doubts, distressing fears,
  Torturing pain and heavy woe.

2 But these days of weeping o'er,
  Passed this scene of toil and pain,
They shall feel distress no more—
  Never, never weep again:
'Mid the chorus of the skies,
  'Mid th' angelic lyres above,
Hark! their songs melodious rise,
  Songs of praise to Jesus' love!

3 All is tranquil and serene,
  Calm and undisturbed repose:
There no cloud can intervene,
  There no angry tempest blows:
Every tear is wiped away,
  Sighs no more shall heave the breast,
Night is lost in endless day,
  Sorrow—in eternal rest.

Raffles.

PARADISE. **P. M.** *J. Barnby.*

446 *"O Paradise."*

1 O Paradise! O Paradise!
Who doth not crave for rest?
Who would not seek the happy land
Where they that loved are blest?
Where loyal hearts and true
Stand ever in the light,
All rapture through and through,
In God's most holy sight.

2 O Paradise, O Paradise,
The world is growing old;
Who would not be at rest and free
Where love is never cold?
Where loyal hearts and true
Stand ever in the light,
All rapture through and through,
In God's most holy sight.

3 O Paradise, O Paradise,
I greatly long to see
The special place my dearest Lord
In love prepares for me;
Where loyal hearts and true
Stand ever in the light,
All rapture through and through,
In God's most holy sight.

4 Lord Jesus, King of Paradise,
Oh, keep me in Thy love,
And guide me to that happy land
Of perfect rest above;
Where loyal hearts and true
Stand ever in the light,
All rapture through and through,
In God's most holy sight.

F. W. Faber.

OAK. 6, 4. *Lowell Mason.*

447 *"Heaven is home."*

1 I'm but a stranger here,—
 Heaven is my home;
Earth is a desert drear,—
 Heaven is my home;
Danger and sorrow stand
Round me on every hand,
Heaven is my Fatherland,
 Heaven is my home.

2 What though the tempests rage?
 Heaven is my home;
Short is my pilgrimage,
 Heaven is my home;
And time's wild, wintry blast,
Soon will be overpast,
I shall reach home at last,—
 Heaven is my home.

3 Therefore I murmur not,—
 Heaven is my home;
Whate'er my earthly lot,
 Heaven is my home;
And I shall surely stand
There, at my Lord's right hand;
Heaven is my Fatherland,
 Heaven is my home.

T. R. Taylor.

JUST OVER THERE. *Geo. C. Stebbins.*

448 *"For there is no night there."*

2 Over there is no more weeping,
Over there all pain is o'er;
I shall rest in Jesus' keeping,
And shall droop and die no more.

3 Over there I'll find my treasure,
Jewels lost, long, long ago;
Love and bliss in fullest measure,
There my heart shall ever know.

4 Over there all are immortal;
Over there is no more night;
And the city's pearly portal
Is almost within my sight.

5 Will you go, dear sinner, with me
Where the Lamb will ever reign;
Where the loved of earth will greet Thee,
Never more to part again?

Anon.

UXBRIDGE. L. M. *Lowell Mason.*

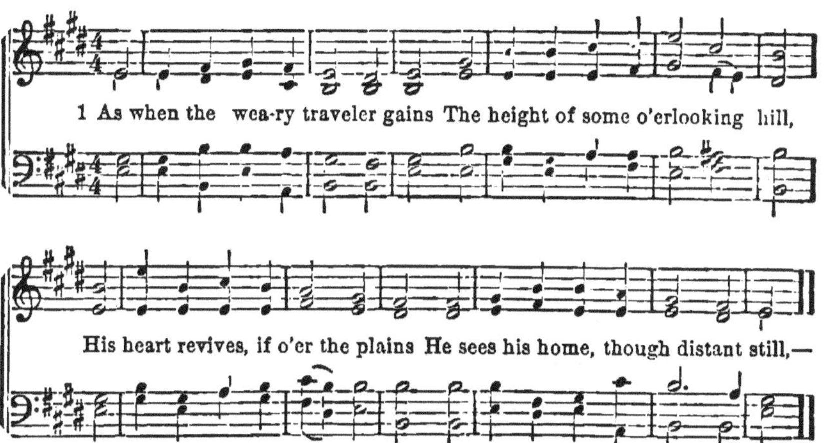

449 *With Christ in Heaven.*

2 So when the Christian pilgrim views,
By faith, his mansion in the skies,
The sight his fainting strength renews,
And wings his speed to reach the prize.

3 "'Tis there," he says, "I am to dwell
With Jesus in the realms of day;
Then shall I bid my cares farewell,
And He will wipe my tears away."

Newton.

4 Holy and heavenly be that soul
Where dwells a hope so high as this;
How should we long to reach the goal;
And seize the prize of endless bliss!

Gibbons.

450 *Eternal Life.*

1 Eternal life! how will it reign,
When, mounting from this breathless clod,
The soul, discharged from sin and pain,
Ascends to enjoy its Father, God!

2 Eternal life! how will it bloom
In beauty, on that blissful day
When, rescued from the imprisoning tomb,
A glory clothes our rising clay!

3 Eternal life! oh, how refined
The joy! the triumph how divine!
When saints, in body and in mind,
Shall in the Saviour's image shine!

451 *"Here have we no continuing city."*

1 "We've no abiding city here:"
Sad truth, were this to be our home;
But let this thought our spirits cheer,
"We seek a city yet to come."

2 "We've no abiding city here;"
We seek a city out of sight:
Zion its name—the Lord is there,
It shines with everlasting light.

3 Oh, sweet abode of peace and love,
Where pilgrims freed from toil are blest!
Had I the pinions of the dove,
I'd fly to Thee, and be at rest.

4 But hush, my soul! nor dare repine;
The time my God appoints is best:
While here, to do His will be mine,
And His to fix my time of rest.

Kelly.

Arranged.

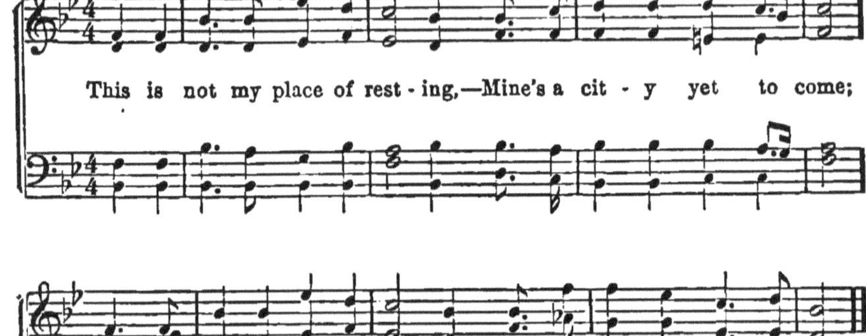

On - ward to it I am hast - ing —On to my e - ter - nal home.

452 *Not our Rest.*

2 In it all is light and glory;
O'er it shines a nightless day:
Every trace of sin's sad story,
All the curse, hath passed away.

3 There the Lamb, our Shepherd, leads us
By the streams of life along,—
On the freshest pastures feeds us,
Turns our sighing into song.

4 Soon we pass this desert dreary,
Soon we bid farewell to pain;
Never more are sad or weary,
Never, never sin again!

H. Bonar.

453 *The City.*

1 Daily, daily sing the praises
Of the City God hath made;
In the beauteous fields of Eden
Its foundation-stones are laid.

2 In the midst of that dear City
Christ is reigning on His seat,
And the angels swing their censers
In a ring about His feet.

3 From the throne a river issues,
Clear as crystal, passing bright,
And it traverses the City
Like a sudden beam of light.

4 There the wind is sweetly fragrant,
And is laden with the song
Of the seraphs, and the elders,
And the great redeemed throng.

5 Oh, I would my ears were open
Here to catch that happy strain!
Oh, I would my eyes some vision
Of that Eden could attain!

S. Baring-Gould.

EWING. 7, 6. D. *Alex. Ewing.*

454 *"Eye hath not seen, nor ear heard."*

2 They stand, those halls of Zion,
All jubilant with song,
And bright with many an angel,
And all the martyr throng;
The Prince is ever in them,
The daylight is serene;
The pastures of the blessed
Are decked in glorious sheen.

3 There is the throne of David;
And there, from care released,
The song of them that triumph,
The shout of them that feast:
And they who, with their Leader,
Have conquered in the fight,
Forever and forever
Are clad in robes of white.

Lat., *Bernard de Morlaix.*

455 *"In my Father's house are many mansions."*

1 For thee, O dear, dear country!
Mine eyes their vigils keep;
For very love, beholding
Thy happy name, they weep:
The mention of Thy glory
Is unction to the breast,
And medicine in sickness,
And love, and life, and rest.

2 Jesus, the Gem of beauty,
True God and Man, they sing;—
The never-failing Garden,
The ever-golden Ring;
The Door, the Pledge, the Husband,
The Guardian of His court;
The Day-star of salvation,
The Porter and the Port.

Lat., *Bernard de Morlaix.*

JORDAN. C. M. D. *W. Billings.*

456 "*Go over this Jordan.*"

2 Sweet fields beyond the swelling flood
Stand dressed in living green;
So to the Jews old Canaan stood,
While Jordan rolled between.
But timorous mortals start and shrink
To cross this narrow sea;
And linger, shivering on the brink,
And fear to launch away.

3 Oh, could we make our doubts remove,
These gloomy doubts that rise,
And see the Canaan that we love
With unbeclouded eyes:—
Could we but climb where Moses stood,
And view the landscape o'er, [flood,
Not Jordan's stream, nor death's cold
Should fright us from the shore.

I. Watts.

457 "*Hold fast.*"

1 The roseate hues of early dawn,
The brightness of the day,
The crimson of the sunset sky,
How fast they fade away!
Oh, for the pearly gates of Heaven!
Oh, for the golden floor!
Oh, for the Sun of Righteousness,
That setteth nevermore!

2 The highest hopes we cherish here,
How soon they tire and faint!
How many a spot defiles the robe
That wraps an earthly saint!
Oh, for a heart that never sins!
Oh, for a soul washed white!
Oh, for a voice to praise our King,
Nor weary day or night!

3 Here faith is ours, and heavenly hope,
And grace to lead us higher;
But there are perfectness and peace,
Beyond our best desire.
Oh, by Thy love and anguish, Lord,
And by Thy life laid down,
Grant that we fall not from Thy grace,
Nor fail to reach our crown!

C. F. Alexander.

458 *"In Thy presence is fulness of joy; at Thy right hand there are pleasures for-evermore."*

1 Heaven is the land where troubles cease,
Where toils and tears are o'er:
The sunny clime of rest and peace,
Where cares distract no more.
Heaven is the home where spirits dwell,
Who wandered here awhile,
And, "seeing things invisible,"
Departed with a smile.

2 Heaven is the place where Jesus lives
To plead His dying blood,
While to His prayers the Father gives
An unknown multitude.
Heaven is the dwelling-place of joy,
The home of light and love,
Where faith and hope in rapture die;
There's perfect bliss above.

Anon.

MT. BLANC. P. M. *Old English Melody.*

459 *"The Holy City.*

2 We can see that distant home,
Though clouds rise dark between;
Faith views the radiant dome,
And a lustre flashes keen
From the new Jerusalem.

3 Oh, holy, heavenly home!
Oh, rest eternal there!
When shall the exiles come,
Where they cease from earthly care,
In the new Jerusalem!

4 Our hearts are breaking now
Those mansions fair to see;
O Lord, Thy heavens bow,
And raise us up with Thee,
To the new Jerusalem.

C. Beecher.

REST FOR THE WEARY. 8, 7. *Rev. William McDonald.*

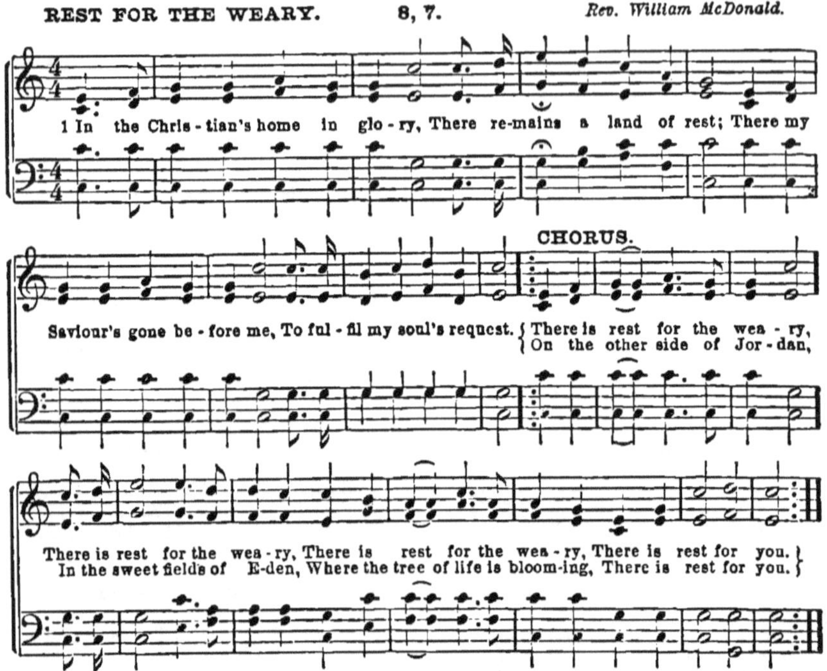

460 *"Rest for the Weary."*

2 He is fitting up my mansion,
Which eternally shall stand;
For my stay shall not be transient
In that holy, happy land.

3 Pain and sickness ne'er shall enter,
Grief nor woe my lot shall share;
But in that celestial centre
I a crown of life shall wear.

4 And the grave shall then be conquer'd,
And the sting of death be lost;
And our bark, all safely anchored,
Never more be tempest-tossed.

5 Sing, oh sing, ye heirs of glory;
Shout your triumph as you go;
Zion's gate will ope before ye,
You shall find an entrance through.

Rev. Samuel Harmer.

461 *The Multitude before the Throne.*
[Omitting the Chorus.]

1 Hark the sound of holy voices,
Chanting at the crystal sea,
Hallelujah, hallelujah,
Hallelujah! Lord, to Thee.

2 Multitude, which none can number,
Like the stars in glory stand,
Clothed in white apparel, holding
Palms of victory in their hand.

3 They have come from tribulation,
And have washed their robes in blood,
Washed them in the blood of Jesus;
Tried they were, and firm they stood.

4 Gladly, Lord, with Thee they suffered,
Gladly, Lord, with Thee they died;
And by death to life immortal
They were born, and glorified.

Anon.

C. M. *N. D. Gould.*

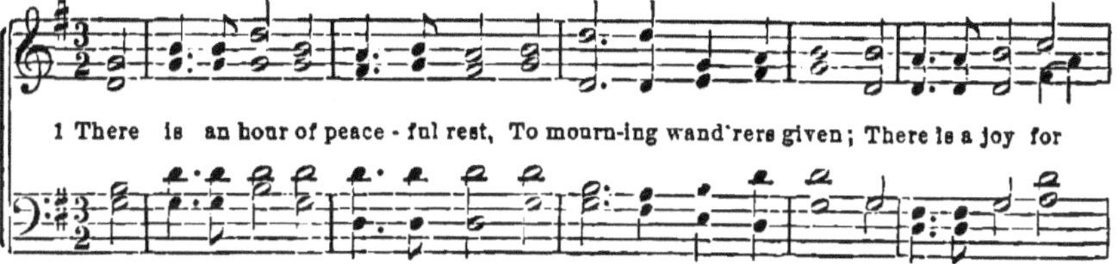

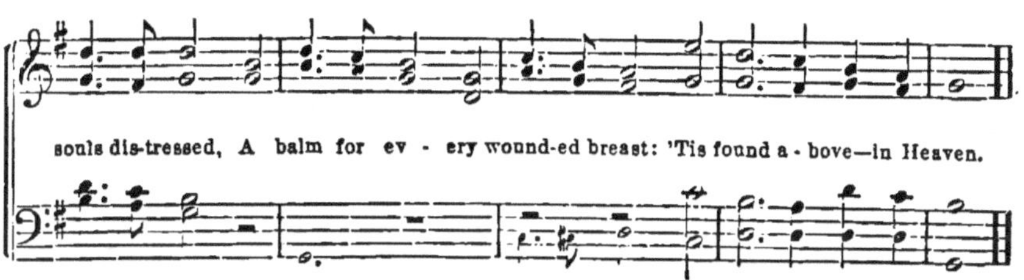

462 *Heaven Anticipated.*

2 There is a home for weary souls,
By sins and sorrows driven;
When tossed on life's tempestuous shoals,
Where storms arise and ocean rolls,
And all is drear but Heaven.

3 There, faith lifts up the tearless eye,
The heart no longer riven,
And views the tempest passing by,
Sees evening shadows quickly fly,
And all serene in Heaven.

4 There, fragrant flowers immortal bloom,
And joys supreme are given;
There, rays divine disperse the gloom;
Beyond the dark and narrow tomb,
Appears the dawn of Heaven.

William B. Tappan.

463 *Rev. 21: 23.*

1 There is a fold where none can stray,
And pastures ever green;
Where sultry sun, or stormy day,
(night is never seen.

2 There is a Shepherd living there,
The first-born from the dead,
Who tends, with sweet, unwearied care,
The flock for which He bled.

3 There congregate the sons of light,
Fair as the morning sky;
And taste of infinite delight,
Beneath their Saviour's eye.

4 Their joy bursts forth in strains of love,
In one harmonious song;
And through the heavenly courts above
The echoes roll along.

5 Oh, may our faith take up that sound,
Though toiling here below!
'Midst trials may our joys abound,
And songs amidst our woe!

6 Until we reach that happy shore,
And join to swell their strain;
And from our God go out no more,
And never weep again.

Anon.

WHAT MUST IT BE TO BE THERE. *Geo. C. Stebbins.*

DUET.

1 We speak of the land of the blest, A country so bright and so fair,

And oft are its glo-ries confessed, but what must it be to be there.

REFRAIN.

To be there, to be there, Oh, what must it be to be there,

to be there, to be there, to be there,

To be there, to be there, Oh, what must it be to be there.

to be there, to be there, to be there.

464 *"There shall be no more death, neither sorrow, nor crying."*

2 We speak of its pathways of gold,
Its walls decked with jewels so rare,
Its wonders and pleasures untold,
But what must it be to be there.

3 We speak of its peace and its love,
The robes which the glorified wear,
The songs of the blessed above,
But what must it be to be there.

4 We speak of its freedom from sin,
From sorrow, temptation and care,
From trials without and within,
But what must it be to be there.

5 Do Thou, Lord, midst pleasure or woe,
For Heaven our spirits prepare,
Then shortly we also shall *know*,
And *feel* what it is to be there.

Mrs. Elizabeth Mills.

TAPPAN. C. M. *Geo. Kingsley.*

465 *The Promised Land.*

2 Oh, the transporting, rapturous scene
  That rises to my sight:
Sweet fields arrayed in living green,
  And rivers of delight.

3 All o'er those wide-extended plains
  Shines one eternal day;
There God, the Son, forever reigns,
  And scatters night away.

4 No chilling winds, or poisonous breath,
  Can reach that healthful shore:
Sickness and sorrow, pain and death,
  Are felt and feared no more.

5 When shall I reach that happy place,
  And be forever blest?
When shall I see my Father's face,
  And in His bosom rest?

6 Filled with delight, my raptured soul
  Can here no longer stay;
Though Jordan's waves around me roll,
  Fearless I'd launch away.

Rev. Samuel Stennett.

466 *"Come, crown and throne; come, robe and palm."*

1 These are the crowns that we shall wear,
  When all Thy saints are crowned;
These are the palms that we shall bear
  On yonder holy ground.

2 These are the robes, unsoiled and white,
  Which we shall then put on,
When, foremost 'mong the sons of light,
  We sit on yonder throne.

3 That is the city of the saints,
  Where we so soon shall stand,
When we shall strike these desert-tents,
  And quit this desert-land.

4 Then welcome toil, and care, and pain!
  And welcome sorrow, too!
All toil is rest, all grief is gain,
  With such a prize in view.

5 Come, crown and throne; come, robe and palm;
  Burst forth, glad stream of peace!
Come, holy city of the Lamb!
  Rise, Sun of righteousness! *Anon.*

WHITNEY. C. M. *Mason.*

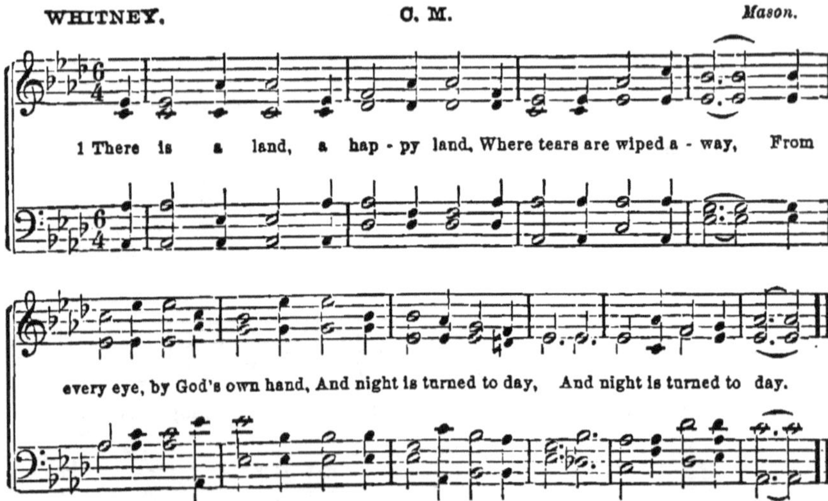

467 *A Better Land.*

2 There is a home, a happy home,
Where way-worn travelers rest,
Where toil and languor never come,
And every mourner's blest.

3 There is a port, a peaceful port,
A safe and quiet shore,
Where weary mariners resort,
When life's rough voyage is o'er.

4 There is a clime, a glorious clime,
A region fair and calm;
Where all around are scenes sublime,
And all the air is balm.

5 There is a crown, a dazzling crown,
Bedecked with jewels fair;
And priests and kings of high renown
That crown of glory wear.

6 That land be mine, that calm retreat,
That crown of glory bright;
Then I'll esteem each bitter sweet,
And every burden light.

468 *"We have a building of God, a house not made with hands, eternal in the heavens."*

1 There is a house not made with hands,
Eternal and on high;
And here my spirit, waiting, stands,
Till God shall bid it fly.

2 Shortly this prison of my clay
May be dissolved and fall;
Then, O my soul, with joy obey
Thy Heavenly Father's call.

3 'Tis He, by His almighty grace,
That forms thee fit for Heaven;
And, as an earnest of the place,
Has His own Spirit given.

4 We walk by faith of joys to come—
Faith lives upon His word;
But while the body is our home,
We're absent from the Lord.

5 'Tis pleasant to believe Thy grace,
But we had rather see;
We would be absent from the flesh,
And present, Lord, with Thee.

Anon.

CALLING US AWAY. C. M. *Walter Kittridge.*

469 *"These are they who have washed their robes and made them white in the blood of the Lamb."*

2 Once they were mourning here below,
And bathed their couch with tears;
They wrestled hard, as we do now,
With sins, and doubts, and fears.

3 I ask them whence their victory came;
They, with united breath,
Ascribe their conquest to the Lamb,
Their triumph to His death.

4 They marked the footsteps that He trod;
His zeal inspired their breast;
And, following their incarnate God,
Possessed the promised rest.

5 Our glorious Leader claims our praise,
For His own pattern given;
While the long crowd of witnesses
Show the same path to Heaven.

I. Watts.

MAY JESUS CHRIST BE PRAISED. *Joseph Barnby.*

470 *"Thou art worthy."*

2 Whene'er the sweet church bell
Peals over hill and dell,
May Jesus Christ be praised:
Oh, hark to what it sings,
As joyously it rings,
May Jesus Christ be praised.

3 Does sadness fill my mind?
A solace here I find,
May Jesus Christ be praised:
Or fades my earthly bliss?
My comfort still is this,
May Jesus Christ be praised.

4 The night becomes as day
When from the heart we say,
May Jesus Christ be praised:
The powers of darkness fear,
When this sweet chant they hear,
May Jesus Christ be praised.

5 In Heaven's eternal bliss
The loveliest strain is this,
Let Jesus Christ be praised:
Let earth, and sea, and sky
From depth to height reply,
May Jesus Christ be praised.

Rev. E. Caswall.

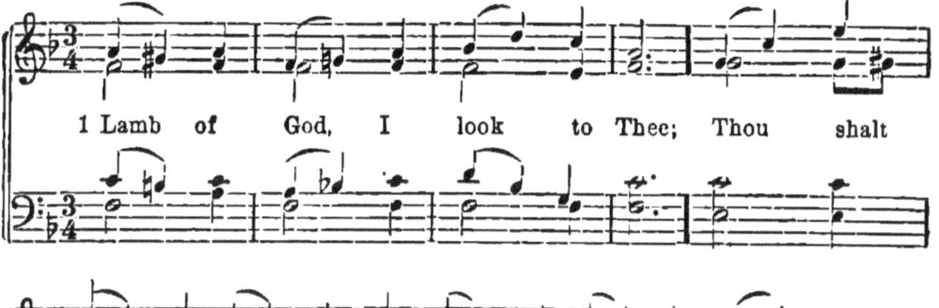

471 *"Speak, Lord, for Thy servant heareth."*

2 Fain I would be as Thou art;
Give me Thy obedient heart!
Thou art pitiful and kind;
Let me have Thy loving mind.

3 Meek and lowly may I be;
Thou art all humility!
Let me to my betters bow;
Subject to Thy parents Thou.

4 Let me above all fulfill
God my heavenly Father's will;
Never His good Spirit grieve;
Only to His glory live!

5 Loving Jesus, gentle Lamb,
In Thy gracious hands I am:
Make me, Saviour, what Thou art!
Live Thyself within my heart.

C. Wesley.

472 *"The Lord is my shepherd."*

1 To Thy pastures green and fair,
Saviour, let a child repair;
I will never stray from Thee,
But Thy fold my home shall be.

2 Like a gentle lamb, I'll stay
In the meadows fresh and gay;
Peaceful and contented there,
Guarded by my Shepherd's care.

3 By the waters still and clear,
I shall wander without fear;
Happy by my Shepherd's side,
All my wants shall be supplied.

4 Lord, wilt Thou my shepherd be?
Help me then to follow Thee;
At Thy feet myself I cast,
Thee to serve while life shall last.

Anon.

ANGRY WORDS.

H. R. Palmer.

473 *"Love one another."*

2 Love is much too pure and holy,
Friendship is too sacred far,
For a moment's reckless folly
Thus to desolate and mar.

3 Angry words are lightly spoken;
Bitterest thoughts are rashly stirred;
Brightest links of life are broken
By a single angry word.

Anon.

HAPPY LAND. *Anon.*

473 *Happy Land.*

2 Come to that happy land,
  Come, come away.
Why will ye doubting stand,
  Why still delay?
Oh, we shall happy be,
When, from sin and sorrow free,
Lord, we shall live with thee,
  Blest, blest for aye.

3 Bright in that happy land
  Beams every eye;
Kept by a Father's hand,
  Love cannot die.
Oh, then, to glory run,
Be a crown and kingdom won,
And bright above the sun
  We reign for aye.

Anon

HAPPY MEETING. *Anon.*

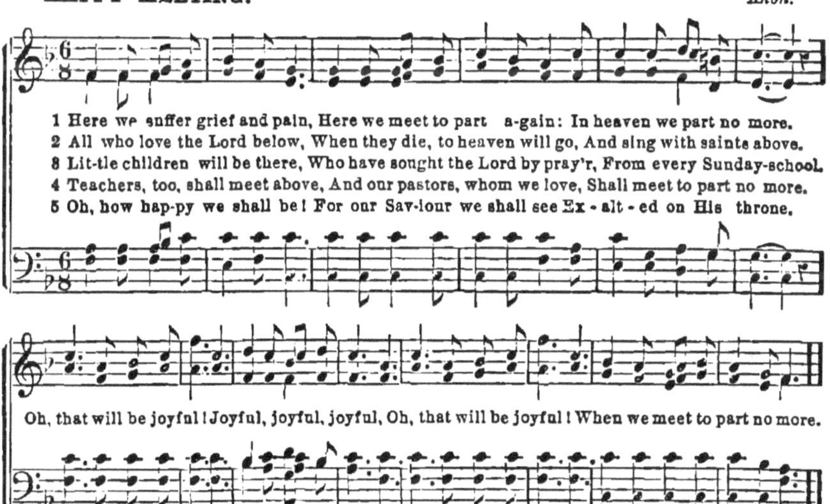

BEAUTIFUL HOME. *H. R. Palmer.*

476 *"The glory of God did lighten it."*

2 Flowers forever are springing
 In that home so fair,
Thousands of children are singing
 Praises to Jesus there;
How they swell the glad anthems
 Ever around the bright throne.

3 Soon shall I join that anthem,
 Far beyond the sky;
Jesus became my ransom
 Why should I fear to die?
Soon my eyes will behold Him
 Seated upon the bright throne.

Frank Forest.

SINGING AS WE JOURNEY. *Lucy J. Rider.*

477 *"Sing forth the honor of His name."*

2 We are traveling to our home,
 Blessed home, blessed home,
We are traveling to our home,
 Singing as we journey,
Toward a city out of sight,
Where will fall no shade of night,
For our Saviour is its light,
 Singing as we journey.

3 Full of joy we onward go,
 Heavenward go, Homeward go,
Full of joy we onward go,
 Singing as we journey,
Singing all the journey thro'—
Singing hearts are brave and true—
Singing till our home we view,
 Singing as we journey.

Lucy J. Rider.

WOODWORTH. L. M. *Wm. B. Bradbury.*

478 *Just as I Am.*

2 Just as I am, and waiting not
To rid my soul of one dark blot,
To Thee, whose blood can cleanse each spot,
O Lamb of God! I come, I come!

3 Just as I am, though tossed about,
With many a conflict, many a doubt,
Fightings and fears within, without,
O Lamb of God! I come, I come!

4 Just as I am, poor, wretched, blind,
Sight, riches, healing of the mind,
Yea, all I need, in Thee to find,
O Lamb of God! I come, I come!

5 Just as I am; Thou wilt receive,
Wilt welcome, pardon, cleanse, relieve,
Because Thy promise I believe,
O Lamb of God! I come, I come!

Miss Charlotte Elliott.

GOD CARES FOR ME. *Emma L. Morton.*

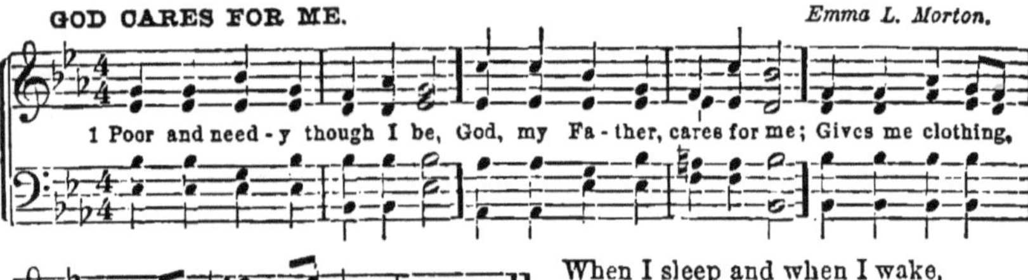

shelter, food, Gives me all I have of good.

479 *Matt. 10: 30.*

2 He will hear me when I pray,
He is with me night and day,
When I sleep and when I wake,
For the Lord my Saviour's sake.

3 He who reigns above the sky,
Once became as poor as I;
He whose blood for me was shed,
Had not where to lay His head.

4 Then to Him I'll tune my song,
Happy as the day is long;
This my joy forever be,
God, my Father, cares for me.

Anon.

480 "*Tell me the old, old story.*"

2 Tell me the story slowly,
That I may take it in—
That wonderful Redemption,
God's remedy for sin!
Tell me the story often,
For I forget so soon!
The "early dew" of morning
Has passed away at noon!

3 Tell me the story softly,
With earnest tones and grave;
Remember, I'm the sinner
Whom Jesus came to save.
Tell me the story always,
If you would really be,
In any time of trouble,
A comforter to me.

4 Tell me the same old story,
When you have cause to fear
That this world's empty glory
Is costing me too dear;
Yes, and when that world's glory
Is dawning on my soul,
Tell me the old, old story,—
"Christ Jesus makes thee whole."

Kate Hankey.

I LOVE TO TELL THE STORY. *Wm. G. Fischer.*

481 *"I love to tell the story."*

2 I love to tell the story;
More wonderful it seems
Than all the golden fancies
Of all our golden dreams.
I love to tell the story:
It did so much for me!
And that is just the reason
I tell it now to thee.

3 I love to tell the story;
'Tis pleasant to repeat
What seems, each time I tell it,
More wonderfully sweet.
I love to tell the story;
For some have never heard
The message of salvation
From God's own holy word.

4 I love to tell the story;
For those who know it best
Seem hungering and thirsting
To hear it like the rest.
And when, in scenes of glory,
I sing the new, new song,
'Twill be the old, old story
That I have loved so long!

Kate Hankey.

482 *"Love Divine."*

2 Breathe, oh, breathe Thy loving Spirit,
Into every troubled breast;
Let us all in Thee inherit,
Let us find that second rest;
Take away our power of sinning,
Alpha and Omega be;
End of faith, as its beginning,
Set our hearts at liberty.

3 Come, Almighty to deliver,
Let us all Thy life receive;
Suddenly return, and never,
Never more Thy temples leave.
Thee we would be always blessing,
Serve Thee as Thy hosts above,
Pray, and praise Thee without ceasing,
Glory in Thy perfect love.

C. Wesley.

483 *Joy.*

1 Take, my soul, thy full salvation,
Rise o'er sin, and fear, and care;
Joy to find in every station
Something still to do or bear.
Think what Spirit dwells within thee;
What a Father's smile is thine;
What a Saviour died to win thee:
Child of Heaven, shouldst thou repine?

2 Haste thee on from grace to glory,
Armed by faith and winged by prayer:
Heaven's eternal day 's before thee,
God's own hand shall guide thee there.
Soon shall close thy earthly mission,
Swift shall pass thy pilgrim days,
Hope soon change to glad fruition,
Faith to sight, and prayer to praise.

Rev. Henry Francis Lyte.

TOUCH NOT, TASTE NOT. *W. S. Marshall.*

484 *Touch not, taste not.*

2 Who hath babblings, who hath strife?
He who leads a drunkard's life,
He who scorns the Lord divine,
He who goes to seek mixed wine.

3 Who hath wounds without a cause?
He who breaks God's holy laws:
He whose lov'd ones weep and pine,
While he tarries at the wine.

4 Who hath redness of the eyes,
Who bring poverty and sighs,
Into homes almost divine,
They who tarry at the wine.

5 Touch not, taste not, handle not,
Wine will make a dark, dark blot;
Like an adder it will sting,
And at last to ruin bring.

Rev. J. B. Atchinson.

THERE IS A FOUNTAIN. *Western Melody*

485 *"A Fountain opened for sin."*

2 The dying thief rejoiced to see
  That fountain in his day;
And there may I, though vile as he,
  Wash all my sins away.

3 E'er since by faith I saw the stream
  Thy flowing wounds supply,
Redeeming love has been my theme,
  And shall be till I die.

4 Then in a nobler, sweeter song
  I'll sing Thy power to save,
When this poor, lisping, stammering tongue
  Lies silent in the grave.

Wm. Cowper.

THE WONDROUS GIFT. *Ira D. Sankey.*

1 Grace! 'tis a charm - ing sound, Har - mo - nious to the ear; Heaven with the ech - o shall re - sound, And all the earth shall hear.

REFRAIN.

Saved by grace a - lone, This is all my plea; Je - sus died for all man - kind, And Je - sus died for me.

486 *"By grace are ye saved."*

2 Grace first contrived a way
To save rebellious man;
And all the steps that grace display,
Which drew the wondrous plan.

3 Grace taught my roving feet
To tread the heavenly road,
And new supplies each hour I meet,
While pressing on to God.

4 Grace all the work shall crown,
Through everlasting days;
It lays in Heaven the topmost stone,
And well deserves our praise.

Philip Doddridge.

STOCKWELL. 8, 7. *D. E. Jones.*

487 *The Evening Blessing.*

2 Though destruction walk around us,
Though the arrow near us fly,
Angel-guards from Thee surround us;
We are safe, if Thou art nigh.

3 Though the night be dark and dreary,
Darkness cannot hide from Thee:
Thou art He who, never weary,
Watcheth where Thy people be.

4 Should swift death this night o'ertake us,
And our couch become our tomb,
May the morn in Heaven awake us,
Clad in light and deathless bloom!

488 *"With you always."*

1 Always with us, always with us—
Words of cheer and words of love;
Thus the risen Saviour whispers,
From His dwelling-place above.

2 With us when we toil in sadness,
Sowing much and reaping none;
Telling us that in the future
Golden harvests shall be won.

3 With us when the storm is sweeping
O'er our pathway dark and drear;
Waking hope within our bosoms,
Stilling every anxious fear.

4 With us in the lonely valley,
When we cross the chilling stream—
Lighting up the steps to glory
With salvation's radiant beam.

E. H. Nevin.

489 *Psalm 127.*

1 Vainly, through night's weary hours,
Keep we watch, lest foes alarm;
Vain our bulwarks, and our towers,
But for God's protecting arm.

2 Vain were all our toil and labor,
Did not God that labor bless;
Vain, without his grace and favor,
Every talent we possess.

3 Vainer still the hope of Heaven,
That on human strength relies;
But to him shall help be given,
Who in humble faith applies.

4 Seek we, then, the Lord's Anointed;
He will grant us peace and rest:
Ne'er was suppliant disappointed,
Who through Christ his prayer addressed.

H. Auber.

CREATION. **L. M. D.** *F. J. Haydn.*

490 *In Nature.*

2 Soon as the evening shades prevail,
The moon takes up the wondrous tale;
And nightly, to the listening earth,
Repeats the story of her birth;
While all the stars that round her burn,
And all the planets in their turn,
Confirm the tidings as they roll,
And spread the truth from pole to pole.

3 What though in solemn silence, all
Move round the dark terrestrial ball,—
What though no real voice nor sound
Amid their radiant orbs be found,—
In reason's ear they all rejoice,
And utter forth a glorious voice,
Forever singing as they shine,—
"The hand that made us is divine."

J. Addison.

6, 4. *H. Carey.*

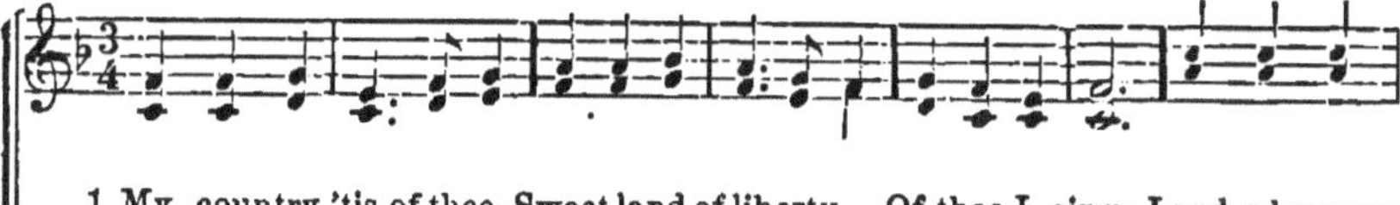

1 My country 'tis of thee, Sweet land of liberty, Of thee I sing; Land where my

491 *National Song.*

2 My native country, thee—
Land of the noble, free—
Thy name I love;
I love thy rocks and rills,
Thy woods and templed hills;
My heart with rapture thrills
Like that above.

3 Let music swell the breeze,
And ring from all the trees
Sweet freedom's song:
Let mortal tongues awake;
Let all that breathe partake;
Let rocks their silence break,—
The sound prolong.

4 Our fathers' God! to thee,
Author of liberty,
To thee we sing:
Long may our land be bright
With freedom's holy light;
Protect us by Thy might,
Great God, our King!

S. F. Smith.

492 *"God save the State."*

1 God bless our native land:
Firm may she ever stand,
Through storm and night;
When the wild tempests rave,
Ruler of wind and wave,
Do Thou our country save
By Thy great might.

2 For her our prayer shall rise
To God, above the skies;
On Him we wait;
Thou who art ever nigh,
Guarding with watchful eye,
To Thee aloud we cry,
God save the State.

Rev. John S. Dwight.

LOOK TO JESUS.

C. E. Pollock.

493 *"Look unto Me and be ye saved."*

2 See the loving Saviour stands,
Pleading for Thy fond embrace;
Trust thyself to Jesus' hands,
In His bosom hide thy face,
All thy sickness He can cure,
All thy sins He will forgive,
He will make His promise sure,
Look to Jesus, look and live.

3 Look to Jesus, not in vain,
Do the weary seek for rest;
Weep away thy tears and pain,
Like a child upon His breast;
Breathe thy sorrow in His ear,
Strength for every day receive;
Light in darkness will appear,
If thou wilt but look and live.

Josephine Pollard.

494 *1 Thess.* 5:16.

2 Rejoice in peace made sure,
No judgment now for thee;
Thy conscience purged, thy life secure,
More safe thou canst not be.

3 Rejoice in joys to come,
The hope of glory near;
He'll soon return to take thee home,
No cause for thee to fear.

4 Now by the Spirit sealed,
Rejoice in God the Lord;
The mighty God is now thy shield,
And He thy great reward.

English.

HEAR THOU MY PRAYER. *Geo. C. Stebbins*

495 *"Hear Thou in Heaven Thy dwelling-place."*

2 Thou knowest all my need,
My inmost thought dost see;
Ah, Lord! from all allurements freed,
Like Thee transformed I'd be.

3 Thou holy blessed One,
To me, I pray, draw near;
My spirit fill, O heavenly Son,
With loving, godly fear.

4 Bind Thou my life to Thine,
To me Thy life is given;
While I my all to Thee resign,
Thou art my all in Heaven.

Rev. Henry C. Graves.

INDEX TO HYMNS.

INDEX TO TUNES.

METRICAL INDEX OF TUNES.

www.ingramcontent.com/pod-product-compliance
Lightning Source LLC
Chambersburg PA
CBHW030407270326
41926CB00009B/1304
9783337243739